CORAL SEA

SOUTH

PACIFIC

OCEAN

GULF OF CARPENTARIA

ERN

ORY

SOUTH AUSTRALIA

QUEENSLAND

NEW SOUTH WALES

VICTORIA

TASMANIA

TASMAN SEA

BASS STRAIT

CW01464615

Cairns

Townsville

Mount Isa

Mackay

Longreach

Rockhampton

Gladstone

Bundaberg

Sunshine Coast

Toowoomba

BRISBANE

Gold Coast

Lismore

Coffs Harbour

Tamworth

Port Macquarie

Broken Hill

Dubbo

Muswellbrook

Orange

Newcastle

Mildura

Gosford

Wagga Wagga

SYDNEY

Renmark

Wollongong

Nowra

ort Augusta

Port Pirie

ncoln

ADELAIDE

Albury-Wodonga

ACT CANBERRA

Horsham

Bendigo

Ballarat

Shepparton

Bega

Mount Gambier

MELBOURNE

Warrnambool

Morwell

Sale

Burnie

Launceston

HOBART

Great Barrier Reef

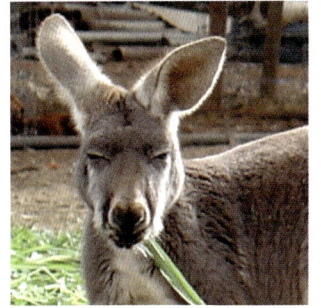

Meet the Locals

The ABC Insider's Guide to Australia

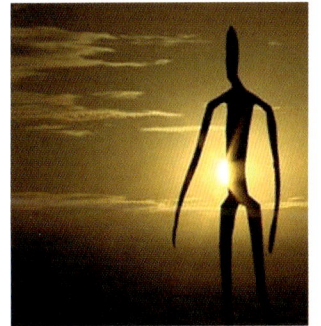

ABC | Local Radio

Contents

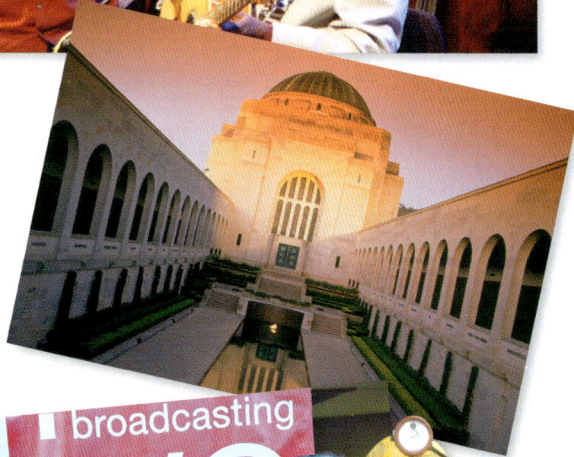

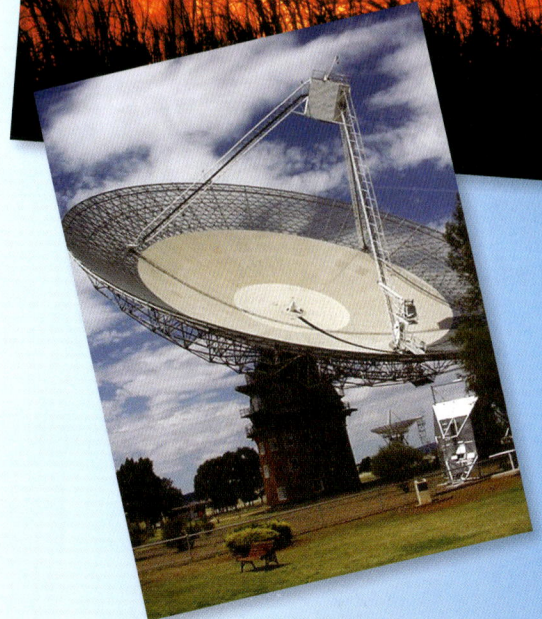

Introduction

Wouldn't it be great if every time you travelled Australia, you knew every place as well as your own backyard? Wouldn't it be great if everywhere you went, you could have the benefit of local knowledge? Well, now you can.

Across Australia the Australian Broadcasting Corporation's Local Radio network provides a unique point of access to every community in every State and Territory, in the towns and in the bush. In compiling this book, we've taken advantage of that access and sought tips and suggestions from the ABC's Local Radio audience for their favourite places, the local identities 'you just have to meet' and those special experiences or locations you won't find in standard guide books.

Meet the Locals will help you to 'be in the know'. We've combined detailed maps with the frequencies for ABC Local Radio stations for every one of the ABC's 45 Local Radio regions. We're quite proud of the result. The country is divided first into State and Territory sections. Then the introduction to each section includes a reference map showing all the regions within each State and Territory. Finally, each region has its own chapter that includes a map of the region, ABC Local Radio frequencies, tourist information, things you shouldn't miss, tourism-authority contacts and of course, local tips and ideas.

And that's not all. Tune in to the extraordinary world of ABC Local Radio and find out what's happening and who's making news in the region. Without ABC Local Radio, you might miss out on the local lizard races (page 222) or the hotel that gets occasional visits from crocodiles (page 169).

Tune in to the extraordinary world of ABC Local Radio and find out what's happening and who's making news in the region …

You might not meet the local belly dancers (page 153), puppeteers (page 69) or the bat lady (page 42). You might never discover the best gardens, scenic lookouts, waterfalls or fish-and-chip shops. In addition, you'll also find your favourite Statewide and nationwide programs such as 'AM', 'PM', 'The World Today', 'The Country Hour', 'Statewide Drive', 'Evenings', 'Nightlife', 'Grandstand', 'Lights Camera Action', 'Coodabeen Champions', 'Saturday Night Country' and 'Australia All Over'.

For those who wish to go even further, ABC Local Radio is also on the Internet at the comprehensive ABC Backyard website (www.abc.net.au/backyard). With a click of the mouse you can check out a region you're about to visit, and find out what's going on before you even get there. In some regions you can even listen in online. Plus there are archived stories from the last few years, great photos and recorded interviews full of colourful characters and yarns.

All of which means you don't have to leave the ABC behind whenever you leave home. Wherever you are in Australia, whether living, working or travelling, with *Meet the Locals* ABC Local Radio is with you – always informative, ever useful and endlessly entertaining.

Tuning Tip

You're listening to a fascinating interview, or the cricket is poised on a knife-edge. But you're covering one of those vast distances between two Australian towns and, as the signal fades, you start hunting the dial, searching for better reception, any reception. We all know what that's like, and that's where this guide can help.

Opposite the maps throughout *Meet the Locals*, you'll see lists of towns that broadcast or can receive the Local Radio station for that region. Some towns (highlighted in green) have transmitters that broadcast on the FM band and, while they provide a high-quality signal, they may only have a range of between 20 and 50 kilometres from town. Other towns (highlighted in red) transmit on the AM band and, in the vast flat spaces of Australia, they can provide quite good reception that covers hundreds of kilometres and many towns. The maps also locate the transmitters in each region by using a green or red symbol. Note the feature on tuning while driving between capital cities (see page 90) for more information.

So when you're near a town listed in green type, check the frequency and tune to the FM band for the best quality local radio. But when you're between two towns, you'll usually get better reception if you scan the region's AM frequencies.

Due to the enormous coverage provided by some AM transmitters, some lucky towns are able to receive broadcasts from two Local Radio regions. In such cases, the town will usually appear on the maps

and in the frequency lists for both (usually adjoining) regions. In each case the alternative frequency or frequencies it can receive follows the town name in the list. And if the town also happens to transmit one of those local radio stations, it will be highlighted in green or red in the appropriate region, as explained above.

Visit www.abc.net.au/reception/ for comprehensive frequency information for all ABC services across Australia.

Local Radio Frequencies		
Alpha	540 AM	105.7 FM ABC Central Queensland 1548 AM ABC Central Queensland
Augathella	540 AM	
Barcaldine	540 AM	
Blackall	540 AM	
Charleville	603 AM	
Corfield	540 AM	
Isisford	540 AM	
Jericho	540 AM	
Longreach	540 AM	
Morven	603 AM	
Muttaburra	540 AM	
Winton	540 AM	
Bedourie	105.9 FM	540 AM
Birdsville	106.1 FM	540 AM
Boulia	106.1 FM	540 AM
Burketown	96.3 FM	567 AM ABC North West Queensland
Camooweal	106.1 FM	567 AM ABC North West Queensland
Collinsville	106.1 FM	540 AM 630 AM ABC North Queensland
Croydon	105.7 FM	567 AM ABC North West Queensland
Doomadgee	97.5 FM	567 AM ABC North West Queensland
Georgetown	106.1 FM	567 AM ABC North West Queensland
Gununa	92.7 FM	
Injune	105.9 FM	711 AM ABC Southern Queensland
Karumba	106.1 FM	567 AM ABC North West Queensland

ABC Local Radio
regions across Australia

New South Wales

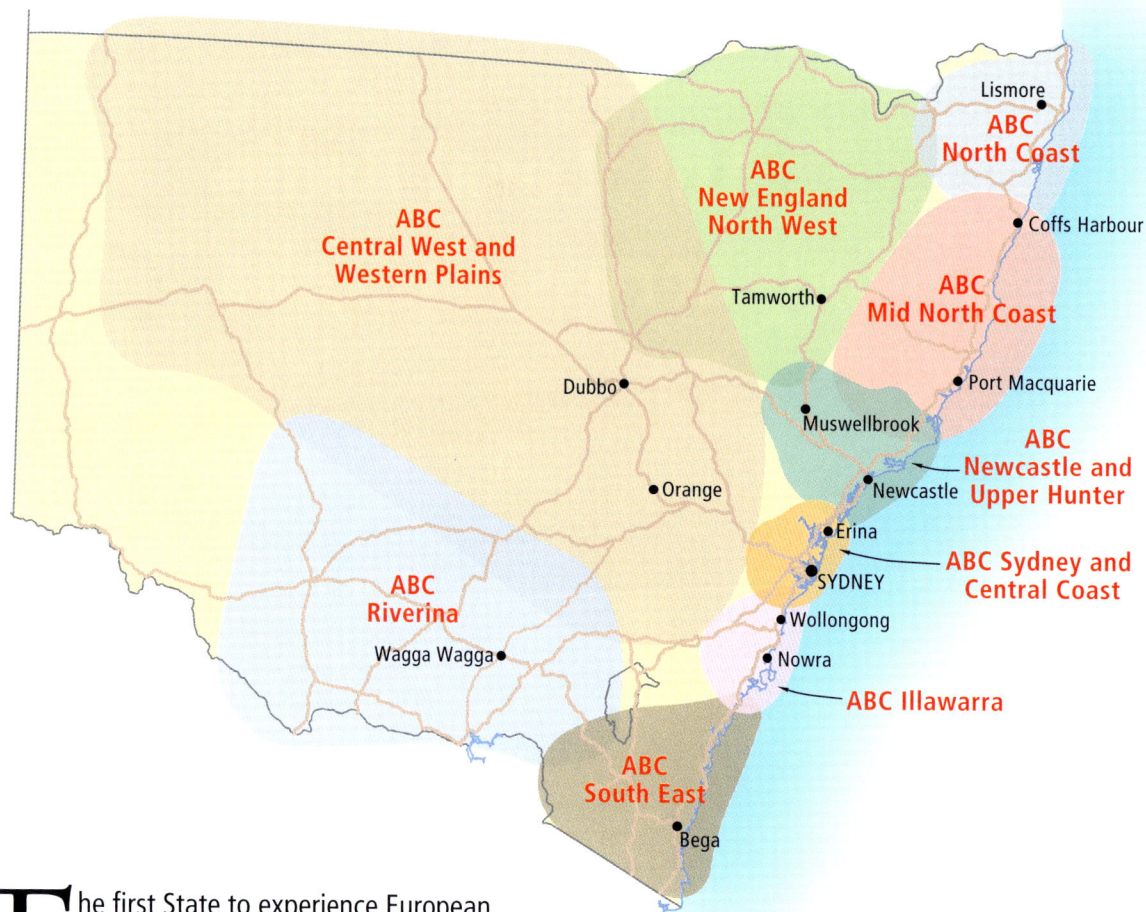

ABC
North Coast

Lismore

Coffs Harbour

ABC
New England
North West

ABC
Central West and
Western Plains

ABC
Mid North Coast

Tamworth

Port Macquarie

Dubbo

Muswellbrook

ABC
Newcastle and
Upper Hunter

Newcastle

Orange

Erina

ABC Sydney and
Central Coast

SYDNEY

ABC
Riverina

Wollongong

Wagga Wagga

Nowra

ABC Illawarra

ABC
South East

Bega

The first State to experience European settlement, New South Wales today is Australia's most visited State. It has a wealth of natural attractions, from the golden beaches that stretch along the entire length of the east coast, to the spectacular mountain ranges that for years limited access to the vast inland plain. The richness of the scenery together with the many attractive towns and villages provide something for everyone. And then, of course, there's one of the world's great cities, Sydney, with its superb harbour and famous Opera House.

Note: As ABC Far West broadcasts in both New South Wales and South Australia, and operates on central standard time, it is included in the South Australian section of this publication. See pages 124–7.

🖧 See inside back cover for a list of ABC Local Radio stations and their frequencies.

ABC Sydney and Central Coast

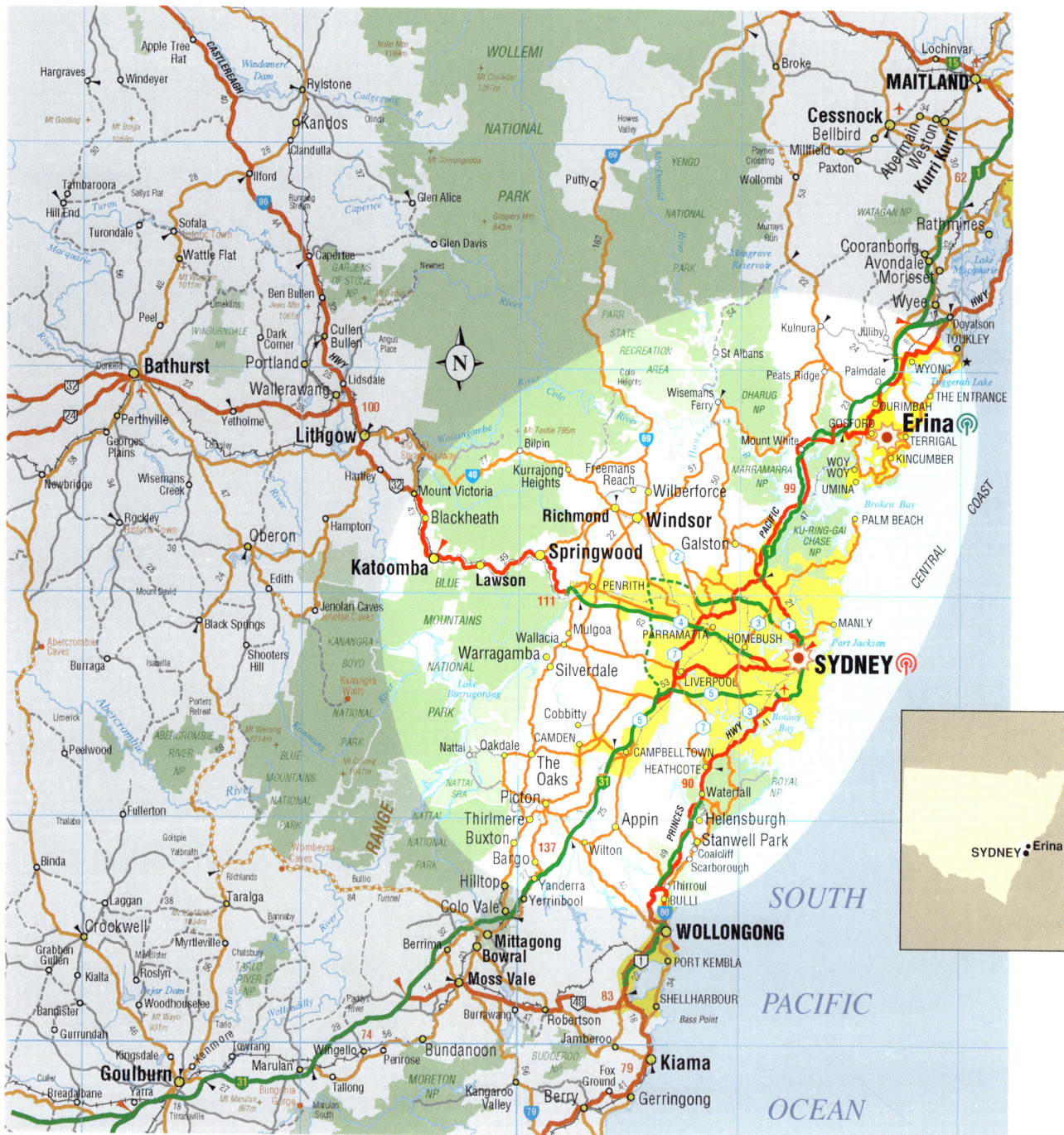

Location of ABC Local Radio studio

Local Radio Frequencies	
Camden	702 AM
Katoomba	702 AM
Picton	702 AM
Richmond	702 AM
Sydney	702 AM
Windsor	702 AM
Gosford (Erina)	92.5 FM
The Entrance	92.5 FM
Wyong	92.5 FM

Sydney has the only AM transmitter in the region
Gosford has the only FM transmitter in the region

Sydney is one of the world's great cities – a lively, cosmopolitan, self-confident metropolis that is blessed with golden beaches, a sparkling harbour, one of the most beautiful buildings on earth and much, much more. On its doorstep there are superb natural wonders, with the spectacular waterways of Pittwater and the Hawkesbury, and the scenic beauty of the Blue Mountains. There are more beautiful waterways, national parks and superb beaches on the Central Coast.

For the visitor, Sydney is an easy city to navigate. Many of its main attractions are concentrated around the central business district, and one of the easiest (and fun) ways to get from place to place is to hop on a ferry. You get to see more of the wonderful harbour while getting to your next sightseeing destination.

With a population of 4.2 million, Sydney is also one of the liveliest places in the country, and there's no better way to keep track of what's happening than the local radio station, 702 ABC Sydney and Central Coast. Whether it's a whale in the harbour, dolphins off Avoca Beach or snow in the Blue Mountains, ABC local radio gives you a unique view of this fabulous part of the world every day.

TOURISM AUSTRALIA

Sydney's two famous icons

NOT TO BE MISSED

- Tour the **Sydney Opera House** to discover its internal architecture or book to see a performance
- Climb the **Harbour Bridge** with BridgeClimb, for the ultimate view of the city and harbour
- Visit **Sydney Olympic Park**, home of the 2000 Olympics
- Take the ferry to **Manly**, followed by a stroll down The Corso to the beach
- See all kinds of wildlife in the postcard setting of **Taronga Zoo**, then visit the denizens of the deep at **Sydney Aquarium**
- Appreciate the finest in Australian and international art at the **Art Gallery of New South Wales**
- For unique insights, visit the **Australian Museum** or the **Powerhouse Museum**
- Swim, sunbathe or watch the beautiful people at Australia's best-known beach, **Bondi**
- Give your credit card a solid workout in the shops of **Double Bay** and **Oxford Street**

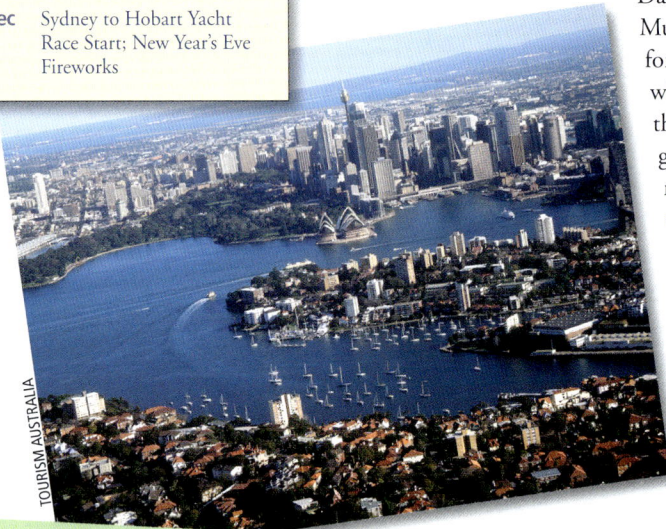

TOURISM AUSTRALIA

City Centre

Bordered by the harbour to the north and west, and by the harbour and parks and gardens to the east, Sydney is one of the most strikingly beautiful cities in Australia. Sightseeing opportunities abound, there is great shopping and dining, and superb museums and art galleries and, if you're fit, they're all within easy walking distance. If not, the Sydney Explorer Bus service takes in all the major attractions (fee applies) or you can hop on the city-circle train line to get from one place to another.

SIGHTS AND ACTIVITIES • Enjoy all manner of attractions at Darling Harbour including IMAX, the Australian Maritime Museum, Sydney Aquarium and numerous restaurants catering for every budget • Take a tour of the State Theatre, a gem whose interiors have to be seen to be believed • Stroll around the Royal Botanic Gardens to Mrs Macquarie's Chair, with great harbour views all the way • Shop in one of Sydney's most beautiful buildings, the Queen Victoria Building • See the foundations of the first Governor's Residence, and discover the city's past in the Museum of Sydney • Dine in the revolving restaurant or see the city at your feet from Sydney Tower and Skytour; back at ground level, don't miss Pitt Street Mall's beautiful Strand Arcade • For the ultimate foodie experience, be dazzled at the David Jones Food Hall or the Sydney Fish Market

VISITOR INFORMATION
106 George Street, The Rocks (02) 9255 1788
Palm Grove, Darling Harbour (02) 9281 0788

MEET THE LOCALS

Seagulls

They were among the stars of *Finding Nemo,* and the anthropomorphic film got it spot on by giving Sydney's seagulls only one word of dialogue: 'Mine!'. They're the very common silver gull (*Larus novaehollandiae*) and if you take the popular ferry trip to Manly, you may wonder why the birds follow the vessel the whole way – the picture makes it pretty obvious.

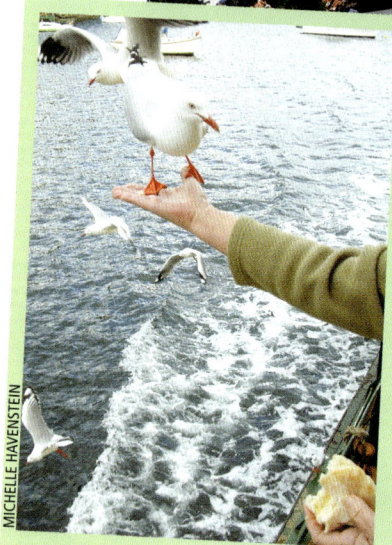

MICHELLE HAVENSTEIN

The Harbour

Described as one of the best harbours in the world, it's paradise for recreational boating; for visitors the spectacle of the harbour covered in sails on weekends is unforgettable. From the wide expanses of the harbour, with the city in the background, to secluded coves and bays surrounded by bushland, it's an enchanted place that's full of surprises.

SIGHTS AND ACTIVITIES • Take one or more of a whole range of cruises available for sightseeing, coffee, dinner or stage shows. The obvious trip is to Manly, but you can also take a RiverCat inland to Parramatta, to Taronga Zoo or to Darling Harbour • Hire a yacht for an idyllic introduction to one of the best sailing venues in the world • Book at the National Parks Office in Cadman's Cottage in The Rocks for tours of various harbour islands including Fort Denison and Goat Island (site of the *Water Rats* TV series) • Get great views of the city on the walk from the Taronga Zoo ferry wharf to Bradleys Head

The Beaches

From Cronulla in the south to Palm Beach in the north, then on to The Entrance on the Central Coast, Sydney is blessed with some of the finest surf beaches in the country. There is quite literally kilometre after kilometre of sun-drenched golden sand, and everything from packed shores where it seems the entire city is sunning itself, to quiet spots where the only footprints are your own.

SIGHTS AND ACTIVITIES • Take a Bondi and Bay Explorer bus to all the sights in the eastern suburbs' harbourside locations, then down the coast to Bondi, Tamarama, Bronte and Coogee beaches • Walk Sydney's best-known and incredibly popular path from Bondi to Bronte (the venue for Sculpture by the Sea in October) • Ride the Manly ferry then stroll through The Corso to the surf beach, turn right and head around to Fairy Bower and Shelly Beach • Jump on the train to Cronulla where there's another good coast walk, or you can take the ferry to Bundeena and enjoy the crystal clear waters of Jibbon Beach

Eastern Suburbs

As urban environments go, this is one of the most concentrated areas of wealth, culture, social diversity and recreational facilities you'll find anywhere. It is bounded by the city on one side, the harbour on another and beaches including Bondi on the other. Within this area you'll find just about everything you could ever want or need. Little wonder the real estate here is among the most expensive in the world.

SIGHTS AND ACTIVITIES • Take a ferry trip to Watsons Bay for a wonderful walk around South Head and back, followed by a sumptuous seafood lunch at one of several restaurants there • Shop for designer clothes and jewellery at the very upmarket Double Bay • Surf, sunbathe or stroll along the seafront taking in the beautiful people at Bondi, with a very enjoyable lunch or dinner an option as well • Seek out style, and discover gay culture, along Paddington's Oxford Street; note, too, the superb Victorian architecture in this suburb, one of the most architecturally consistent anywhere • Enjoy fine dining on the waterfront at several restaurants on Woolloomooloo's finger wharf

Manly

Bondi

Bondi's South American Festival

In a city with an incredibly diverse mix of cultures, you should expect anything anywhere. Every February, for example, the surfers and sunbathers of Bondi make way for the spectacle, music and flavours of the South American Festival. It's been running for 25 years, and involves dance, music, art and food from nearly every country in Latin America. It's also a great place to find out where to get lessons in, say, the samba or *capoiera*.

Inner West

Sydney has a remarkably diverse multicultural population, and much of it can be found in the inner west. Also in this area there are elegant harbourside suburbs that still retain the flavour of their working-class origins.

SIGHTS AND ACTIVITIES ● Take a ferry to Balmain, where you'll find gentrification rubbing shoulders with the working port ● Marvel at the diversity of people in Newtown's bohemian King Street – this is the place for second-hand clothes and books, and top-notch cheap- and cheerful-dining ● Get a taste of Italy in Leichhardt's Norton Street, of Vietnam and Thailand in Marrickville's Marrickville Road, and of Korea in Campsie's Beamish Street

North Shore

On the northern shore of the harbour the city is less developed, in part due to the fact that access was restricted until the Harbour Bridge was completed in the 1930s. However, there are now several burgeoning commercial centres, but much of the area is typified by large comfortable homes in bushland settings.

SIGHTS AND ACTIVITIES ● Glimpse the life of Australia's first 'saint' at Mary MacKillop Place ● Cruise Middle Harbour, one of the most beautiful waterways of Sydney Harbour, passing sheltered Balmoral Beach, which you can return to for swimming, dining and boat hire ● Take a spectacular seaplane flight from Rose Bay to Palm Beach for lunch

Blue Mountains

To the west of the city lies the section of the Great Dividing Range known as the Blue Mountains. For years they formed a barrier to settlement, but now they're a place of spectacular beauty dotted with attractive towns and villages.

SIGHTS AND ACTIVITIES ● See the iconic Three Sisters at Echo Point, and in the same area ride a cable car or the incredibly steep Scenic Railway ● Hike to the Blue Gum Forest in the Grose Valley ● Explore places normally restricted to the most adventurous via the giant screen presentation on the Blue Mountains at The Edge cinema ● Enjoy the charm of Leura, the mountain village where time has stood still ● Ride the steam trains and diesel locos of the Zigzag Railway on Bells Line of Road ● See the flowers or colours of the many European-style gardens in spring and autumn

VISITOR INFORMATION
Blue Mountains Visitor Information Centre, Katoomba; local freecall 1300 653 408

TOURISM AUSTRALIA

Blue Mountains

Central Coast

As if Sydney didn't have enough beaches and enviable stretches of water, just to its north there's more, and some would argue, better ones. Pittwater and the Hawkesbury is an enclosed waterway that rivals Sydney Harbour. It extends across Broken Bay up to Gosford and Brisbane Water. On the north side of Broken Bay there are some superb and rarely visited ocean beaches in Bouddi National Park, and the resorts and holiday destinations of Avoca, Terrigal and The Entrance.

SIGHTS AND ACTIVITIES • See reptiles of all shapes and sizes at the renowned Australian Reptile Park at Somersby • Hire a houseboat and escape into the untouched corners of the national parks along Pittwater and the Hawkesbury; ferry cruises are also available • Take a break at one of the most exclusive and beautiful beaches in the Sydney region, Pearl Beach • Admire the sweeping ocean views from The Skillion at Terrigal • Fish in the quiet waters of Tuggerah, Budgewoi and Munmorah lakes, near The Entrance

VISITOR INFORMATION
Rotary Park, Terrigal Drive, Terrigal (02) 4385 4430
Memorial Park, Marine Parade, The Entrance (02) 4334 4213

MEET THE LOCALS

The local boar

His name is Il Porcellino, a replica of the boar in the Mercato Nuovo (new market) in Florence. You can find him outside the Sydney Hospital in Macquarie Street. Watch for a while and you'll notice Sydneysiders coming up to rub his nose for luck, which is why it's shiny. They also bring good fortune to the hospital as Il Porcellino also accepts donations.

MEET THE LOCALS

ABC Sydney fun moment

The place: Leichhardt oval in May 2003. The task: Commentators Tim Gavel and former rugby league international Mark Geyer were preparing to preview a football game between the local Wests Tigers and the Brisbane Broncos. The outcome: Just before they went to air, they were distracted by an under-6's game being played in pouring rain, featuring a player who was more footy jumper than footballer, but made up for it by tackling everyone, including his own team. Instead of doing the preview, they began commentating on this game and tears of laughter ensued. It's immortalised on the web at www.abc.net.au/sydney/stories/s850261.htm

MEET THE LOCALS

An immortal local

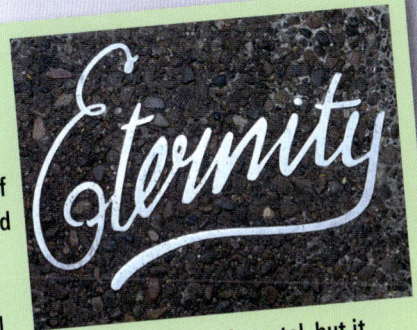

Search the ground of the sunken courtyard between Sydney's Town Hall and St Andrew's Cathedral and you'll find the Eternity symbol. It's cast in metal, but it emulates the copperplate of Arthur Stace (1885–1967) who chalked it on pavements all over the city in the latter years of his life, to remind people that's there more to life than their immediate concerns. Appropriately, it was emblazoned on the Sydney Harbour Bridge to mark the millennium celebrations in 2000.

ABC Newcastle and Upper Hunter

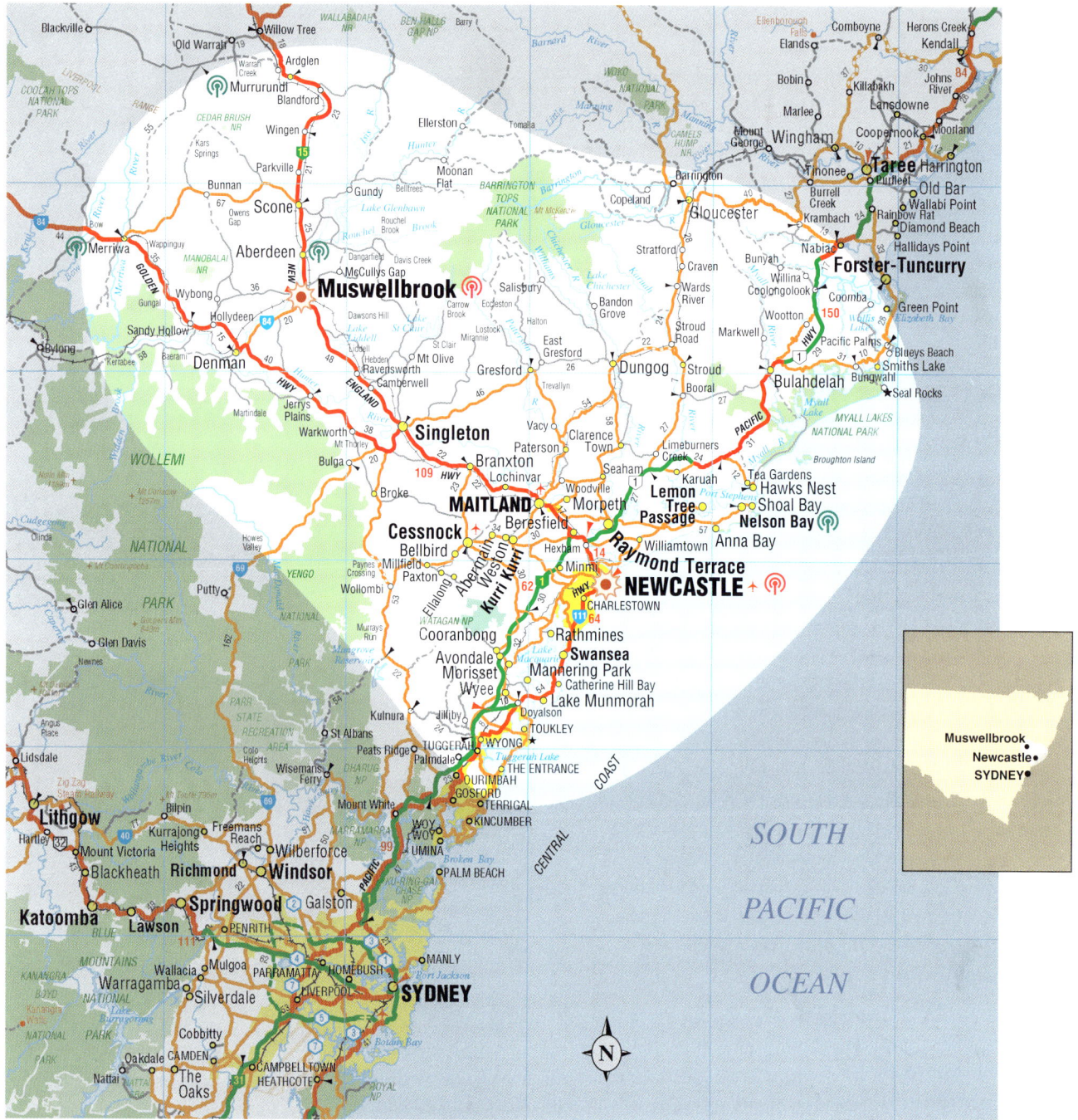

Location of ABC Local Radio studio

Local Radio Frequencies

Cessnock	1044 AM 1233 AM	
Dungog	1044 AM 1233 AM	
Gloucester	1044 AM	100.9 FM ABC Mid North Coast
Hawks Nest	1233 AM	
Lake Macquarie	1233 AM	
Maitland	1233 AM	
Muswellbrook	1044 AM	105.7 FM
Newcastle	1233 AM	
Raymond Terrace	1233 AM	
Singleton	1044 AM	105.7 FM
Stroud	1233 AM	
The Entrance	1233 AM	92.5 FM ABC Central Coast
Tuggerah	1233 AM	92.5 FM ABC Central Coast
Wyong	1233 AM	92.5 FM ABC Central Coast
Aberdeen	105.7 FM	
Merriwa	101.9 FM	
Murrurundi	96.9 FM	
Port Stephens/ Nelson Bay	95.7 FM	
Scone	105.7 FM	1044 AM

Towns in red have their own AM transmitter
Towns in green have their own FM transmitter

Hunter Valley sunrise

Extending from Wyong in the south to beyond Nelson Bay in the north, Merriwa in the west and Muswellbrook in the north-west, the Newcastle and Upper Hunter region combines superb beaches and coastal scenery with idyllic rural towns and settings, and has some of the finest wineries in the world. Little wonder that the locals regard their lifestyle as among the best in the country.

Add to this the extensive inland waterways and you have a recreational paradise. There are also national parks on both sides of the broad expanse of the Hunter Valley, featuring superb mountain scenery and opportunities for bushwalking and bird-watching.

Serving this community and the large numbers of visitors from all over the world, ABC Newcastle and Upper Hunter covers an area with a population of more than 692 000 people, and has been broadcasting to the people of the Hunter for more than six decades. The station has covered the highs and the lows of the local community – from the Newcastle earthquake and the end of steel production at BHP to the Grand Final win of the local football team, the Knights.

NOT TO BE MISSED

- Watch ships come and go while you dine at **Newcastle**'s refurbished Wharf Precinct
- Sample the many fine wines of the **Hunter Valley**'s numerous wineries
- Shop for antiques in charming rural villages like **Dungog**, **Merriwa** and **Scone**
- Enjoy the superb (and vast) waterways of **Lake Macquarie** and **Port Stephens**
- Savour the beautiful scenic drive to **Wollombi**; there are convict-built roads along the way

TOURISM AUSTRALIA

LOCAL EVENTS

Jan **Lower Hunter:** Vintage Festival

Mar **Newcastle:** Beaumont Street Jazz and Arts Festival

Apr **Lake Macquarie:** Heritage Afloat **Maitland:** Heritage Month

May **Lovedale (near Cessnock):** Lovedale Long Lunch **Morpeth:** Jazz Festival

Aug– Newcastle: Cathedral **Sept** Flower Festival

Sept **Maitland:** Garden Ramble **Wollombi:** Folk Festival

Oct **Cessnock:** Jazz in the Vines; Opera in the Vineyards **Newcastle:** Mattara Festival **Singleton:** Festival of Wine and Roses

Dec **Newcastle:** King Street Fair

MEET THE LOCALS

River stories

From bustling Newcastle to the tiniest towns and rural communities, everyone in the region has one thing in common, the Hunter River. As part of its community, ABC Newcastle and Upper Hunter has collected stories of the river all the way from its source to the sea. They're featured in a special section of the ABC Backyard website. Stories of wine pioneers, working boats, steelworks and the working port abound. This image is of Moonan Flat, the place where creeks coming down from the Barrington Tops join to form the river.

Newcastle

The city of Newcastle (population 270 324) is the second-largest in New South Wales. It has had its fair share of setbacks, having suffered earthquake and the closure of its steel operation. But Newcastle is a resilient place. It has enjoyed a revival in recent years with its waterfront areas becoming less industrialised and more devoted to recreation. The city has a thriving arts scene, the local footy team is idolised and it has some of the best surf beaches in the country.

SIGHTS AND ACTIVITIES • Enjoy a meal or a stroll along the waterfront at Queens Wharf; visit its boutique brewery and the observation tower which is linked by walkway to the City Mall • Visit King Edward Park, also on the waterfront, with its gardens, views, rotunda, public pool and more • See native animals in their natural habitat, bird-watch and picnic in the 182 hectares of bushland at Blackbutt Reserve • Marvel at the tales of shipwrecks and the town's military history in the museums at Fort Scratchley, above Newcastle Harbour • Cruise nearby Lake Macquarie, four times the size of Sydney Harbour, and in the waterside suburb of Wangi Wangi visit artist William Dobell's house • Delve into aviation history at Fighter World at the Williamtown Air Base

VISITOR INFORMATION
Wheeler Place, 363 Hunter Street (02) 4974 2999

Cessnock

The gateway to the vineyards of the Hunter Valley, Cessnock (population 14 860) is a charming country town. Other industries include mining and beef cattle, but wine, gourmet produce and tourism are the mainstays. The wineries literally start where the suburbs end.

SIGHTS AND ACTIVITIES • Tour some of the more than 60 wineries in the immediate vicinity of town • Play golf at one of the several first-rate courses on the outskirts of town and nearby • Take an early-morning balloon flight over the vineyards • Hire a bike and ride the mostly undulating country roads • Trail ride (horses for hire) through the Brokenback Range • Shop for antiques and artworks in town

VISITOR INFORMATION
Lot 111, Main Road, Pokolbin (02) 4990 4477

TOURISM AUSTRALIA

Muswellbrook

The main centre of the Upper Hunter Valley, Muswellbrook (population 10 541) is surrounded by large open-cut coalmines and is also a focus for the region's agricultural industry. Nearby, there are plenty of fine wineries, extending west and south towards Denman and Broke.

SIGHTS AND ACTIVITIES • Visit the art gallery in the old Town Hall, or take a self-guide historic town tour (brochure available) • Find out about wineries, tastings and sales at the Upper Hunter Wine Centre • Hike the Wollemi National Park, with its rugged scenery and the famed Wollemi pine, one of the oldest tree species on earth • Take the back road through Denman to Rylstone, for excellent scenery and access to the wineries of Mudgee, then return to Sydney via the Blue Mountains

VISITOR INFORMATION
87 Hill Street (02) 6541 4050

Nelson Bay

Situated on a peninsula with the wide, beautiful bay of Port Stephens on one side and the ocean on the other, this pleasant coastal town of 7001 people is an ideal location for every kind of water sport. Little wonder that this area is an immensely popular visitor destination, especially as Newcastle and the Hunter Valley are just a short drive away.

SIGHTS AND ACTIVITIES • Visit the restored Inner Lighthouse, which includes a museum of local history • Walk the heritage trail between Dutchmans Bay and Little Beach (brochure available) • Cruise on dolphin- and whale-watching tours, or around Port Stephens itself • Tour by four-wheel drive along the immense coastal dune system, charter a dive boat, hire a canoe or bike • Amuse the kids at Toboggan Hill Park with toboggan runs, minigolf, indoor rock-climbing and more

VISITOR INFORMATION
Victoria Parade (02) 4981 1579

LOCAL TIPS

- **Scone**, the world's second-largest horse-breeding centre, boasts a Gabriel Sterk sculpture of a mare and foal, and the Australian Stock Horse Museum
- There are numerous historic sandstone buildings along the convict-built Flags Road, near **Merriwa**
- Pass the time at the giant sundial on the riverbank in **Singleton**'s James Cook Park
- **Lake St Clair**, north of Singleton, is a haven for water sports and offers lakeside camping and fine views of the Mount Royal Range
- Visit the superb Hunter Region Botanic Gardens at **Raymond Terrace**

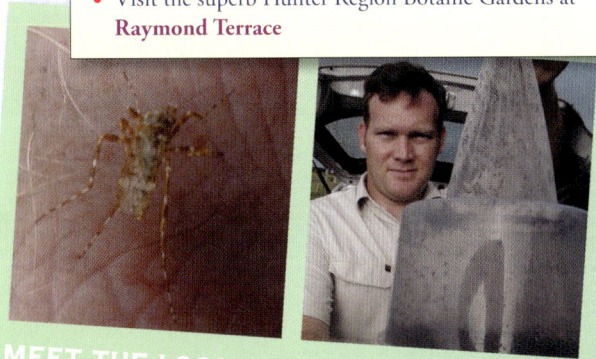

MEET THE LOCALS

The mozzie hunter

His name is Dr Cameron Webb and he's an entomologist who hunts for mosquitoes as part of his work for the Hunter Catchment Management Trust 'to better understand the ecology of the mosquitoes in the Hunter region and to help plan for mosquito control'. And you would, considering the area is home to the Hexham grey, 'probably one of the biggest you'll see, up to three or five times larger than the common mosquito', Dr Webb says. 'The immature stage of that mosquito is predatory – it's kind of like the shark of the mosquito world.'

LOCAL KNOWLEDGE

Shipwrecks

The coastline around Newcastle is full of extraordinary tales of navigational mishaps, and ships and lives lost in storms. They include the loss of the SS *Cawarra* in the Great Gale of 1866. However, a more recent disaster was the *Sygna*, swept ashore by a powerful storm 30 years ago. The crew were saved in a daring rescue and, while much of the ship was salvaged, the stern section remains a grim reminder of the dangers of the sea.

ABC Illawarra

Location of ABC Local Radio studio

Local Radio Frequencies		
Bowral	97.3 FM	
Helensburgh	97.3 FM	702 AM ABC Sydney
Huskisson	97.3 FM	
Kiama	97.3 FM	
Mittagong	97.3 FM	
Moss Vale	97.3 FM	
Nowra	97.3 FM	
Picton	97.3 FM	
Ulladulla	97.3 FM	
Wollongong	97.3 FM	

Wollongong has the only transmitter (FM) in the region

Coastline near Wollongong

E xtending south from the Royal National Park along the coast to Shoalhaven, and inland to the Southern Highlands, this region has a more temperate climate, unlike much of the New South Wales coast. There are four distinct seasons to the year here, and summer is often milder than further north.

As a consequence, the vegetation is often lush and the fields verdant. Added to this is the marvellous terrain, with a coastal plain abutting the majestic slopes and peaks of the Illawarra escarpment, where scenic lookouts and spectacular waterfalls abound. On the coast, dairy farms proliferate, and a wealth of cheeses can be found in the gourmet delis of the towns. Up in the highlands, cool-climate gardens are one of the major attractions.

Serving the coastal and highlands communities, ABC Illawarra presents morning and afternoon programming that addresses the agricultural, social and recreational issues affecting the people who live in or visit this multi-faceted region. Programming is also shared with ABC South East New South Wales.

NOT TO BE MISSED

- Fish, swim or stroll one of the Illawarra's finest beaches at **Seven Mile Beach National Park**
- Delve into one of Australia's most extensive cave systems at **Wombeyan Caves**
- Windsurf or sail the smooth waters of **Lake Illawarra**
- Dive or snorkel in the clear waters of Bass Point, **Shellharbour**

TOURISM AUSTRALIA

Tulip Time, Bowral

- See the superb displays of tulips in **Bowral** and other highland towns during September and October

MEET THE LOCALS
Little terns

One good turn deserves another, the saying goes, and on the beaches of the Illawarra and Shoalhaven, one good turn can save several. Little terns nest on the ground, usually in the sand dunes, which makes them particularly vulnerable to disturbance. National Parks officers monitor colonies, some of which have been devastated by things as unpredictable as hailstorms. Keeping an eye out when walking in the dunes and turning away from nests can make a difference, too.

MEET THE LOCALS
The fish buoy

They're a fab fad on the south coast of New South Wales (that's FAD for 'fish attracting buoys', not fad as in a 'temporary, irrational pursuit'). Funded by recreational fishing licences, the buoys have ropes suspended beneath them. Certain species of blue-water fish are attracted by objects in the ocean that stay in one place, and tend to loiter around them. Ten have been installed to date and have improved the chances of hooking a big one.

Wollongong

This big, busy industrial city, centred on the steelworks and coal-loading facility, is set in a spectacular location between the sea and the escarpment, which provides some of the best scenery in the State. Its award-winning university is putting Wollongong on the map with its work in Nano technologies. Wollongong (population 219 761) also offers great surfing, opportunities for four-wheel-drive adventures, wonderful lookouts and much more.

SIGHTS AND ACTIVITIES • Enjoy several excellent beaches • Stroll among the fishing fleet at Wollongong Harbour or visit the lighthouse that dates from 1872 • Try a walk or four-wheel-drive tour of the city or surrounds (brochures available) • See the Nan Tien Temple, just south of town; it's the largest Buddhist temple in the Southern Hemisphere • Let loose with boating, sailboarding or fishing at the large sheltered waterway of Lake Illawarra • Take in the superb combination of coastal and mountain scenery from lookouts at Stanwell Tops, Sublime Point, Mount Keira, Mount Kembla and Bulli Pass

VISITOR INFORMATION
93 Crown Street (02) 4227 5545

Kiama

The main attraction is the famous blowhole, which can spout up to 60 metres when the sea is particularly boisterous. However, even without its tourist drawcard, this dairying and mixed farming town (population 11 711) has plenty of charm to attract visitors.

SIGHTS AND ACTIVITIES

• Trace your family history at the Family History Centre, which has a collection of records from around the world • At Blowhole Point, feed the pelicans, visit the Pilots Cottage Historical Museum or enjoy a coffee • Drive to nearby Jamberoo, located in one of the most picturesque areas of the coast • Visit the award-winning Minnamurra Rainforest Centre, just west of Jamberoo • Watch or go sailboarding at superb Seven Mile Beach, just south of Kiama • Further south, browse the antique shops, cafes and restaurants at picture-postcard Berry

VISITOR INFORMATION
Blowhole Point Road (02) 4232 3322

Mittagong

Considered the gateway to the Southern Highlands, Mittagong (population 6088) has many historic buildings, but the cool-climate gardens are the main attraction.

SIGHTS AND ACTIVITIES • Take a stroll along the stunning Box Vale Walking Track • Tour the Wombeyan Caves after taking the 60-kilometre scenic drive along a narrow winding road • Visit the Bradman Museum or enjoy the floral displays during Tulip Time in Bowral • In nearby Berrima, tour the many historic buildings and antique shops, browse for books or lunch in the historic pub

VISITOR INFORMATION
62–70 Main Street (02) 4871 2888

Moss Vale

Considered the industrial and agricultural centre of the Southern Highlands, Moss Vale (population 6108) is also a charming town that retains much of the character of times gone by.

SIGHTS AND ACTIVITIES • Take a walk around the town's many historic buildings (brochure available) • Go bird-watching at Cecil Hoskins Nature Reserve • Discover A Little Piece of Scotland at nearby Sutton Forest • Walk or drive via the charming towns of Exeter and Bundanoon to several spectacular lookouts in Morton National Park

VISITOR INFORMATION
See Mittagong above.

Nowra

The major centre in the Shoalhaven district, Nowra (population 17 614) is a gateway to a number of popular holiday destinations, and also an excellent place to sample some of the district's fine dairy produce and seafood, especially oysters.

SIGHTS AND ACTIVITIES • Visit significant historic buildings including the Historic Houses Trust's Meroogal (in town) and Bundanon, the latter a gift to the nation from artist Arthur Boyd, west of town • Fish, canoe, sail or cruise along the Shoalhaven River • Enjoy the Australian Naval Aviation Museum at HMAS *Albatross* • Take in the wonderful scenery at nearby Kangaroo Valley, which has several historic pubs, buildings and bridges • See some of the whitest sands in the world at nearby Huskisson, on Jervis Bay, which has a wonderful enclosed waterway, several first-rate museums and exhibitions, and dolphin and whale-watching tours

VISITOR INFORMATION
Cnr Princes Highway and Pleasant Way (02) 4421 0778

LOCAL TIPS

- Near **Bundanoon**, see glow worms at night in the Glow Worm Glen, reached after a 25-minute walk from the end of William Street
- Berkelouw's Book Barn, 3 kilometres south of **Berrima**, has more than 200 000 second-hand books to browse
- **Robertson**, at the top of the Macquarie Pass, has some extraordinary scenery, and was the site for many of the locations in the film *Babe*
- The Cockatoo Run is a superb scenic train journey from **Port Kembla** to **Robertson** (Tuesday, Thursday and weekends, March to November)
- Catch prawns, fish, surf or swim at **Culburra** and **Lake Wollumboola**

MEET THE LOCALS

The fish girl

That's Bonita 'Snagger' Brown. Normally the presenter of ABC Illawarra's 'Afternoon Show', every Wednesday from 3pm it becomes 'The Big Fish', with all the news and issues on fishing along the South Coast of New South Wales. Like all good reporters, Bonita (not to be confused with bonito, a fish) knows the importance of hooking a big story. So lured by the tales on 'The Big Fish', and breaming with enthusiasm, she's taken to fishing like bait to water.

LOCAL KNOWLEDGE

Apocalypse daily

While holidaying in the Shoalhaven, don't be surprised if you feel you're about to be attacked. Near Nowra is HMAS Albatross, a naval aviation centre (which includes a Naval Aviation Museum) where training for everything from sea rescues to parachute jumps is carried out. It's the base for such aircraft as the new Seasprite (pictured) and the workhorse Seakings, which also saw action during the 1998 Sydney to Hobart Yacht Race, rescuing crews from yachts in distress.

ABC North Coast

Location of ABC Local Radio studio

Local Radio Frequencies	
Grafton	738 AM
Maclean	738 AM
Murwillumbah	720 AM
Tweed Heads	720 AM
Woolgoolga	738 AM
Yamba	738 AM
Alstonville	94.5 FM
Ballina	94.5 FM
Bangalow	94.5 FM
Bonalbo	91.3 FM
Byron Bay	94.5 FM
Casino	94.5 FM
Coraki	94.5 FM
Kyogle	94.5 FM
Lennox Head	94.5 FM
Lismore	94.5 FM
Nimbin	94.5 FM
Tenterfield	88.9 FM
Wollongbar	94.5 FM
Woodburn	94.5 FM

Towns in red have their own AM transmitter
Towns in green have their own FM transmitter

Cape Byron Lighthouse

The far north coast of New South Wales has long been a highly evocative region in the State. It's widely considered to be paradise, with a superb climate, magnificent beaches, relaxed pace of life and delectable local produce – this against a backdrop of spectacularly rugged mountain ranges.

The area is dotted with idyllic seaside fishing villages, pleasant country towns and scenic mountain hamlets. The many drives through the area can be breathtaking, the waterways almost boundless, the activities endless. On the coast you can go surfing, fishing, whale-watching, boating, hang-gliding and camping. Inland you can go white-water rafting, bird-watching, hiking or simply antique-shopping. The region is also renowned for its strong arts, music and film industries.

ABC North Coast began broadcasting from Grafton in the Clarence Valley in 1936 and later moved to new studios in Lismore in 1989. Local programming extends through the morning from 6am, with additional local production between 2pm and 4pm.

NOT TO BE MISSED

- Surf one of New South Wales' most famous breaks at **Watego**'s, Byron Bay
- Climb to the summit of the spectacular **Mount Warning**, for incredible views of the Border Ranges, Murwillumbah and the coast
- Take a scenic drive through the **Tweed Range** and through the **Border Ranges'** World Heritage forests
- Go on a Woollool Woollool Aboriginal Cultural Tour from **Tenterfield** to the striking Bald Rock monolith

TOURISM AUSTRALIA
Surfing off Watego's

Stall at The Channon market

TOURISM AUSTRALIA

Lismore

The major centre in the north-east of the State, Lismore (population 28 380) is the centre of a lush farming area with dairy cattle, beef cattle, macadamias, mangoes and a wide range of other produce. It's also a university town, and surrounded by spectacular national parks with incredibly rugged rainforest ranges. And then there's the fascinating alternative lifestyle community that is dotted throughout the area.

SIGHTS AND ACTIVITIES • Take in the rainforest on Lismore's doorstep, at the 6-hectare Rotary Rainforest Reserve and boardwalk or at the information centre • Cruise the Richmond River on the MV *Bennelong* • Visit the Regional Art Gallery or the Richmond River Historical Museum • Sample alternative culture in the fascinating town of Nimbin, or at the markets at The Channon, the second Sunday of each month • Tour Rocky Creek Dam (platypus-viewing), Minyon Falls and Nightcap National Park, north of town

VISITOR INFORMATION
Cnr Ballina and Molesworth streets (02) 6622 0122

Byron Bay

Situated at the most easterly point of Australia, Byron Bay (population 6130) is the capital of the northern New South Wales holiday coast. Superb surfing beaches and lovely coastal townships stretch away to the north and south, in an area regarded as having one of the most liveable climates in the world. Byron itself is a cosmopolitan centre with a dazzling range of shopping, dining and pampering opportunities. Accommodation ranges from sumptuous five-star to cosy B&Bs and budget backpackers.

SIGHTS AND ACTIVITIES • Shop in town for New-Age products, discount surfboards, locally made jewellery and timber products • Bushwalk, hang-glide, fish, swim, dive and skydive in the surrounding area • Watch for dolphins (year-round) and whales (June to July and September to October) at Cape Byron Lighthouse, where there's also a visitor centre • For a pleasant break from Byron's hustle and bustle, nearby Bangalow has pleasant cafes, antique shops and more

VISITOR INFORMATION
80 Jonson Street (02) 6685 8050

LOCAL KNOWLEDGE
Lying down for what you believe in

In a region renowned for its strong support for a variety of causes, be they environmental, social or political, it's no surprise that when it chooses to the New South Wales north coast can send a message that's heard around the world. Take the anti-war protest in early 2003. Organisers hoped up to 100 women would bare all to send a message to the federal government. Instead, 750 women lay down in a secluded field near the village of Federal to make a heart symbol and spell out 'No War' using nothing but their bodies – acting locally, the media attention was global.

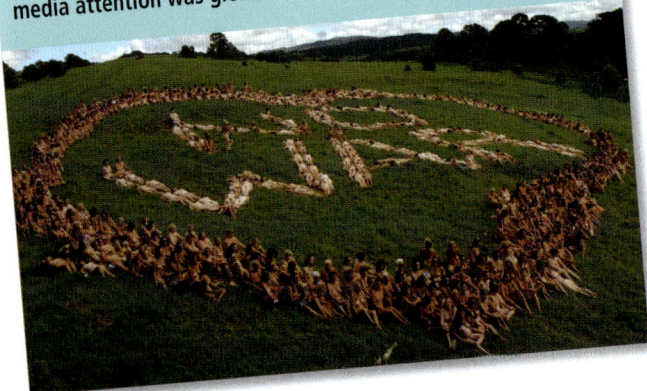

Grafton

This lovely garden city (population 16 562) on the Clarence River was the first city on the North Coast. Today it is the centre of a beef cattle and sugarcane region.

SIGHTS AND ACTIVITIES • Be impressed by the city's beautiful historic buildings, including the cathedral • Hire a RiverCat for a self-drive or skippered cruise • Admire the superb tree-lined streets and numerous parks and gardens • Canoe or raft the rivers of the nearby national parks • Enjoy fresh prawns from Yamba, or take a refreshing plunge at its ocean beaches

VISITOR INFORMATION
Pacific Highway, South Grafton
(02) 6642 4677

Murwillumbah

Set among sugarcane fields on the Tweed River just a few kilometres from the coast, this charming town (population 7657) in the beautiful Tweed Valley (actually the core of a gigantic extinct volcano) offers access to numerous coastal and inland activities.

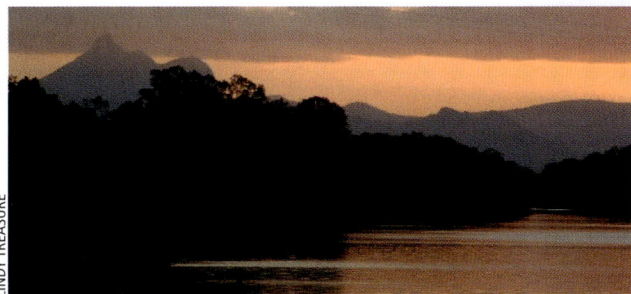
White-water rafting near Grafton
TOURISM AUSTRALIA

SIGHTS AND ACTIVITIES • Visit the World Heritage Rainforest Centre • Head for Mount Warning National Park, in the centre of the Mount Warning caldera, and if you're fit follow the track to the top for great views of the area • Hire a houseboat for a relaxing cruise on the Tweed • Head north to sample tea at Madura Estates and tour a sugar mill (at Condong, July to November) • Take a six-wheel-drive trip to the top of Banana Mountain at Pioneer Plantation

VISITOR INFORMATION
World Heritage Rainforest Centre, cnr Pacific Highway and Alma Street (02) 6672 1340

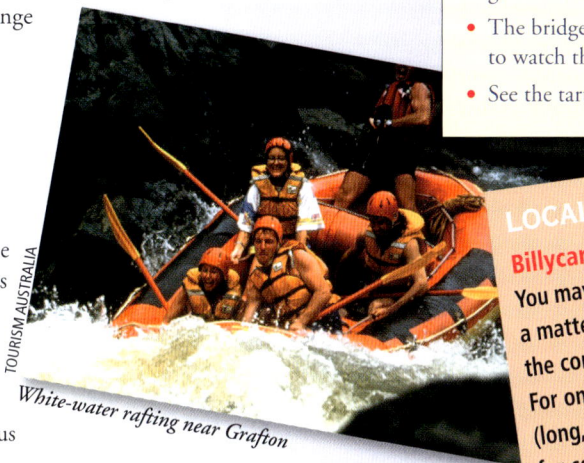
LINDY TREASURE
Tweed River and Mount Warning

LOCAL TIPS

- Try fossicking for gold, quartz and labradorite at **Casino**
- Enjoy a pub lunch at the classic New Brighton Hotel, 7 kilometres from Brunswick Heads at **Billinudgel**
- Another great surfing location is **The Point**, below Pat Morton Lookout near Lennox Head
- Catch up with the prawning fleet at **Evans Head** for freshly caught seafood
- The World Heritage **Bundjalung National Park** is great for fishing, swimming, canoeing and hiking
- The bridge over the Clarence in **Grafton** is a great spot to watch the sunset
- See the tartan power poles in **Maclean**

LOCAL KNOWLEDGE

Billycart races

You may find it hard to take seriously, but it's actually a matter of some gravity. For it's gravity that powers the contestants in Bangalow's annual Billycart Derby. For one day in May, the charming town's main street (long, straight and quite steep) becomes the racetrack for contestants of all ages. There are local and open competitions, with competitors coming from interstate trying to roll the opposition.

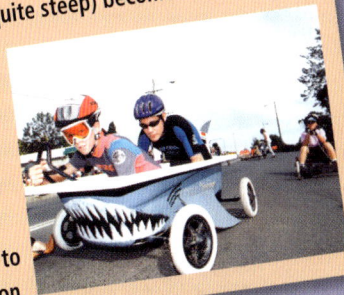

LOCAL KNOWLEDGE

Enlightenment!

Every year it shines brighter and brighter. It's Lismore's annual Rivers of Light lantern festival. The culmination of months of lantern-making workshops comes with a massive street parade, where everything from tiny lanterns to giant creatures, people and objects bring a warm inner glow to the night of the winter solstice in late June.

ABC Mid North Coast

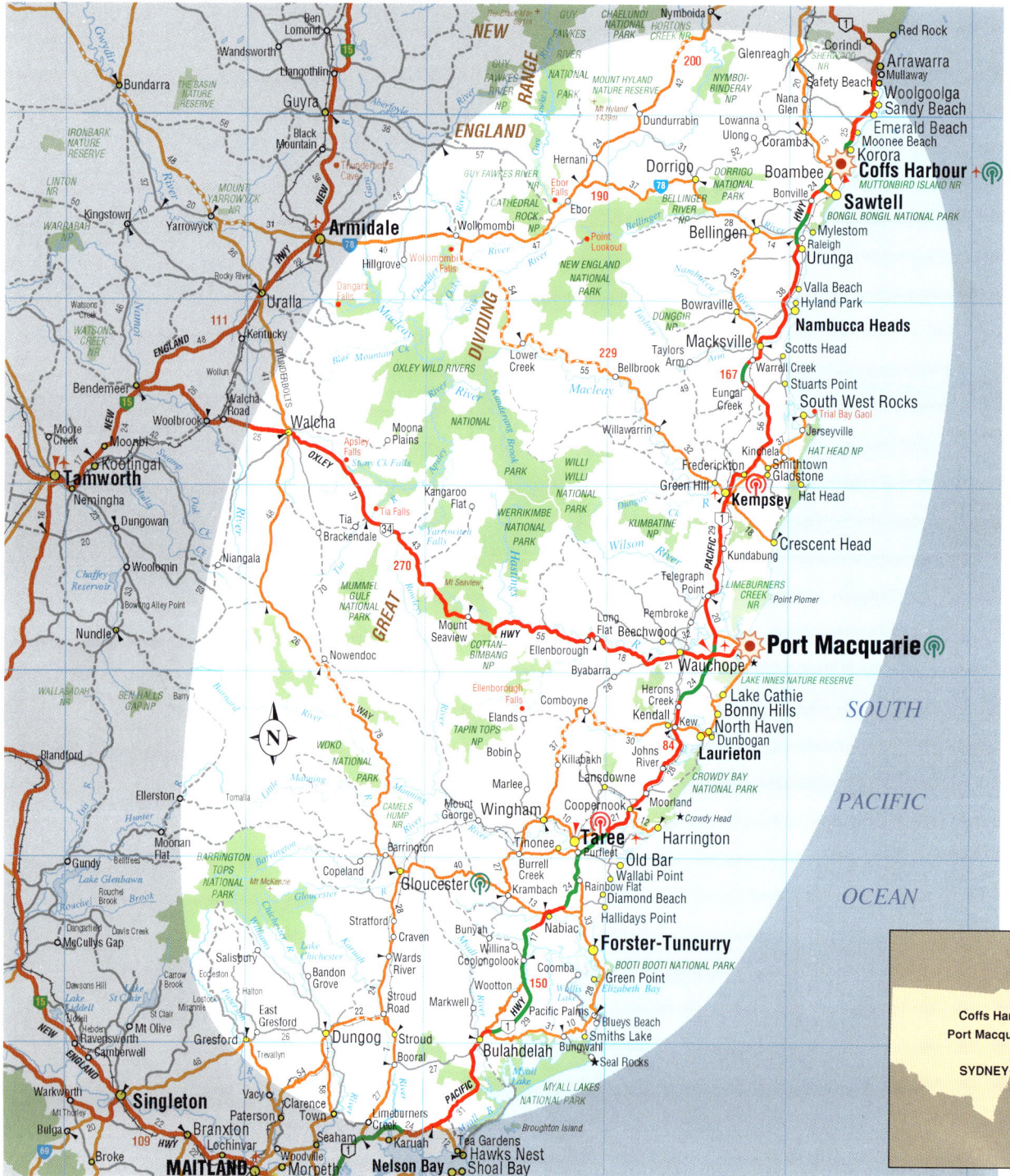

Location of ABC Local Radio studio

Local Radio Frequencies		
Kempsey	684 AM	92.3 FM
South West Rocks	684 AM	92.3 FM
Taree	756 AM	95.5 FM
Wingham	756 AM	95.5 FM
Bellingen	92.3 FM	738 AM ABC North Coast
Bulahdelah	95.5 FM	756 AM
Coffs Harbour	92.3 FM	
Comboyne	95.5 FM	756 AM
Dorrigo	92.3 FM	
Forster-Tuncurry	95.5 FM	756 AM
Gloucester	100.9 FM	
Kendall	95.5 FM	756 AM
Laurieton	95.5 FM	756 AM
Macksville	92.3 FM	684 AM
Nambucca Heads	92.3 FM	684 AM
Port Macquarie	95.5 FM	
Wauchope	95.5 FM	
Woolgoolga	92.3 FM	

Towns in red have their own AM transmitter
Towns in green have their own FM transmitter

Sunrise, Boambee

There are three distinct strips in this beautiful region of coastal New South Wales. First there are several hundred kilometres of near-perfect beaches, studded with pleasant fishing ports and seaside villages. Just inland of the beaches is a vast region of rich farmland producing dairy products, vegetables, beef and timber. And behind them is the unbroken line of mountain ranges of the Great Divide. Taken altogether, it's an incredibly popular holiday destination in summer, and a pleasant place to escape to year-round.

The locals, however, will tell you that the best thing about their region is the lifestyle. There's plenty of diversity, a great sense of community and a relaxed unhurried pace that's the envy of most visitors to the area.

ABC Radio's Mid North Coast studios were first opened in Kempsey in 1956 and an additional outpost opened at Coffs Harbour in 1997. In February 2004 the Kempsey studio moved to new state-of-art premises in Port Macquarie.

NOT TO BE MISSED

- Scuba dive at Broughton Island in the **Myall Lakes National Park**
- Hook a big one off the rocks at **Hat Head**, a renowned fishing spot
- Enjoy the fresh catch of the day at the Fisherman's Wharf in **Coffs Harbour**
- Shop for antiques or just enjoy the relaxed ambience of the mountain towns of **Bellingen** and **Dorrigo**

Graffiti Rocks, Nambucca Heads

Coffs Harbour

One of the main centres on the Mid North Coast, Coffs Harbour (population 22 177) is studded with resorts and excellent beaches. It is also the centre of a thriving agricultural and fishing industry. Banana plantations cling to the steep hillsides near town. Coffs Harbour is also famous as the training base for the Australian Wallabies rugby team.

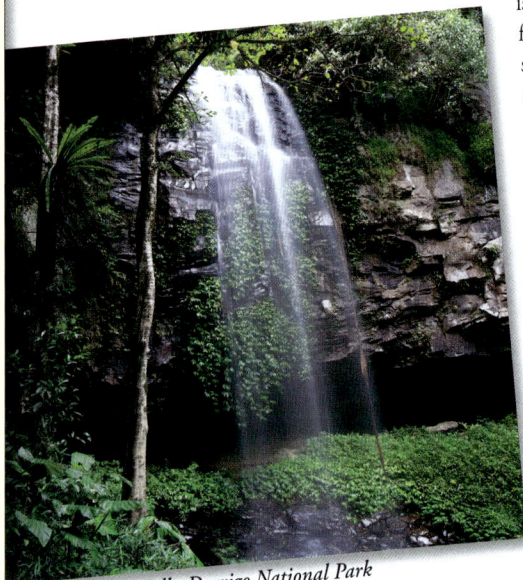
Crystal Shower Falls, Dorrigo National Park

SIGHTS AND ACTIVITIES • Take a fishing charter, scuba course or whale-watching tour (June to November) from The Marina, or view passing whales from nearby Muttonbird Island Nature Reserve • See porpoises and seals at the Pet Porpoise Pool, a research and nursery facility • Visit the Big Banana, signature attraction of the town • Enjoy the bird life and superb rainforest at the North Coast Regional Botanical Gardens • Go white-water rafting on the Nymboida River • Take a Gambaari Aboriginal Cultural Tour of the coastal area

VISITOR INFORMATION
Cnr Pacific Highway and McLean Street
(02) 6652 1522

LOCAL KNOWLEDGE

Preserving a way of life

Drive to the seaside village of Seal Rocks and along the dusty track you may see a sign that says 'We want to keep our dirt road and keep development out'. With developers eager to swoop on this idyllic spot, the locals believe a sealed road would seal their fate. Meanwhile this place has an atmosphere that's reminiscent of an earlier age, and visitors can enjoy such simple attractions as swimming, fishing and visiting historic sites like the exquisitely beautiful Sugarloaf Lighthouse, which has operated continuously since 1875.

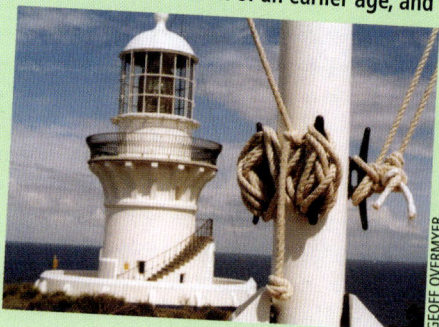
GEOFF OVERMYER

Bellingen

One of the most attractive towns in the region, Bellingen (population 2690) was formerly a timber and shipbuilding town. More recently, it has become a haven for artists and alternative lifestylers. Much of the town has been classified by the Australian Heritage Commission.

SIGHTS AND ACTIVITIES • Stroll alongside the Bellinger River, hire a canoe, or take a bike ride into the nearby forest areas • Enjoy the fine buildings along the main street while shopping for antiques and artworks – several good cafes are standing by with good coffee • Pack a picnic and take a scenic drive north-east across Never Never Creek to the Promised Land (brochure available); the road continues to Dorrigo National Park which features a Skywalk offering magnificent views, the fascinating Rainforest Centre and splendid waterfalls

VISITOR INFORMATION
Pacific Highway, Urunga (02) 6655 5711

Kempsey

The commercial centre of the incredibly fertile Macleay Valley, Kempsey (population 8630) is surrounded by dairy and horticultural operations. The town is also home to light industries, including the Akubra hat factory, and was the birthplace of country-music icon, the late Slim Dusty. Located just a little inland, it is close to two coastal towns, South West Rocks and Crescent Head, both of which have great beaches and recreational facilities.

SIGHTS AND ACTIVITIES • Visit the Cultural Centre which incorporates the Macleay River Historical Society Museum and a settler's cottage, as well as displays on Akubra hats and Slim Dusty • Watch a video of Akubra hat-making at the visitor information centre • Take a walk or scenic drive through the coastal and inland areas (brochures available); there are some interesting wineries in the area • Learn about maritime and convict history at the Boatman's Cottage (at South West Rocks) and Trial Bay Gaol (nearby); enjoy the incredible views from the headland where Smoky Cape Lighthouse is located • Surf the excellent break at Crescent Head

VISITOR INFORMATION
Cultural Centre, Pacific Highway, South Kempsey (02) 6563 1555

Port Macquarie

One of the oldest towns in the State, Port (population 33 709) has leapt ahead in recent years to become one of the most populous and popular holiday and retirement destinations on this stretch of coast. Among its attractions are its mix of surfing and safe swimming beaches.

SIGHTS AND ACTIVITIES • Visit the Hastings Historical Museum and the Mid-North Coast Maritime Museum, and don't miss the convict-built St Thomas Church, the third-oldest surviving church in Australia • Observe coastal vegetation and wildlife in the heart of town at Kooloonbung Creek Nature Reserve • Walk along an elevated boardwalk through a canopy of coastal rainforest at Sea Acres Rainforest Centre • Watch the patients being fed and talk to the volunteer carers at the Koala Hospital • Take the walk from the breakwall to the lighthouse (8 kilometres) • Surf at one end of Town Beach, or swim safely in the coves at the other end

VISITOR INFORMATION
Clarence Street (02) 6581 8000

LOCAL TIPS

- Enjoy a great pub lunch or dinner overlooking the river at the hotel in **Macksville**
- Discover the fascinating Sikh culture in **Woolgoolga**
- Feast on Wallis Lakes **oysters** while soaking up the view on **Forster** Main Beach
- The **Barrington Tops Forest Drive** from Gloucester to Scone provides great scenery and access to rainforest walks and picnic spots

Steam train at Timbertown

- Near Wauchope you'll find **Timbertown**, a re-creation of an 1880s sawmillers' village
- Hire a houseboat for an idyllic cruise on the expansive waterways of the **Myall Lakes**
- **Ocean Drive**, between Kew and Port Macquarie, offers 50 kilometres of stunning coastal scenery

MEET THE LOCALS
The one that didn't get away

If you have any doubts about the reputation of Hat Head (near Kempsey) for great fishing, doubt no more. This is typical of the monsters that are regularly landed by anglers on the rocks. It's a 35-kilogram jewfish caught by local, Dave Leeder. It was so big he couldn't carry it alone, so around midnight he called his mates for help. Obviously there was plenty of fresh fish to reward their efforts.

ABC New England North West

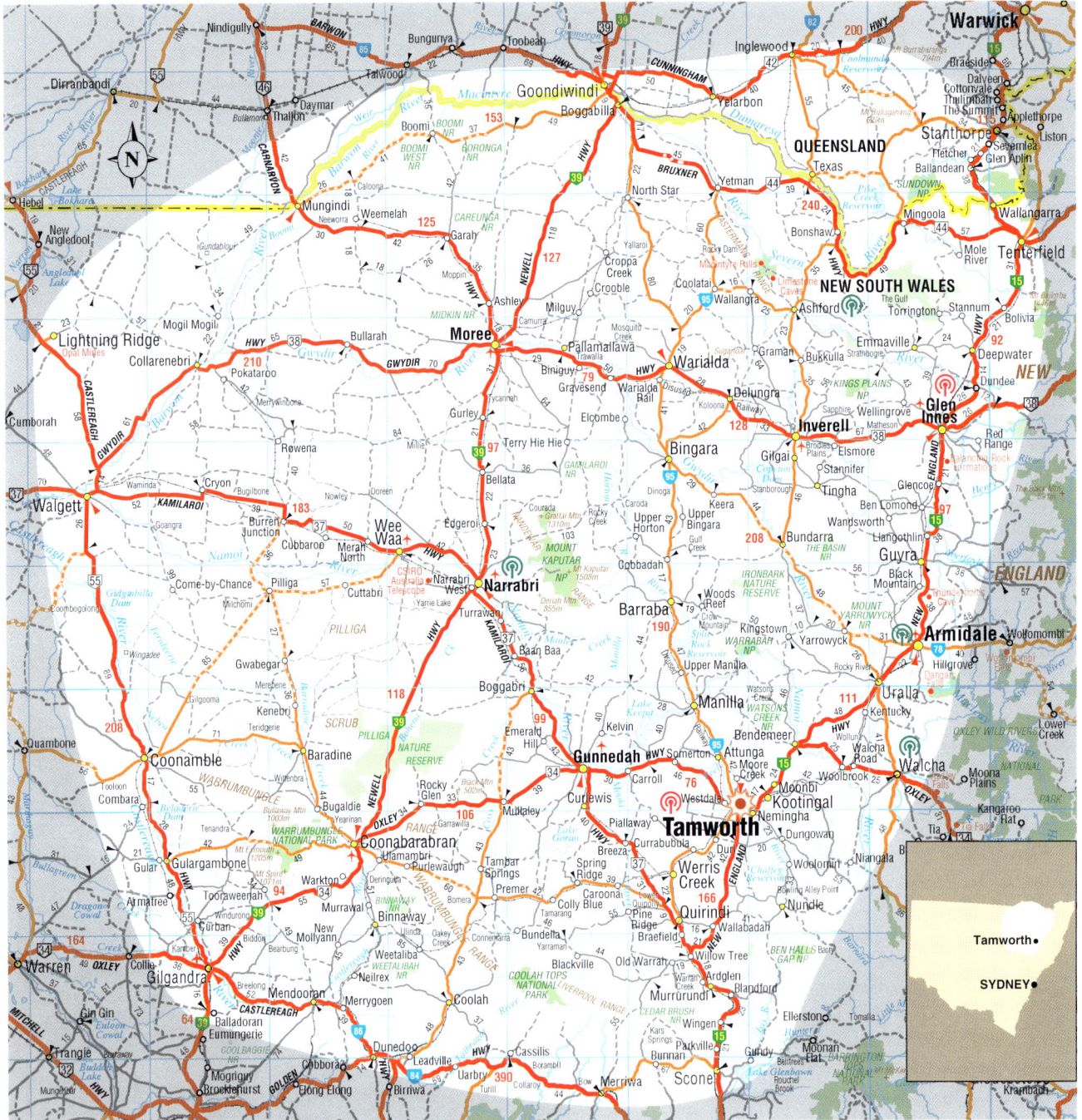

☀ Location of ABC Local Radio studio

Local Radio Frequencies

Town	AM	FM
Barraba	648 AM	
Bingara	819 AM	
Glen Innes	819 AM	
Gunnedah	648 AM	
Inverell	819 AM	
Murrurundi	648 AM	96.9 FM ABC Newcastle
Quirindi	648 AM	
Tamworth	648 AM	
Tenterfield	819 AM	88.9 FM ABC North Coast
Wee Waa	648 AM	99.1 FM
Armidale		101.9 FM
Ashford		107.9 FM
Guyra		101.9 FM
Moree		99.1 FM
Narrabri		99.1 FM
Walcha		88.5 FM

Towns in red have their own AM transmitter
Towns in green have their own FM transmitter

The territory covered by ABC New England North West is as diverse as its name is long. It ranges from the temperate high-altitude climes along the snaking line of the Great Dividing Range, to the north-western flatlands that look toward the country's sunburnt heart.

There is a diverse range of Aboriginal cultures thriving in the region, alongside European and other cultures, forming a colourful assembly of farmers and graziers, writers and artists and famous figures. Tamworth, where the ABC studios are located, is perhaps best known as Australia's home of country music.

Rural industries form an integral part of the region's economy and way of life. Cotton and grains, prime beef and wool are the mainstays of a diverse agricultural landscape. The ABC New England North West region is also notable for its natural beauty.

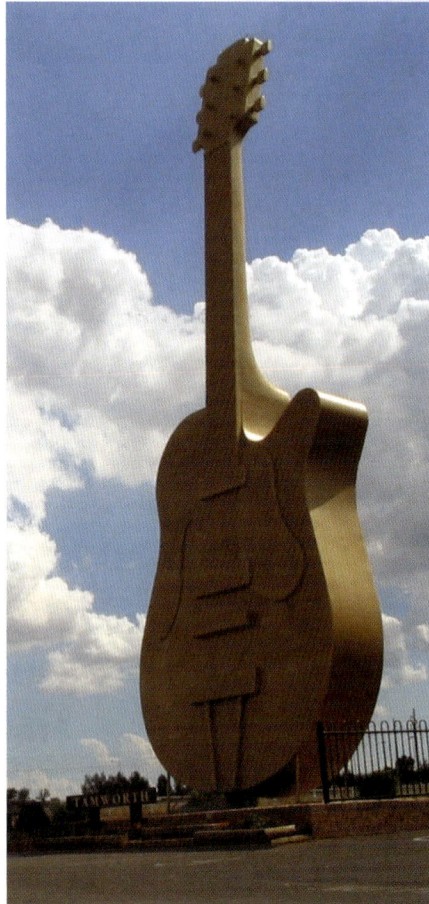

The 12-metre golden guitar, Tamworth

NOT TO BE MISSED

- Head for **Tamworth**'s annual Australian Country Music Festival, even if you're only a 'little bit country'
- See the Wollomombi Falls plunge 220 metres at **Oxley Wild Rivers National Park**
- Catch the view from the summit of **Mount Kaputar** (1508 metres); on a clear day you can see a tenth of the entire state of New South Wales
- Marvel at Australia's most significant provincial art holding, the Hinton Collection, in **Armidale**
- Fossick for everything from jasper, serpentine and crystal to diamonds, sapphires and gold on the signposted **Fossickers Way** between Nundle and Glen Innes
- From Tenterfield take a Woollool Woollool Aboriginal Tour to the extraordinary **Bald Rock Monolith**

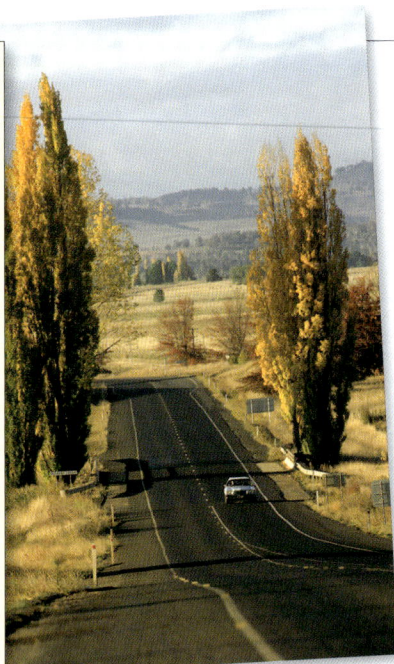
New England Highway near Armidale

MEET THE LOCALS

The pocket admirals

Don't be alarmed if you find yourself witnessing a major naval engagement in the vicinity of Armidale. It just means you've happened on the dam where members of the local squadron of the Australian Battle Group are trying to sink each other. Battleships from World War I and World War II (built at a scale of 1:144) exchange fire (ball bearings) while hunting the opposing side's freighters, all operated by remote control. The ships are sunk when holed below the waterline. More information on this growing sport (and some great photos) can be found at www.ausbg.org. Here HMS *Lion* has sunk a freighter.

Tamworth

The country-music capital of Australia, Tamworth (population 31 865) is also the main commercial centre of the thriving agricultural and mining areas of the north-west of New South Wales.

SIGHTS AND ACTIVITIES • Don't miss the Country Music Festival (January) • Visit the Golden Guitar, just south of town, and the Country Music Roll of Renown at the Radio Centre • See the hand imprints of famous country-music stars at Hands of Fame Park • Trace Tamworth's history as the first city in the Southern Hemisphere to have electric street lighting at the Power Station Museum • Visit the new Art Gallery and Library complex • Head to Oxley Lookout for views of the town and surrounding Peel Valley, and from there you can take the six-kilometre Kamilaroi Walking Track • Try line dancing at the RSL club's country-music jamboree (Thursdays), or other line-dancing venues around town

VISITOR INFORMATION
Cnr Murray and Peel streets
(02) 6755 4300

Armidale

This delightful city (population 21 330) is notable for its cold-climate gardens as it sits at 980 metres in the New England Ranges. The local architecture is remarkable and there are more than 30 National Trust-classified buildings.

SIGHTS AND ACTIVITIES • Orient yourself with a two-hour Heritage Trolley Tour • Visit the New England Regional Art Museum, which includes the famous Hinton Collection • Absorb indigenous culture at the Aboriginal Cultural Centre and Keeping Place • Discover old ways from the old days at the National Trust-classified Folk Museum • Take a tour of the university (Mondays), in particular historic Booloominbah Homestead, plus the Antiquities and Zoology museums

VISITOR INFORMATION
82 Marsh Street (02) 6772 4655

Glen Innes

Another of the lovely 'mountain towns' of the New England Ranges, Glenn Innes (population 6101) was the scene of many famous bushrangers' exploits. Today, it is the centre of a prosperous farming and sapphire-mining area.

Celtic monument

SIGHTS AND ACTIVITIES • Take a self-guide tour of the town's many historic buildings (brochure available) • See the Australian Standing Stones Celtic monument in Centennial Parklands • Visit the Land of the Beardies History House, a folk museum in extensive grounds with a slab hut and pioneer relics • Take a fishing tour to Deepwater • Fossick for sapphire, topaz and quartz around Emmaville and Torrington

VISITOR INFORMATION
152 Church Street (02) 6732 2397

Inverell

Known as Sapphire City, this lovely town (population 9378) is surrounded by fertile farming land. Zircon, sapphire, industrial diamonds and tin are mined in the area.

SIGHTS AND ACTIVITIES • Fossick at sites outside of town • Visit a working mine at DeJon Sapphire Centre • Step back into colonial times at the Pioneer Village • See working-horse memorabilia at the Draught Horse Centre • Visit the memorial to the Myall Creek Massacre, 35 kilometres south-west on the Delungra–Bingara Road

VISITOR INFORMATION
Campbell Street (02) 6722 1693

Narrabri

Located between the Nandewar Range and the Pilliga scrub, Narrabri (population 6419) is one of the north-west's major cotton towns. It's here that the mountain ranges end and the vast plains of western New South Wales begin.

SIGHTS AND ACTIVITIES • Take a tour of the cotton fields and processing plants between April and June • Visit the CSIRO Australia Telescope, an array of six large radio telescopes, and its visitor centre (open weekdays) • See the spectacular views from the summit of Mount Kaputar

VISITOR INFORMATION
Newell Highway (02) 6799 6760

LOCAL TIPS

- Don't forget your fishing rod: trout, perch and cod abound in the mountain streams around such towns as **Armidale** and **Glen Innes**
- Go bird-watching, waterskiing or sailboarding at **Lake Yarrie**, 30 kilometres west of Narrabri
- There's more great water-sport opportunities at **Copeton Dam** near Inverell
- Relieve your arthritis and rheumatism in the artesian baths at **Moree**
- **Paradise Park** in Murrurundi is surrounded by mountains and has kangaroos appearing at dusk, plus nearby you can walk through The Eye of The Needle, a small gap in the boulders with a scenic view from the top of the rock formation

MEET THE LOCALS

The yarn spinner

In an area full of great local history, there are plenty of fascinating stories doing the rounds of the north-west. One of the best storytellers is Bingara Historical Society's Bob Kirk. His stories can often be heard on ABC New England North West's 'Breakfast Postcard' segment, like the one about the truckie carrying a load of caged birds. Unable to climb the Moonbi Ranges, he went around and banged on the cages until all the birds flew off their perches. Having thus lightened his load, he climbed the mountains with ease.

MEET THE LOCALS

The gentleman bushranger

On the highway at Uralla, you can meet the man known as the Gentleman Bushranger, Fred 'Thunderbolt' Ward. He operated around the New England region in the 1860s, before being shot dead in May 1870 at Uralla. His statue can be seen there, but in Walcha, you'll also find an interesting relic thought to belong to him. Thunderbolt was a small man, weighing around 55 kilograms. In the 1890s a young lad found a saddle in a cave in the area that clearly belonged to someone quite small. The suspicion is that it was Thunderbolt's and the saddle can still be seen in the Walcha Pioneer Cottage.

ABC Central West and Western Plains

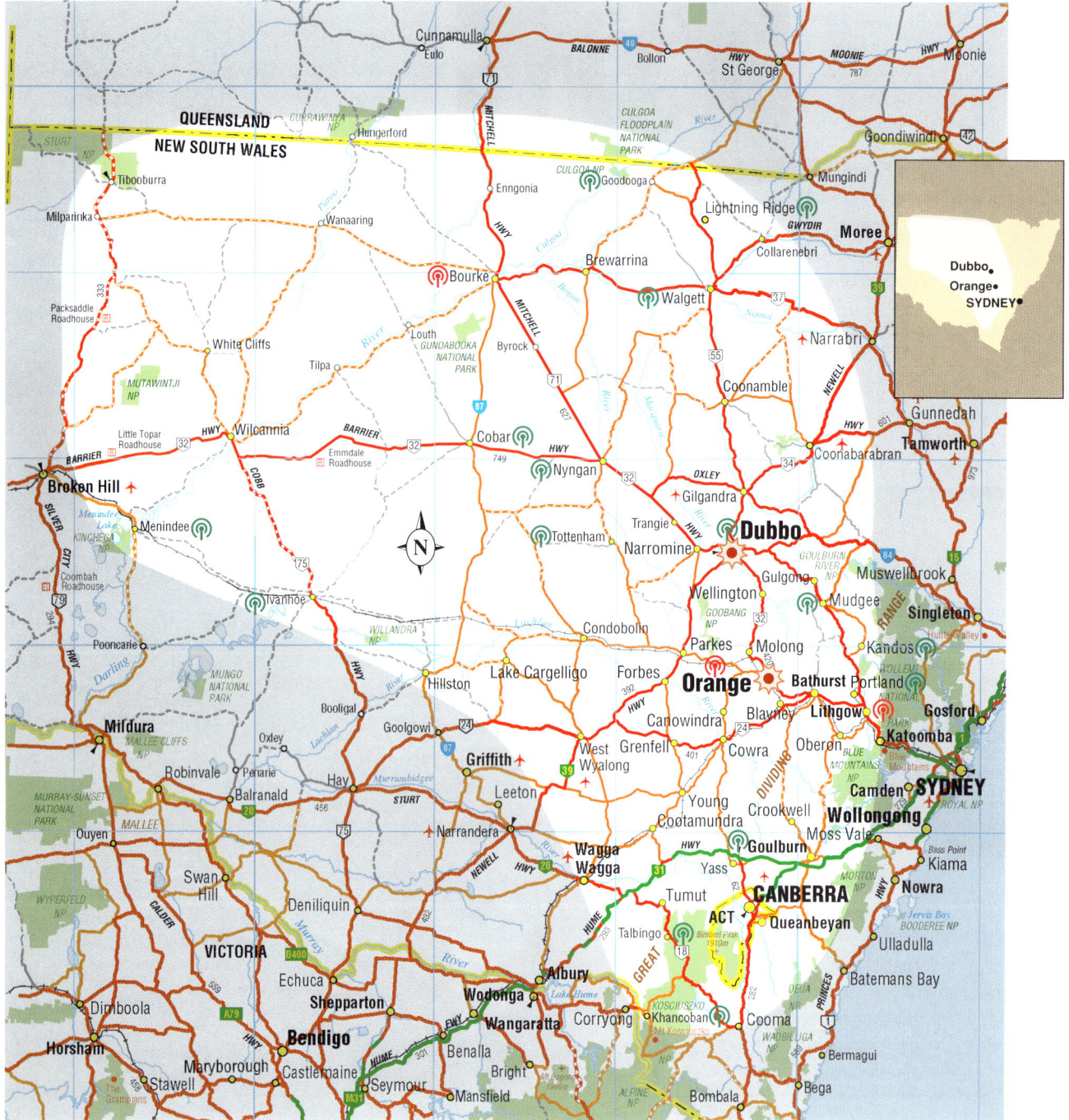

⊙ Location of ABC Local Radio studio

The ABC's Central West and Western Plains studios cover an area of approximately 400 000 square kilometers – half the State of New South Wales! The Central West studio based in Orange reaches about 230 000 people, while the Western Plains studio in Dubbo reaches about 100 000 people.

The station has three major transmitters at Byrock, near Bourke, Mount Cenn Cruaich, near Coonabarabran and Cumnock to the north-west of Orange. The Cumnock transmitter pumps out 50 kilowatts of power and was installed in1937 to get radio to as many people as possible. People often report hearing it all over eastern Australia

Radio telescope, Parkes

and even as far away as Sweden! There are also sixteen other smaller transmitters across the region, which fill in some of the radio blackspots. Coverage extends from White Cliffs, Tilpa and Menindee in the State's far west, up to the Queensland border and beyond, through Walgett and Coonabarabran, and around to Mudgeee and Lithgow in the east. The stations cover as far south as Goulburn and West Wyalong, and out as far as Hillston and Ivanhoe in the south-west of the state. One quirk of the service is that it is broadcast into Norfolk Island (95.9FM) via satellite, so you may hear the occasional warning about high seas while your landlocked in the middle of New South Wales.

Local Radio Frequencies

Bathurst	549 AM	
Blayney	549 AM	
Bourke	657 AM	
Brewarrina	657 AM	549 AM
Byrock	657 AM	
Canowindra	549 AM	
Condobolin	657 AM	549 AM
Cowra	549 AM	
Forbes	549 AM	
Grenfell	549 AM	
Gulgong	549 AM	
Lake Cargelligo	549 AM	
Lithgow	1395 AM	
Molong	549 AM	
Oberon	549 AM	
Orange	549 AM	
Parkes	549 AM	
Wellington	549 AM	
Cobar	106.1 FM	
Coonabarabran	107.1 FM	
Coonamble	107.1 FM	
Crookwell	106.9 FM	
Dubbo	107.1 FM	
Gilgandra	107.1 FM	
Goodooga	99.3 FM	
Goulburn	90.3 FM	
Ivanhoe	106.1 FM	
Kandos/ Rylstone	96.3 FM	
Khancoban	89.7 FM	
Lightning Ridge	92.1 FM	
Menindee	97.3 FM	
Mudgee	99.5 FM	
Narromine	107.1 FM	
Nyngan	95.1 FM	
Portland/ Wallerawang	94.1 FM	
Talbingo	88.9 FM	
Tottenham	98.9 FM	
Trangie	107.1 FM	
Walgett	105.9 FM	

Towns in red have their own AM transmitter
Towns in green have their own FM transmitter

Norfolk Island receives ABC Central West and Western Plains via satellite.

Orange

The base for the ABC in the west of New South Wales, Orange is a prosperous town of 30 705 and, along with nearby Bathurst, forms the heart of the Central West. The area around Orange is blessed with rich volcanic soils that support a variety of agricultural industries, notably wineries. The town itself preserves a fascinating gold-mining history and much of the charm of times gone by.

SIGHTS AND ACTIVITIES • Visit the birthplace of poet Banjo Paterson, marked by an obelisk and celebrated with an annual festival (February or March) • See a variety of beautiful cold-climate plants at Cook Park and the Botanic Gardens • Take a self-guide walk around the town's many historic buildings (brochure available) • See the historic diggings at Ophir, or the largest gold and copper operation in the State at Cadia Mines • Enjoy a picnic and a visit to the bird and animal sanctuary at Mount Canobolas Park • Taste wines at several cellar doors in the district

VISITOR INFORMATION
Cnr Byng and Peisley streets (02) 6393 8226

Countryside near Orange

MICHELLE HAVENSTEIN

Bathurst

Established in 1815 and the oldest town in New South Wales west of the Great Dividing Range, Bathurst enjoys a great reputation for its cattle, sheep, grain and fruit. The town of 26 029 has an abundance of classic Georgian and Victorian architecture, is the birthplace of former prime minister, Ben Chifley, and the home of Australia's most famous motor-racing circuit, Mount Panorama.

SIGHTS AND ACTIVITIES • Embrace local history at Ben Chifley's Home, the Historical Society Museum and Miss Traill's House (1845) • Drive to Mount Panorama to learn all about car racing at the National Motor Racing Museum; nearby are Bathurst Goldfields (gold-mining reconstruction) and Joseph Banks Nature Reserve • Visit Oberon in March for the Kowmung Music Festival (with chamber music in caves, sheds and other locations) • Fossick for gold at Sofala and Hill End, or be inspired by the scenery as were the artists Russell Drysdale, Donald Friend, John Olsen and Brett Whiteley • See shearing demonstrations and performing sheep, cattle and sheepdogs at Bathurst Sheep and Cattle Drome

VISITOR INFORMATION
1 Kendell Avenue (02) 6332 1444

Bourke

The centre of a vast sheep-grazing area (and more recently fruit and cotton thanks to irrigation), Bourke (population 2775) was once a major paddle-steamer port on the Darling. It is famed as the town where the outback truly begins, and poet Henry Lawson once said of it, 'If you know Bourke, you know Australia'.

SIGHTS AND ACTIVITIES • Tour the historic buildings and sites in the town and surrounding area (brochure available) • On and around the river, see the first lift-up bridge in New South Wales (1883), the Darling's only lock and weir, paddle-steamers offering trips and a replica of the historic wharf • Fly over the town and surrounds on an ultralight flight

VISITOR INFORMATION
Old Railway Station, Anson Street (02) 6872 2280

Coonabarabran

A typical New South Wales agricultural town, Coonabarabran (population 3012) is blessed with a great variety of attractions that make it a perfect base for exploring the surrounding area.

SIGHTS AND ACTIVITIES • See the massive skeleton of a diprotodon found in the area at the Australian Museum Diprotodon Display in the town's visitor information centre • Discover the wonders of space at the Skywatch Night and Day Observatory; it also has space-themed minigolf • Visit the Siding Springs Observatory, site of the Southern Hemisphere's largest optical telescope • Hike, picnic, bird-watch, spot wildflowers, rock-climb and more in the spectacular Warrumbungle National Park • Take a guided Aboriginal cultural and ecological tour to find out more about the area • Go koala spotting at The Alloes in the nearby Pilliga Scrub

VISITOR INFORMATION
Newell Highway (02) 6842 1441

LOCAL TIPS

- Bird-watchers flock to the **Macquarie Marshes**, a superb wetland area with one of the best inland bird habitats in the State
- Near Condobolin is **Mount Tilga**, considered the geographical centre of New South Wales; a steep 2-kilometre climb to the summit provides magnificent views
- **Kandos** has one of the most highly rated golf courses in inland New South Wales
- **Grenfell** is poet Henry Lawson's birthplace – there's an obelisk on the site on the road south to Young (a Henry Lawson festival is held in June)
- **Cobar** is something of an oasis in the arid far west, its Great Cobar Outback Heritage Centre a fascinating insight into the pastoral and mining industries
- **Parkes** is surrounded by superb wheat country, and is home to the radio telescope featured in the film *The Dish*

MEET THE LOCALS

The jailhouse pups

If you happen to be passing Kirconnell Correctional Centre near Bathurst and see puppies behind bars, don't worry. It's not that they've been bad to the bone or fallen foul of the long arm of the paw. They're actually part of a unique program where selected prisoners train the dogs from puppyhood to become companion animals for disabled people. There are no 'hangdog' looks, and the program is reaping benefits in prisoner attitudes as well.

MEET THE LOCALS

The amazing egg cleaner

Visit the charming central-west town of Millthorpe and among its many attractions you may find the amazing hand-operated egg cleaner. It's one of the exhibits at the Millthorpe Museum, among a vast array of historic agricultural machinery, including an 1840s wool press and Australia's oldest plough.

LOCAL KNOWLEDGE

Mount Panorama

For some people, the word Bathurst doesn't conjure images of a New South Wales country town. Instead they think of V8 super cars roaring up the famous Mount Panorama, of the famous battles between Holdens and Fords, and of household names like Brock, Moffatt, Skaife, Richards and Johnson. For ABC Central West, Bathurst can mean all these things, but at certain times of the year, the revhead takes the forefront. Regular reports on the drama at the mountain, with updates on all the action, are posted on a special section of the Backyard website: www.abc.net.au/centralwest/bathurst/

Dubbo

Considered the regional capital of western New South Wales (and the base for the ABC Western Plains studio), Dubbo is a thriving city of 30 102 with a range of attractions in town and the renowned open-range Western Plains Zoo on its outskirts.

SIGHTS AND ACTIVITIES • Spend a night with the animals at Western Plains Zoo's accommodation, or visit during the day for keeper talks and tours of some 1400 animals from five continents on the 300-hectare site • For more animals, the Dubbo Art Gallery has a constantly expanding collection of Animals in Art • Listen as animatronics convicts tell their story at the Old Dubbo Gaol • Take a cruise on the Macquarie River, or enjoy a picnic at nearby Burrendong Dam

VISITOR INFORMATION
Cnr Newell Highway and Macquarie Street (02) 6884 1422

LOCAL KNOWLEDGE

Usually sunken treasure

In Bourke, they've found that drought does have one advantage. Falling water levels present an opportunity to clean the bed of the Darling River. But what do you do with the trash? Treasure it, is the answer, and around town artworks have been commissioned using the recovered debris.

Lightning Ridge

For a little town of 1814 people, Lightning Ridge is one of the best known in outback New South Wales, and it has plenty to keep visitors entertained. The main reason for its fame is the presence of black opal, and the friendly, outgoing people who mine it.

SIGHTS AND ACTIVITIES • Shop for opals, fossick for opals, take underground mine tours or watch videos on the lives of the miners – both in town and at sites such as the Big Opal and the Walk-in-Mine • Marvel at the superb collection of cacti at the Cactus Nursery • Refresh yourself and wash off the dust at the Hot Artesian Bore Baths • Take a 'car-door tour' following painted car-door signposts to several interesting sites around town (brochure available)

VISITOR INFORMATION
Bill O'Brien Way (02) 6829 0565

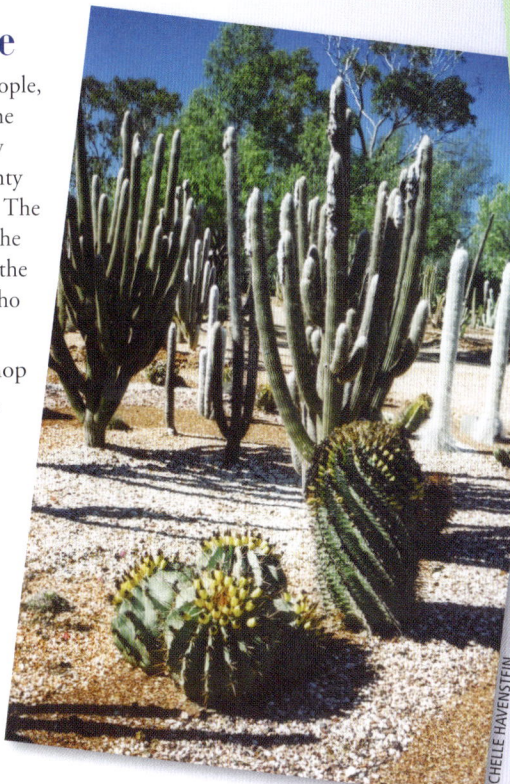
Cactus Nursery
MICHELLE HAVENSTEIN

Mudgee

An attractive town with 8195 people, Mudgee has really come into its own in recent years as its premium wine industry has gone ahead by leaps and bounds. It has also developed boutique and gourmet food lines such as game, breads and olives. The town itself has numerous classic Victorian buildings and some spectacular old pubs.

SIGHTS AND ACTIVITIES • Walk or drive on a historic tour of the town's many fine buildings (brochure available) • Take a winery tour • Purchase or learn about honey, another major product of the region, at Honey Haven and Mount Vincent Mead • Visit the historic town of Gulgong, once featured on the ten-dollar note, and home of the largest collection of memorabilia for the locally born and raised poet, Henry Lawson

VISITOR INFORMATION
84 Market Street (02) 6372 1020

MEET THE LOCALS

A committed conservationist

If you sometimes wonder how you can make a difference for the environment, the efforts of the late Judie Peet of Dubbo can help you. Thinking globally but acting locally, she documented the plants and birds of her region for 20 years, among them glossy black cockatoos in Goonoo State Forest. In recognition of her contribution, a dam in the area has been named after her, a good spot for seeing the spectacular birds she helped protect.

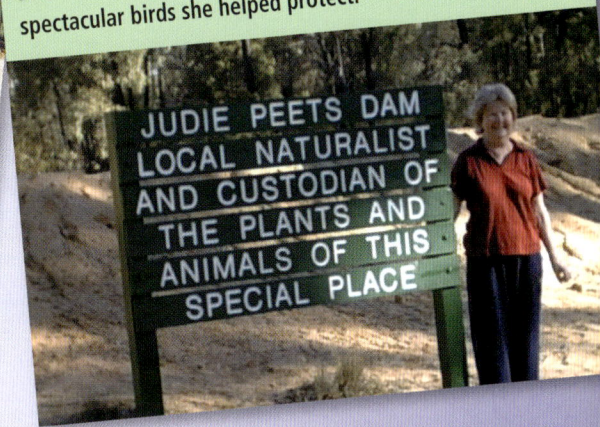

MEET THE LOCALS

Cheetahs?

Not to mention the lions, tigers, elephants, maned wolves, African wild dogs, echidnas, kangaroos, gibbons and many more at Dubbo's Western Plains Zoo. It's a great place to visit, but it's also a tremendous repository of expertise on the care and breeding of many species. ABC Western Plains taps that expertise on a regular basis with its 'Zoo Tales', interviews with keepers, vets and other experts at the zoo. You can hear them on the radio, or visit the ABC Backyard website's Zoo Tales page at www.abc.net.au/westernplains/breakfast/features/zootales.htm

ABC Riverina

Location of ABC Local Radio studio

Towns in red have their own AM transmitter
Towns in green have their own FM transmitter

JO MAZZOCHI

Some of the Riverina's finest

The Riverina broadcast area includes the hugely productive Murrumbidgee Irrigation Area, as well as the famous merino wool-growing region and the high-rainfall south-west slopes and plains. Industries include forestry, agriculture, horticulture, tourism, food processing, education, defence and light manufacturing.

Sport and the arts play a large role in the recreational activities of the region, which is home to a number of national sporting identities, as well as the only full-time professional theatre company in regional New South Wales.

On 16 December 1931 the ABC opened a radio station called 2CO in Albury to service the south of New South Wales and the north-east of Victoria. The first rural reporter based in regional New South Wales, Brian Gwin-Jones, was appointed to Wagga Wagga in 1953. In 1991, 2CO moved to new studios in Wagga. Ever since, ABC Riverina has reflected the interests and concerns of both the urban and rural residents of this diverse region.

NOT TO BE MISSED

- Fly-fish in the excellent trout streams on the western side of the **Snowy Mountains**
- Meet the Dog on the Tuckerbox, 5 miles (8 kilometres) from **Gundagai**
- Discover why the **Riverina** has earnt a reputation for great wines
- Enjoy the 'beach', as the sandy stretches of the **Murrumbidgee** are called locally
- Pick cherries in the many orchards around **Young** (late spring to early summer)
- Devour delicious, crispy apples fresh from a roadside stall around **Batlow**
- Tour the wineries around **Griffith**

Wagga Wagga

The major centre for the Riverina is also the largest inland city in New South Wales, with a population of 56 729. It is a centre for the agricultural industry, and supports light industry, educational institutions and a large military presence. It is also home to a regional performing arts group and an ideal base for exploring the surrounding region, especially its wineries.

SIGHTS AND ACTIVITIES • Ride the miniature train around the Botanic Gardens and mini zoo • Combine a visit to the Regional Art Gallery, which features the National Art Glass Collection, with the adjacent Museum of the Riverina • Sample some of the region's excellent produce at Charles Sturt University • Visit the RAAF Museum near town at Forest Hill • Walk to the top of The Rock, at the nearby town of The Rock, to view the area's unusual scenery • Swim at Wagga Beach (taking care of the river's sometimes strong current) • Ask a local about the 'five o'clock wave'

VISITOR INFORMATION
Tarcutta Street (02) 6926 9621

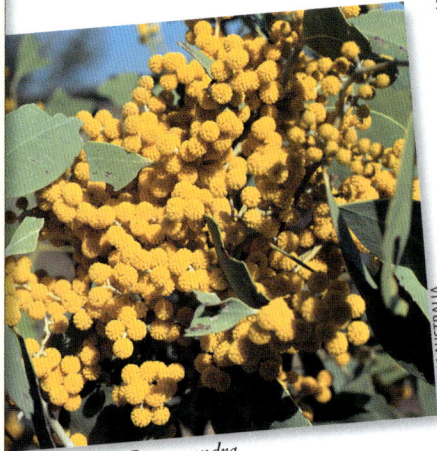
Wattle Time, Cootamundra
TOURISM AUSTRALIA

Deniliquin

Located in the centre of Australia's most extensive irrigation area, where rice is one of the major crops, this lively town (population 7816) has also played a prominent part in the development of fine merino wool, with two of Australia's best-known studs, Wanganella and Boonoke, nearby.

SIGHTS AND ACTIVITIES • Learn about the development of the merino-wool industry at Peppin Heritage Centre in the Old George Street Public School; the Peppin family played a key role in the industry in the nineteenth century • Take a self-guide historic and nature walk around several National Trust buildings and Blake Botanic Reserve and Island Sanctuary (brochure available) • Head north of town to the Pioneer Tourist Park which features art galleries, a blacksmith shop, steam engines and a mini rural museum • For a bush pub experience, head to Conargo Pub, 25 kilometres north-east

VISITOR INFORMATION
Peppin Heritage Centre, George Street (03) 5881 2878

MEET THE LOCALS

The bush oar-maker

If you've heard the story of the sailor who survived a terrible storm, turned his back on the sea and carried an oar inland until he found a town where no-one knew what it was, it turns out he could have settled in Wagga Wagga. For sure enough, 500 kilometres from the sea, that's where master oar-maker Rod Cullen has his workshop. Yes, he's a long way from his customers, who include fussy professional anglers, but he's close to his raw materials, especially mountain ash and alpine ash from the nearby Snowy Mountains.

Gundagai

There's quite a bit more to Gundagai than the famous Dog on the Tuckerbox. There are several sites of historical significance, and the town was the scene of Australia's worst flood in 1852, when 89 people drowned. These days the town (population 2064, services wool, wheat, fruit and vegetable industries.

SIGHTS AND ACTIVITIES • Pore over photos, letters and possessions of Henry Lawson at Gabriel Gallery • Visit the National Trust-listed Gundagai Courthouse (1859), the scene of the trials of notorious bushrangers such as Captain Moonlite • Sit with the Dog on the Tuckerbox, 8 kilometres out of town, and see statues of Dad and Dave as well • Fly-fish the mountain streams at nearby Tumut and Tumbarumba, and explore the adjacent high country

VISITOR INFORMATION
249 Sheridan Street (02) 6944 1341

Shear Outback Centre, Hay

Hay

Set among some of the most extraordinary semi-arid grazing land in the country, Hay, on the banks of the Murrumbidgee, has a population of 2896 and is on a vast plain that provides plenty of big-sky scenery and some great sunsets. The area is increasingly becoming irrigated, and is home to several famous sheep stations. It is also well known for its World War II POW internment camps.

SIGHTS AND ACTIVITIES • Visit the spectacular Shear Outback Centre, comprising The Australian Shearers' Hall of Fame and Murray Downs Woolshed • Take a self-guide walk around the town's historic buildings, dating from the 1880s (brochure available) • Explore the stories of 3000 POWs at the restored railway station that houses the POW Internment Camp Interpretive Centre • Picnic and swim at the town's Murrumbidgee beaches then watch the amazing sunset • Stop at Booligal, the town mentioned in the Banjo Patterson poem 'Hay and Hell and Booligal'

VISITOR INFORMATION
407 Moppett Street (02) 6993 4045

LOCAL TIPS

- In **Cootamundra**, visit the birthplace of Australia's most famous cricketer, Sir Donald Bradman
- In **Young** you can try cherries, cherry pie or cherry jam, or just take a walk through the cherry blossoms in spring
- Experience gliding at **Temora**, considered one of the best places in the country for this exhilarating sport
- Admire **Griffith**'s idyllic location, surrounded by low hills, vineyards, rice paddies and citrus orchards, from Sir Dudley de Chair's Lookout in town

MEET THE LOCALS

The wonder pigs

What do you do when you move to the country? Georgia Gowanloch of Adelong did what she thought was normal, she bought a piglet, a lamb and a calf. Fair enough, but then she started dressing up the pet pig, Holly-Honey, and putting make-up on her. Soon the pig was a star attraction at country shows around the Riverina, along with the late Hoover the Wonder Pig (pictured). And Holly-Honey got married to Hoover on national television. Ask around and you can still see Georgia's perky pig perform with perfect panache, along with Porky Pig and Hoover Junior.

GEORGIA GOWANLOCH

LOCAL KNOWLEDGE

Forgotten journeys

As part of the National Trust's Heritage Festival, ABC listeners around the country were invited to take photos that celebrated their built environment. This photo by Stephen Taylor shows all that remains of a train station at Burrandana, south-east of Wagga Wagga, just one of the relics of a bygone time.

ABC South East

Tumut · Adelong · Mount Horeb · Mount Adrah · Oberne · Wondalga · Batlow · Talbingo · Kunama · Rosewood · Laurel Hill · Tumbarumba · Tooma · Cabramurra · Mt Selwyn · Adaminaby · Anglers Reach · Old Adaminaby · Eucumbene · Buckenderra

Tintaldra · Corryong · Towong · Towong Upper · Khancoban · Berridale · East Jindabyne · Jindabyne · Thredbo · Smiggin Holes · Perisher · Charlotte Pass · Guthega · Mt Kosciuszko 2228m

CANBERRA · A C T · Queanbeyan · Bungendore · Hoskinstown · Rossi · Braidwood · Mongarlowe · Tharwa · Williamsdale · Captains Flat · Ballalaba · Majors Creek · Araluen · Michelago · Anembo · Bredbo · Bunyan · Cooma · Cooma West · Numeralla · Nimmitabel

Batemans Bay · Mogo · Malua Bay · Mossy Point · Broulee · Moruya · Moruya Heads · Congo · Bodalla · Tuross Head · Dalmeny · Narooma · Central Tilba · Tilba Tilba · Cobargo · Bermagui · Bermagui South · Quaama · Bemboka · Bega · Tathra · Kalaru · Kameruka · Candelo · Wolumla · Tura Beach · Merimbula · Pambula · Pambula Beach · Eden · East Boyd · Kiah · Wonboyn Lake

Ulladulla · Kings Point · Burrill Lake · Lake Tabourie · Termeil · Bawley Point · Kioloa · East Lynne · Nelligen · Durras · Long Beach · Cullendulla · Swanhaven · Conjola · Lake Conjola · Yatte Yattah · Milton

Bombala · Delegate · Delegate River · Haydens Bog · Craigie · Bonang · Bendoc · Bibbenluke · Cathcart · Rocky Hall · Wyndham · Nethercote · Towamba · Boydtown · Genoa · Gipsy Point · Mallacoota

Ensay North · Ensay · Tambo Crossing · Murrindal · Buchan · Butchers Ridge · Goongerah · Noorinbee North · Noorinbee · Club Terrace · Bellbird Creek · Bruthen · Orbost · Cann River · Wangarabell

Tumut Power Station · Talbingo Reservoir · Blowering Reservoir · KOSCIUSZKO NATIONAL PARK · Tumut Pond Res · Eucumbene · Lake Eucumbene · NEW SOUTH WALES · VICTORIA · SNOWY RIVER NATIONAL PARK · ALPINE NATIONAL PARK · EAST GIPPSLAND · DEUA NATIONAL PARK · WADBILLIGA NATIONAL PARK · SOUTH EAST FOREST NP · BEN BOYD NP · CROAJINGOLONG NATIONAL PARK · COOPRACAMBRA NATIONAL PARK · MURRAMARANG NP · EUROBODALLA NP · MIMOSA ROCKS NP · MONTAGUE ISLAND NR

SYDNEY · Bega

SOUTH PACIFIC OCEAN

☀ Towns with ABC Local Radio studio

Bega Valley

You could be forgiven for thinking that this corner of New South Wales is a little slice of paradise because, basically, it has just about everything. There are beautiful, seldom-visited beaches, delightful coastal fishing villages, wonderful produce to sample, some of the best rolling-plains sheep country in Australia, brilliant trout-fishing streams and rugged mountain scenery rising to the alpine regions of the Kosciuszko National Park and the New South Wales skifields.

This is one of the most charming regions you'll find anywhere, and it should come as no surprise that one of the towns is named Eden. As well, its distance from the major centres of Sydney and Melbourne makes it less pressured than other regions, and a pleasant place to visit at any time of year.

The main industries include fishing, tourism, dairying, timber, sheep and cattle farming, and a burgeoning wine industry. The main studio of ABC South East is at Bega, and there are numerous transmitters along the coast, on the Monaro and in the mountains, to ensure as broad a coverage as possible.

NOT TO BE MISSED

- In winter, schuss downhill or cross-country ski at **Perisher** and **Thredbo**; in summer, you can mountain-bike downhill then take a chairlift back to the top

- Visit the tiny National Trust village of **Central Tilba**, a showpiece for late nineteenth-century rural architecture

- See penguins, fur seals and several seabird species on a tour of **Montague Island**

- In spring, go hiking in **Kosciuszko National Park** and enjoy the wonderful alpine wildflowers

- In **Cooma** see films and displays on the hydro scheme at the Snowy Mountains Authority Information Centre

- Take a trip to **Dalgety**, once considered for the site of the nation's capital

MEET THE LOCALS

Tin-can pelicans

Don't be surprised if the ubiquitous pelicans of the South Coast look so attached to their roosts that they seem to be rusted on. Some of them are. In Bega, local artist Richard Moffatt was commissioned by Bega Valley Shire to produce a number of life-size pelicans from recycled metal. The results now adorn the fish-pen area in Merimbula, where their beaks can hold more than the jerry cans.

MEET THE LOCALS

Bat lady

The usual reaction to bats is one of horror, as they tend to be the sidekicks of villainous vampires. But flying foxes are a different story, winning the hearts of people everywhere, especially as their habitats come under threat and their numbers decline. Pambula local, and Wildlife Information and Rescue Service (WIRES) member, Alexandra Seddon saw an opportunity to protect a local colony when the land around it came up for sale. With a small inheritance she purchased the 10-hectare block adjoining a friend's 5 hectares, thus assuring the future of Pambula's colony of eastern grey-headed flying foxes.

Bega

Located between the ocean and the mountains, Bega (population 4190) is renowned for the fact that it's possible to leave town to ski in the morning then surf in the afternoon. Another of its major claims is the quality of the local cheeses, as this is the centre of a thriving dairy region. It even has a Cheese Pro-Am (golf) in March.

SIGHTS AND ACTIVITIES • Explore local history at the Bega Family Museum • Learn about all things cheesy at the Bega Cheese Heritage Centre • Swim, slide on natural waterslides, walk and bird-watch at Mumbulla Falls • Sportfish from the town of Bermagui, which has the safest harbour on this section of coast and is near the deep waters of the continental shelf • Explore the historic sea wharf in Tathra which dates from the 1860s, enjoy a coffee there, or swim and surf at the nearby patrolled beach

VISITOR INFORMATION
Princes Highway (02) 6492 2045

Batemans Bay

The first town for holiday-makers coming from Canberra, Batemans Bay (population 9568) is also the first port of call for public servants seeking their sea change. The town's real claims to fame, though, are its crayfish and oysters, and the sheltered waters of the Clyde River.

SIGHTS AND ACTIVITIES • Take a cruise on the Clyde aboard the *Clyde Princess* or MV *Merinda* • Hire a houseboat and cruise the quiet waters; fish for some of the Clyde's giant flathead • Bathe at the many fine beaches, to the south and north, that offer surf or sheltered swimming • Explore the undisturbed coastline of Murramarang National Park • Wander through the pleasant coastal towns of Ulladulla (north) and Narooma (south), and the river town of Moruya, near Tuross Head, renowned for its excellent fishing

VISITOR INFORMATION
Cnr Princes Highway and Beach Road (02) 4472 6900

Eden

This stunning town (population 3106) on the shores of Twofold Bay with the bulk of Mount Imlay towering in the background, has a long and fascinating history. It was the site of an early whaling station and since the decline of whaling, the town has been a busy fishing centre. Its proximity to the northern side of Bass Strait means it is often used as a refuge for yachts in the Sydney to Hobart Yacht Race.

Scene near Merimbula

SIGHTS AND ACTIVITIES • See the skeleton of Tom the killer whale in the Eden Killer Whale Museum in town (Tom helped many early whalers find their prey) • Take a whale-watching cruise from October to November • Walk, swim, fish or dive the many wrecks of Disaster Bay in Ben Boyd National Park, north and south of town • In nearby Boydtown, visit the convict-built Seahorse Inn, or swim at the safe beach • Experience Aboriginal culture and bush tucker at Monarroo Bubbaroo Guddoo Keeping Place • Enjoy fresh oysters from the nearby fishing town of Merimbula

VISITOR INFORMATION
Princes Highway (02) 6496 1953

Jindabyne

This is the main town (population 1670) servicing the ski fields of the Snowy Mountains, but the wealth of attractions and activities in the area ensures that the town is lively all year round.

SIGHTS AND ACTIVITIES • Stay in town during the ski season and take your pick of resorts to visit each day – by car to Thredbo or the SkiTube to Perisher Blue • Take the scenic drive (when the Alpine Way is open) via Thredbo to Khancoban • Fish for trout in the well-stocked Lake Jindabyne (Gaden Trout Hatchery is nearby and has tours) or hire one of the catamarans • Take to the mountains on two wheels; lifts open in summer to carry mountain bikes for downhill or cross-country adventures, or hike to Mount Kosciuszko enjoying mountain scenery and alpine wildflowers

VISITOR INFORMATION
Kosciuszko Road (02) 6450 5600

MEET THE LOCALS

The photo album

In a region of extraordinary scenic beauty everywhere you turn, it's little wonder that the ABC Local Radio invitation to send in snaps of favourite weather, places and creatures would result in a flood of great photography to the Backyard website. It's no surprise that weather snaps featured prominently in an area on the northern side of Bass Strait, where huge storms batter ships and keep fishing fleets tucked in their harbours. This shot by listener Jon Poyner is of a front rolling out to sea near Dalmeny.

TOURISM AUSTRALIA

Bushwalking, near Mount Kosciuszko

The National Broadcaster

A potted history

It was in the years between the two World Wars that the Australian government first recognised the importance of broadcasting information quickly to almost the entire population. From the 1920s, State and Federal governments had been building a network of stations in the capital cities in a piecemeal fashion. However, in the early 1930s the need for a national broadcaster became clear, and at 8pm on 1 July 1932, with then Prime Minister Joe Lyons doing the honours, the Australian Broadcasting Commission (now the Australian Broadcasting Corporation) went to air.

The new ABC's opening-day programs were broadcast live, and included a children's session with Bobby Bluegum, 'Racing Notes' with W. A. Ferry calling the Randwick races, 'British Wireless News' sent by cable from London, local news, weather, stock reports, shipping news, a Women's Association session (topics were commonsense housekeeping and needlecraft), a talk on goldfish and their care, 'Morning Devotions' and music.

Within a year the Sydney and Melbourne studios were taking turns to produce a nightly national program, followed by regular relays between all the major capitals. Live performance also became the basis for the ABC's long involvement in nurturing performing arts – everything from classical music to dance bands and live drama. Listeners were also able to hear talks by world leaders, philosophers, writers and sports people. In the first year these included King George V, Pope Pius XI, the Prime Minister of England Ramsay MacDonald, the newly elected Chancellor of the German Reich Adolph Hitler, authors J.B. Priestley and G.K. Chesterton, and the Captain of the English cricket team D.R. Jardine.

Initially, the ABC controlled twelve stations: two in Sydney (2FC and 2BL), two in Melbourne (3AR and 3LO), one in Brisbane (4GQ), one in Adelaide (5CL), one in Perth (6WF) and one in Hobart (7ZL). There were relay stations at Newcastle (2NC), Corowa (2CO), Rockhampton (4RK) and Crystal Brook (5CK). Between them these covered all the major population centres, and a substantial percentage of the population.

However, to further extend the coverage, five extremely powerful transmitters were added prior to World War II. Some of these

covered enormous areas of their respective States (and other States as well). They included: Wagin (558 AM) and Dalwallinu (531 AM) in Western Australia, Longreach (540 AM) in Queensland, Horsham (594 AM) in Victoria and Cumnock (549 AM) in New South Wales, all of which are still operating. Generally the transmission buildings – huge buildings housing both the transmitter equipment and the enormous generators needed to provide enough power to run them – were located outside the towns. Keeping them operational involved up to 12 staff at each station.

The idea behind these transmitters was to permit emergency broadcasts to most of the Australian population, and it was to prove a remarkably prescient decision. The start of World War II saw the value of the powerful transmitters quickly realised, although in the first months of the war censorship meant very little escaped the heavy hand of official secrecy. Even weather reports were cancelled, for fear of giving some aid to the enemy. At the end of June 1940, the Department of Information took control of the 7.00pm nightly national news. However, after listeners expressed their preference for independent news presented by the Commission, control of the news was returned to the ABC in September 1940.

When Japan entered the war in 1942, radio was being described as a 'major instrument of national policy'. By then, 20 per cent of the ABC's broadcast time was devoted to war matters, and in the ensuing war years that level was destined to grow. By the end of the war the ABC's role as a source of public information on a wide range of matters was well established in the national culture.

Today, with everything from rural reports, sports broadcasts, talkback, news, weather, current affairs and much more, ABC Local Radio continues to be the source of information on what's going on – in our own backyard and on the world stage.

Opposite: *Announcer Newton Hobbs in 1933 reading an ABC news bulletin from a newspaper. This arrangement was sanctioned by a 'gentlemen's agreement' with the Australian Newspaper Proprieters' Association. In 1934, however, the ABC hired its first journalist.*

Above: *Studio at Horsham in Victoria*

This page: *The powerful transmitter built at Horsham in Victoria prior to World War II*

Australian Capital Territory

ABC
Canberra

CANBERRA

The nation's capital and surrounding Territory may be the smallest of Australia's States and Territories, but there's more than enough to cater for every taste and interest. The city is the headquarters for some of Australia's most important cultural, social and academic institutions, which means you'll find art galleries, museums, political institutions and much more. Around the city, you'll also find attractive scenery, intriguing wildlife and a blossoming wine and produce industry.

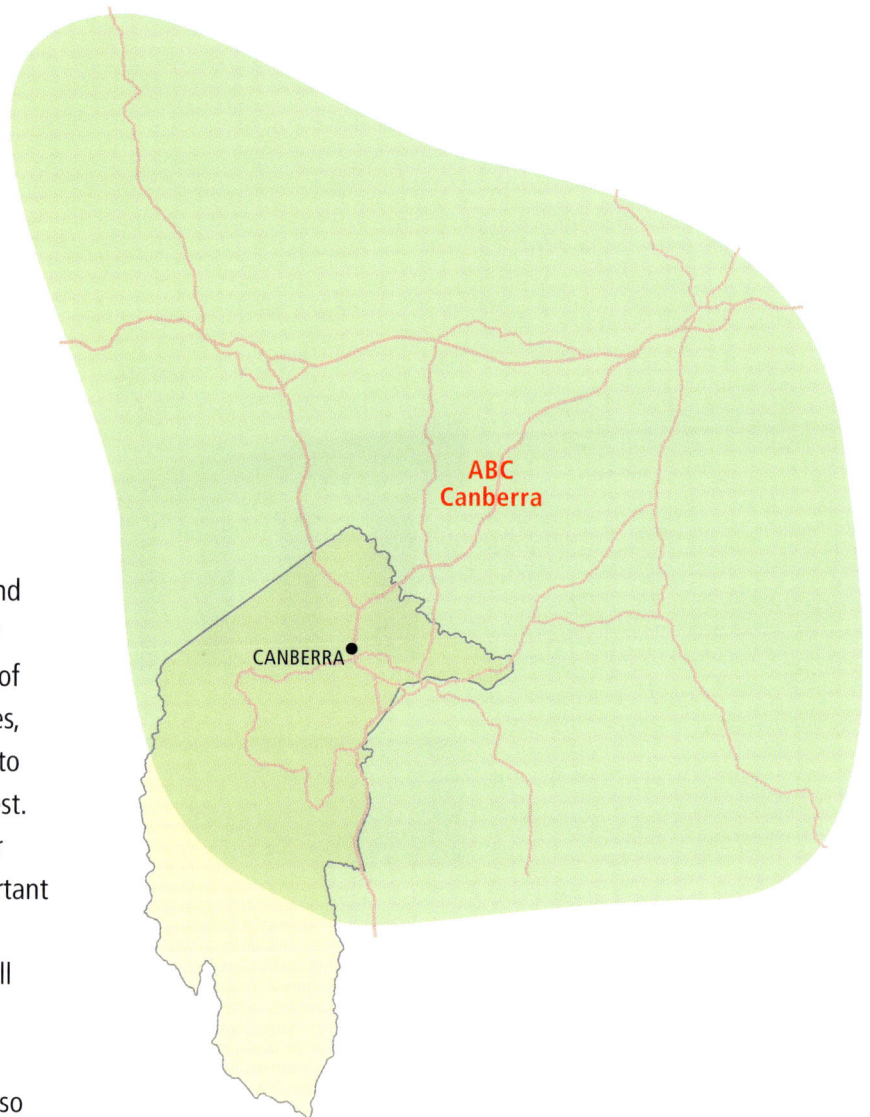

See inside back cover for a list of ABC Local Radio stations and their frequencies.

ABC Canberra

Canberra

48

ABC Canberra

☀ Location of ABC Local Radio studio

Local Radio Frequencies	
Boorowa	666 AM
Braidwood	666 AM
Bungendore	666 AM
Canberra	666 AM
Collector	666 AM
Gunning	666 AM
Michelago	666 AM
Queanbeyan	666 AM
Yass	666 AM

Canberra has the only transmitter (AM) in the region

The seat of Australia's Federal Government, Canberra is the youngest of Australia's capital cities (established early in the twentieth century), yet now home to a diverse population of some 350 000. Originally designed to an urban plan by architect Walter Burley Griffin, it has become known as the Bush Capital, a place where the city and the natural environment are closely entwined. Native bushland combines with parks, gardens, lakes and wetlands to create an atmosphere of spaciousness and style.

Many of the country's major institutions are based in Canberra, and while the city sprawls over a large area, within the confines of the Parliamentary Triangle visitors can find an extraordinary number of places to see and things to do. However, one of Canberra's best-kept secrets is the superb rural and natural scenery that lies within the borders of the Australian Capital Territory and the surrounding district. There are wineries, rugged mountain ranges and historic towns just waiting to be explored.

Having begun broadcasting in January 1953, when Canberra's population was a mere 25 000, ABC Canberra has been part of the development of the national capital for more than half a century. It has reported on the day-to-day lives of the locals at the same time as it has described the national dramas being played out on its very doorstep.

The Bush Capital

NOT TO BE MISSED

- See some of the finest art by national and international artists at the **National Gallery of Australia**
- Appreciate the sacrifices of our forebears at the **Australian War Memorial**
- Witness democracy in action at **Parliament House**
- Soak up the history and texture of **Old Parliament House** and its National Portrait Gallery
- Take in the spectacular views (plus coffee or lunch) from the **Telstra Tower Lookout**
- Discover the nation's history from the **National Museum of Australia**'s perspective

Parliament House

TOURISM AUSTRALIA

Display at Floriade

The Parliamentary Triangle

The area bounded by Commonwealth Avenue, Constitution Avenue and Kings Avenue is referred to as the Parliamentary Triangle. Within it can be found much of the machinery of the Australian Government and some of the nation's most important institutions. It's an extremely compact focal point for any visit to Canberra.

SIGHTS AND ACTIVITIES • Take a tour of Parliament House • See the sound and light exhibition and the National Portrait Gallery at Old Parliament House • Visit the High Court of Australia • See great and controversial works at the National Gallery of Australia • Discover the workings of the National Library and its constantly changing exhibitions • Learn about Australians at war at the Australian War Memorial • Get hands-on experience of science at the award-winning Questacon – the National Science and Technology Centre • Learn about Canberra's development at the National Capital Exhibition • Stroll around the Lake Burley Griffin foreshore, which affords some of the best views of the major public buildings, access to the Carillon (with regular performances), views of the Captain Cook Memorial Water Jet and the superb gardens of Commonwealth Park (where Floriade is held in September and October)

City Centre

Adjacent to the Parliamentary Triangle is the city centre and its immediate surrounds. While this is the major commercial and shopping centre of the city, it is also the site of the Territory's local government and many federal government offices.

SIGHTS AND ACTIVITIES • Visit the Canberra Museum and Gallery in Civic Square, seat of the Australian Capital Territory Legislative Assembly • Wander through the National Museum of Australia with its state-of-the-art technology and interactive displays • View some of Australia's audio and visual heritage at the museum of ScreenSound Australia • Stroll through one of the country's best collections of flora at the Australian National Botanic Gardens • Get incredible views over Canberra and the surrounding area from the Telstra Tower atop Black Mountain • See the fascinating local and overseas creatures at the National Zoo and Aquarium

VISITOR INFORMATION
330 Northbourne Avenue, Dickson (02) 6205 0044

Australian War Memorial

LOCAL TIPS

- Although a relatively new city, Canberra has several old buildings built by original settlers, including **Blundell's Cottage** (1858), **St John the Baptist Church and the Schoolhouse Museum** (1840s) and **Duntroon House** (parts date from 1833)

- One of the best ways to see **Lake Burley Griffin** is to hire a bicycle and ride around it

- In summer a swim in the **Murrumbidgee** can be very refreshing. The waters are usually cleanest at Point Hutt (good swimming) and Coppins Crossing (shallow but a good spot for picnics)

- For a taste of history, **Gus' Cafe** in town pioneered outdoor dining in Canberra

- The best weekend markets can be found on the south side at **Kingston**'s Old Bus Depot, and on the north side at the township of **Hall**

MEET THE LOCALS

Pick the local blueberries

Some years ago Murrumbateman locals Howard and Carol Patrick (pictured) started blueberry farming just to try something different. Later, with several thousand bushes planted, they invited the public to come and pick the berries for them. Now, during the season from late December to mid-February, up to 100 people turn up on weekends to do just that. You buy what you pick, at a reduced rate, or you can buy them picked fresh. With so many pickers though, it pays to call (02) 6230 2346 and check that there's enough ripe berries available.

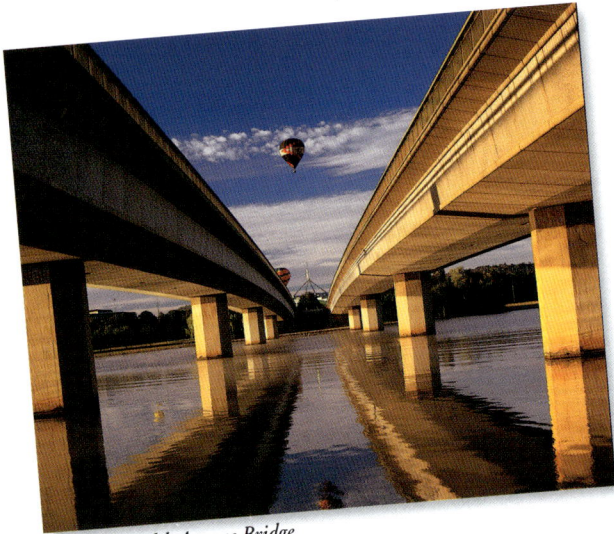
Commonwealth Avenue Bridge

Inner South

South of the Parliamentary Triangle, Canberra's suburbia begins. However, the neighbourhood is fairly upmarket, with the embassies of many nations dotting the suburbs of Yarralumla, Deakin, Forrest and Red Hill.

SIGHTS AND ACTIVITIES • See two of the Canberra's most famous addresses: the Prime Minister's residence, The Lodge; and Government House, Yarralumla, the residence of the Governor General • Watch money being made before your eyes at the Royal Australian Mint • Enjoy a pleasant picnic with a range of recreational facilities for children at Weston Park, on the shores of the lake

Inner North

Within the city's northern precincts and just beyond, you'll find a number of fascinating exhibits that range from the highly competitive to the charming and whimsical.

SIGHTS AND ACTIVITIES • Meet some of Australia's best athletes on a tour of the Australian Institute of Sport, then test your skills at Sportex, which lets you try to match the performances of some of the country's record breakers • Probe the depths of space at the Canberra Planetarium and Observatory • Gape at the National Dinosaur Museum's 30 life-size skeletons at Gold Creek on the Barton Highway • Experience Australia in times gone by at Ginninderra Village • View the world in small scale at Cockington Green; then see scales of a different kind at the Australian Reptile Centre

MEET THE LOCALS

Designer swamps

One suspects that not everything in Canberra was part of the original plan. Parliament Houses? Sure. Government offices? Absolutely. Homes for pampered pollies? You bet. But swamps? Nevertheless, they're now building, err … wetlands small and large in the national capital, and they're extremely proud of them. The Jerrabombera Wetlands on the eastern side of Lake Burley Griffin, for example, are the habitat for more than 100 species of birds, such as spoonbills (pictured), and many species of frogs. A dozen suburbs have also initiated wetlands projects, adding a watery dimension to the Bush Capital that the planners never dreamed of.

MEET THE LOCALS

The powerhouse

Among the many treasures in the National Museum of Australia you'll find the engine that built Canberra, or at least significant parts of it. The Fowler steam traction engine, which dates from 1925, was the workhorse that built Old Parliament House and the nearby Cotter Dam. The museum's engineering consultant, Colin Ogilvie works with the team that restores and conserves many of the museum's vehicles.

Southern ACT

South of the city you'll find the Murrumbidgee River and numerous picnic and swimming areas, and increasingly rugged scenery as the mountains of Brindabella Range rear to altitudes that almost rival the Snowy Mountains. The area is well worth a visit for its scenic beauty, pleasant picnic spots and opportunities to see the region's flora and fauna close at hand.

SIGHTS AND ACTIVITIES • Take Tourist Drive 5 to see the Mount Stromlo Observatory (currently closed due to the 2003 bushfires), and the swimming and picnic areas of the Cotter Reserve • Beyond the Cotter, visit the Canberra Deep Space Communications Complex, which has exhibits on its key role in NASA's interplanetary expeditions • Experience nature first-hand in the wonderfully scenic Tidbinbilla Nature Reserve • Take an 800-metre alpine slide or other snow pursuits at Corin Forest • Head south to Lanyon, a beautiful historic homestead that includes a gallery of Sidney Nolan's paintings • Visit the charming town of Tharwa and the renowned craft complex at Cuppacumbalong • Drive further south to Namadgi National Park with its superb alpine scenery, trout fishing, four-wheel-drive adventures and great rock-climbing at Booroomba Rocks

Beyond ACT

Beyond the borders of the Australian Capital Territory, but within the area covered by ABC Canberra and contained within what is known as Capital Country, you'll find a number of charming villages and towns offering a wide range of rural scenery, adventure experiences, wineries and more.

SIGHTS AND ACTIVITIES • Head north along the Barton Highway and try the superb local wines along the way to Murrumbateman, which has several good restaurants and cafes • At Yass visit the explorer Hamilton Hume's museum, Cooma Cottage, where he lived, and his grave site at the local cemetery • Take the turnoff near Yass to Wee Jasper, a fascinating locality with bird-watching, swimming, scenery and caves for experienced speleologists • On the Kings Highway heading towards the coast, stop off at the wineries on the way to historic Bungendore and Braidwood (setting for the film *The Year My Voice Broke*) • For more wine-tasting, try the wineries just off the Federal Highway near Collector, which also has a highly regarded cafe

LOCAL KNOWLEDGE
Roads to nowhere
Canberra is a planned city, a city of roads, but some plans go awry, while others go nowhere. So take care when driving that the road you're on doesn't come to an abrupt end. Out in the suburbs you'll find plenty of these roads to nowhere, and even for the locals it can be a mystery as to where they were ever intended to go, despite the fact that some involved immense earthworks that have never been completed. This one in Devonport Street, Lyons, ends in a horse paddock, and has done so for more than 30 years.

TOURISM AUSTRALIA

Madew winery, near Collector

Victoria

I t may be the second smallest State in Australia, but Victoria certainly packs a lot in. It has one of the most liveable cities on earth and many beautiful historic towns. As well, it also has deserts, temperate rainforests, rugged coastlines and lofty alpine regions. Its architecture reflects the incredible wealth generated by its many gold rushes. It all adds up to a State that combines great natural beauty with fascinating history and charming regional centres with a modern cosmopolitan lifestyle. It's a place where you can enjoy high culture one day, and wide open spaces the next.

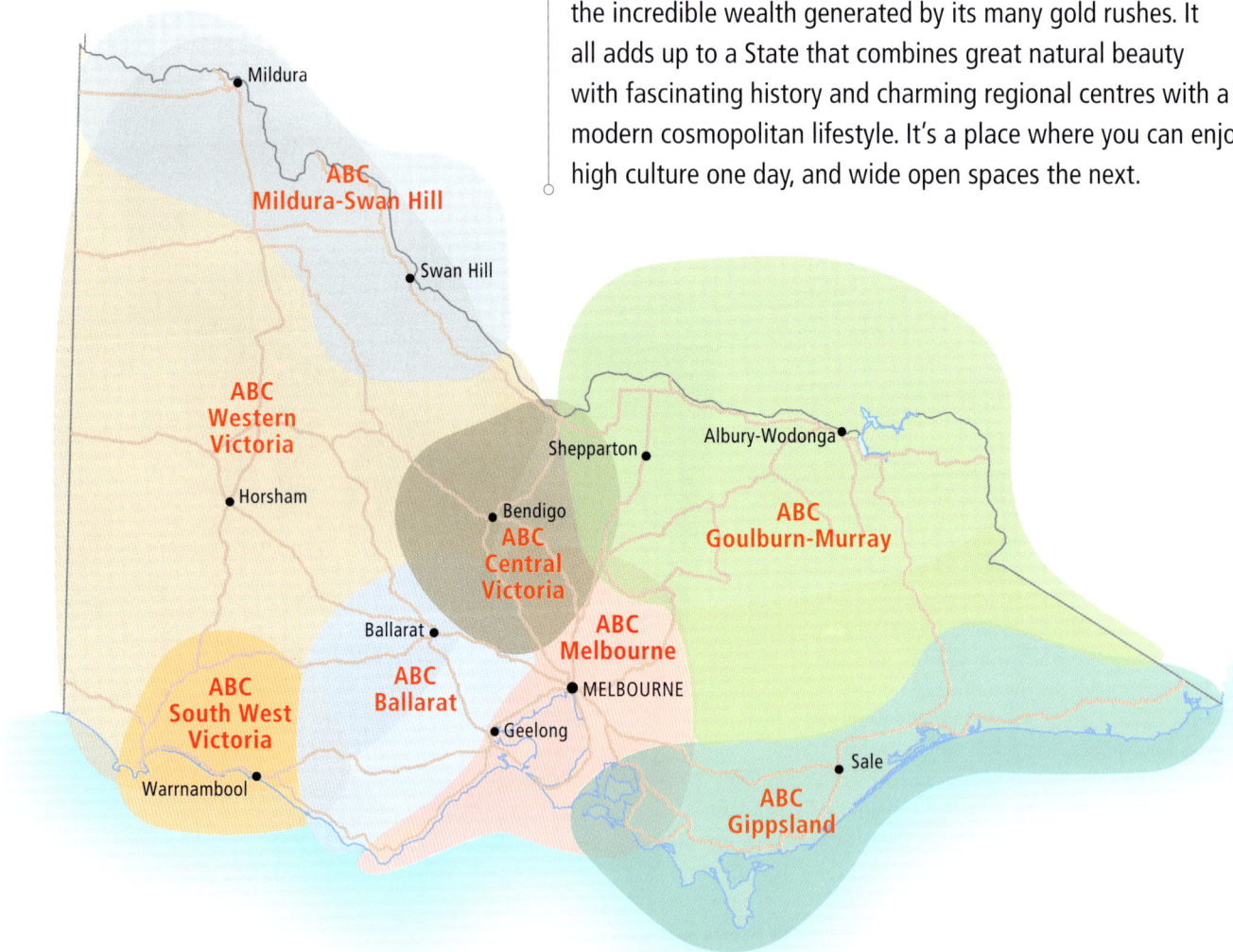

Mildura

ABC Mildura-Swan Hill

Swan Hill

ABC Western Victoria

Horsham

Shepparton

Albury-Wodonga

ABC Goulburn-Murray

Bendigo

ABC Central Victoria

Ballarat

ABC Melbourne

ABC Ballarat

MELBOURNE

ABC South West Victoria

Geelong

Warrnambool

Sale

ABC Gippsland

See inside back cover for a list of ABC Local Radio stations and their frequencies.

ABC Melbourne

Location of ABC Local Radio studio

The capital of Victoria and one of the most cultured and liveable cities in the country, if not the world, Melbourne manages a fine balance between a cosmopolitan outlook and a friendly, Australian character – all this despite a large proportion of the population having come from somewhere else. Indeed, the city has the largest Greek population outside Greece.

The area covered by 774 ABC Melbourne extends around Port Phillip, taking in the busy port city of Geelong, and the Bellarine and Mornington peninsulas. It also takes in the Dandenong Ranges and Yarra Valley. As such, it encompasses wonderful mountain scenery, no less than three wine-growing districts, beaches, national parks and much more.

The station first went to air on 13 October 1924 (as 774 3LO) with an outside broadcast of a performance of *La Boheme* which featured Dame Nellie Melba. Named after 2LO London, 3LO was initially owned by the Broadcasting Company of Australia. The first manager was Major W. T. Conder, a former governor of Pentridge Prison. In 1928 control of 3LO passed to the Sydney-based Australian Broadcasting Company. In 1932 the Australian Broadcasting Commission (ABC) was established and was given control of Melbourne's 3LO and 3AR.

Committed to standards of fairness, accuracy and impartiality, 774 ABC Melbourne is also renowned for its innovation in broadcasting – outside broadcasts have come from a moving tram, an operating theatre during heart surgery, a suburban living room and underwater in Port Phillip – and for being the emergency services network.

TOURISM AUSTRALIA

Classic Melbourne

NOT TO BE MISSED

- Admire the city's latest architectural masterpiece, **Federation Square**
- Discover natural history, social history and much more at the **Melbourne Museum**
- Get a bird's-eye view of the city and surrounds from the Australia's tallest building, the **Rialto Towers**
- Appreciate local and exotic animals in the beautiful parkland setting of **Melbourne Zoo**
- Find just about everything at the **Queen Victoria Market**
- Enjoy the superb displays of indigenous and introduced plants at the **Royal Botanic Gardens**
- Join one of Australia's coolest **cafe societies** in places like Carlton, South Yarra, Fitzroy and St Kilda
- For something different, take a ferry to the historic suburb of **Williamstown**
- Head to **Mornington** or the **Yarra Valley** for cellar-door tastings of fine wines

TOURISM AUSTRALIA

City Centre

Bounded by the Yarra on one side, parks and gardens on two more sides, and the Docklands on the other, the centre of Melbourne is a compact grid of streets that are very easy to navigate. Getting around on foot is usually possible, but there's also a free tram that circles the city which you can board and alight at leisure. There's more to Melbourne than just the central business district but, as the centre of politics, commerce, business, arts, culture and shopping, you can be forgiven if you don't get more than a few blocks away from your hotel. When you do, though, you'll find even more places of interest close by.

SIGHTS AND ACTIVITIES • Spot the amazing architecture at Flinders Street Station and surrounds: St Paul's Anglican Cathedral, Federation Square, St James' Old Cathedral, Royal Mint Building, St Patrick's Cathedral, Tasma Terrace, Parliament of Victoria, Melbourne Town Hall and the Gothic revival ANZ Bank building • Take a break at Birrarung Marr, 8.3 hectares of riverside parkland including a carillon, or any one of the city's beautiful parks • Marvel at the Immigration Museum in the Old Customs House, the Melbourne Aquarium, Victoria Police Museum, State Library of Victoria (beautiful reading room), Old Melbourne Gaol, and the Chinese Museum • Shop 'til you drop at Melbourne Central, Collins Place, the Block Arcade, the Royal Arcade and the Bourke Street Mall

VISITOR INFORMATION
Federation Square, Cnr Flinders Street and St Kilda Road
(03) 9658 9658

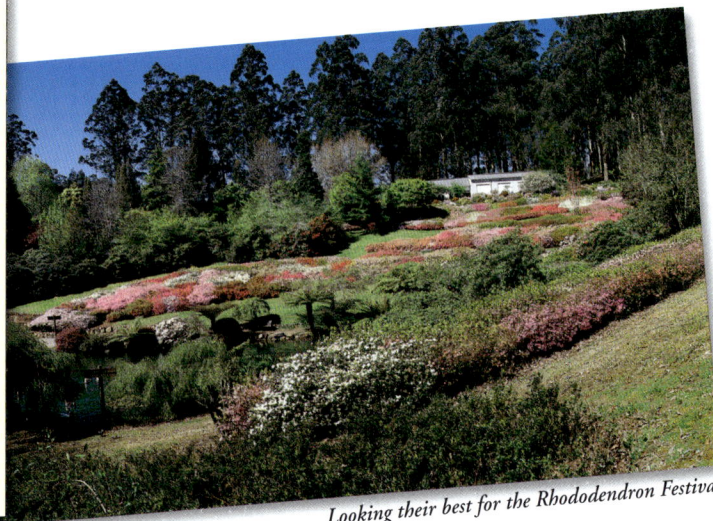

Looking their best for the Rhododendron Festival

South of the Yarra

Across the river the city stretches around the shore of Port Phillip and the commercial buildings give way to suburbs renowned for their style and elegance, such as Toorak and South Yarra. Here, too, you'll find vibrant shopping precincts and cafe strips, plus several cultural institutions.

SIGHTS AND ACTIVITIES • Get your sea legs at the *Polly Woodside* Melbourne Maritime Museum • Have a flutter at the casino in the Crown Entertainment Complex • Shop or dine alfresco at Southgate, with great views of the city skyline • Enjoy the finest in live performance at the Victorian Arts Centre • See a great collection of world art at the National Gallery of Victoria's International Collection, and more art at the Australian Centre for Contemporary Art • Take in the fresh air at the 35-hectare Botanic Gardens, established in 1846 • Walk, cycle or take a ferry along the Yarra • Visit Prahran Market (Tuesday, and Thursday to Saturday) • Wander along the pier at St Kilda, followed by coffee and cake in Acland Street

Inner North

The Victorian-influenced terrace houses and the presence of major educational institutions gives the area just north of the central business district a distinctly bohemian atmosphere. And here you'll find the cafe culture is a way of life.

SIGHTS AND ACTIVITIES • Find the perfect gift in Brunswick Street, Fitzroy or Lygon Street, Carlton, then enjoy a top-notch coffee in one of the excellent cafes • Catch a larger-than-life flick at IMAX then wander through the forest in the Melbourne Museum • Walk through the immaculate grounds of the University of Melbourne and the nearby Ian Potter Museum of Art • Set aside a day for the amazing Melbourne Zoo

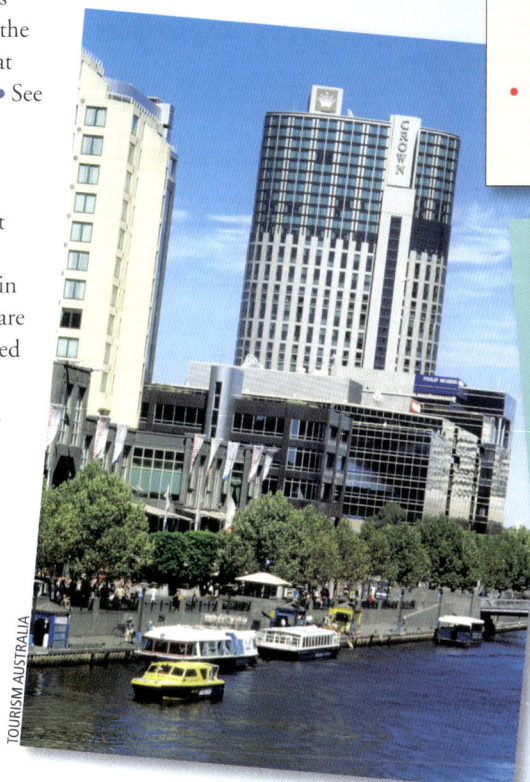

TOURISM AUSTRALIA

Southbank

LOCAL TIPS

- Take the **free tram** around the city streets for a quick and informative city tour
- Enjoy the **live music scene** at a pub in Brunswick Street, Fitzroy
- Discover that Melbourne (not Sydney) is the **alfresco dining** capital of Australia, as you wend your way among the acres of outdoor tables on Fitzroy Street, St Kilda
- Watch a footy match at the **Melbourne Cricket Ground** (MCG); if you're not interested in sport, go there anyway – it's one of the world's great stadiums, and an architectural and historic icon
- Take the fascinating **Williamstown ferry** from Southgate – there are great views along the way and Williamstown is a lovely spot for lunch

MEET THE LOCALS

The buskers

Hold an arts event, and they instantly appear. In a city like Melbourne, where arts events are happening almost all year round, buskers are a permanent fixture in the city's streets. They range in ability from truly awful to absolutely brilliant. Be on the lookout for the best of the best during the International Comedy Festival (April) and the Melbourne International Arts Festival (October).

The hit list

Red Symonds became a national institution as the curmudgeonly judge on Red Faces (the *Hey Hey, It's Saturday* talent quest). 'Gong 'im, Red' has become part of the national lexicon. The world has moved on and, now he is the 774 ABC Melbourne morning presenter, he has a new target in his sights – starfish. Northern Pacific sea stars have invaded Port Phillip, probably having stowed away on visiting ships up to 20 years ago. They threaten local shellfish populations, and it'll take more than a gong to be rid of them. If you go diving in the bay, you may see these (bad) starfish as well as local species of starfish (good). Hear Red's discussion at www.abc.net.au/melbourne/stories/s1055726.htm

Eastern Suburbs

Heading east from the city there are the premier sporting venues of the city, the Yarra's upper reaches and more great shopping and dining experiences.

SIGHTS AND ACTIVITIES • Relive some of Australian sports' finest moments with a guided tour of the magnificent Melbourne Cricket Ground (MCG) • Hunt for bargains in the shops on Swan Street, find fashion for the stylish on Bridge Road, and if you blow your budget, head for Victoria Street's cheap and cheerful Vietnamese strip for a meal • Take in the scenery of Yarra Bend Park or hire a canoe at Studley Park Boathouse

Yarra Valley and Dandenongs

A little over an hour from the hustle and bustle of the city you can find yourself in a completely different world of renowned wineries, excellent country restaurants, stunning ancient forests and superb rural scenery. The Yarra Valley is famous for its cool-climate wines and great eating experiences. The Dandenongs feature superb forests and the whole area is an ideal place for a short break from city life.

SIGHTS AND ACTIVITIES • Follow the Yarra Valley Regional Food Trail to discover berries, trout, chocolates, cheeses and more • Ride the Puffing Billy Steam Train for a unique experience and see the wonderful fern gullies and mountain-ash forest scenery between Belgrave and Gembrook • Visit some of the many cool-climate gardens that are open daily throughout the Dandenongs • Float above the vineyards on an early morning balloon flight • See Australian animals in their natural habitats at the multi-award winning Healesville Sanctuary

VISITOR INFORMATION
Yarra Valley: Old Courthouse, Harker Street, Healesville (03) 5962 2600
Dandenongs: 1211 Burwood Highway, Upper Ferntree Gully (03) 9758 7522

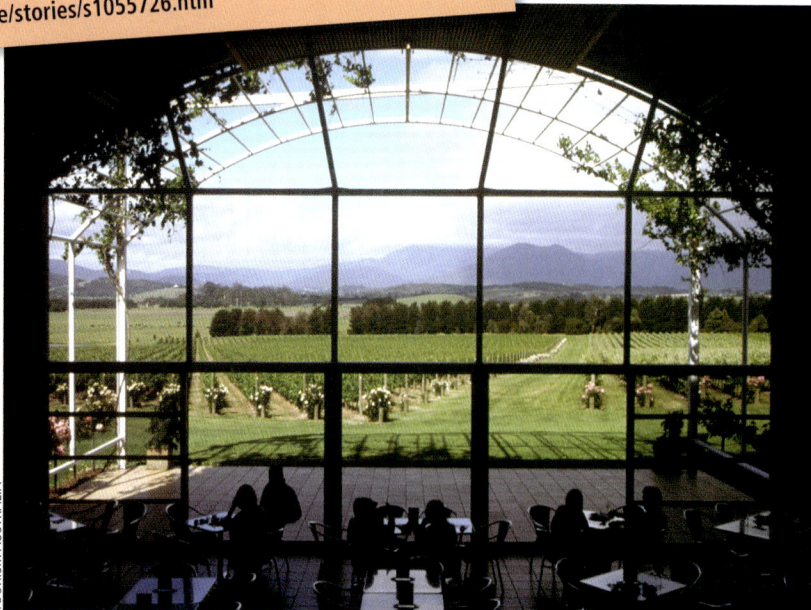

TOURISM AUSTRALIA

Restaurant at Domaine Chandon winery

Mornington Peninsula

This area has long been the seaside holiday destination for many Melburnians, with the sheltered waters of Port Phillip on one side, and the surf beaches facing Bass Strait on the other. In recent years it has also come into its own as a wine-growing area. And for those seeking more active pursuits, it's a golfers' paradise.

SIGHTS AND ACTIVITIES • Stay in the elegant hotels, B&Bs or motels of stylish Portsea, which also has a legendary pub. Note that from nearby Sorrento you can hop across to the Bellarine Peninsula by ferry • Get great views across the bay towards Melbourne from Arthurs Seat, then visit the themed gardens and mazes nearby, including a Maize Maze • Combine a trail ride with a winery tour at Rye • Take an energetic hike through the Mornington Peninsula National Park, with fine coastal scenery and an historic lighthouse (1858) at Cape Schanck

VISITOR INFORMATION
Point Nepean Road, Dromana (03) 5987 3078

Geelong and Bellarine Peninsula

Geelong (population 125 382) is Melbourne's second-oldest city and the largest provincial town in the State. It retains many fine old buildings – symbols of its long-established prosperity – and is the gateway to a region of spectacular coastal scenery, fine sheltered waterways and excellent wineries.

SIGHTS AND ACTIVITIES • Stroll along Geelong's waterfront with its colourful bollards or enjoy a dip in the restored sea baths that date from the 1930s • Play a round of golf at Barwon Heads, one of the State's top three public courses • Sample the Pinot Noirs and Chardonnays that are the mainstays of some 20 local wineries • Dine or stay in some of the elegant Victorian-era hotels of the former fishing village of Queenscliff • For a *Seachange*, look no further than Ocean Grove and Barwon Heads, setting for the hugely popular television series

LOCAL KNOWLEDGE

The book club

As is well known, on the first Tuesday in November the Melbourne Cup is run. But on the first Tuesday of every month, just after the 2pm news, 774 ABC Melbourne runs the Book Club. Books for the whole year are nominated so listeners have time to read them, then listeners and selected guests join the monthly discussion of each month's volume. Interesting, lively and erudite radio ensues. Pictured is the Afternoon team, Tracey Strong (Producer), Lynne Haultain (Presenter) and Kat Perdriau (Producer). Find out what books are being read and discussed, and hear audio of previous discussions at www.abc.net.au/melbourne/stories/s814809.htm

MEET THE LOCALS

Barefoot fisherman

He's in his eighties, never wears shoes, has let 40 years pass between visits to nearby Melbourne and is the last of the 'Couta boat fisherman operating out of Queenscliff. Lewis Ferrier also remembers when they were making the film *On the Beach* – he took the film stars Ava Gardner, Fred Astaire, Gregory Peck and Anthony Perkins out for a day on his boat. His life story is quite extraordinary and, if you can't meet him in Queenscliff, you can hear his story at www.abc.net.au/melbourne/stories/s1049861.htm

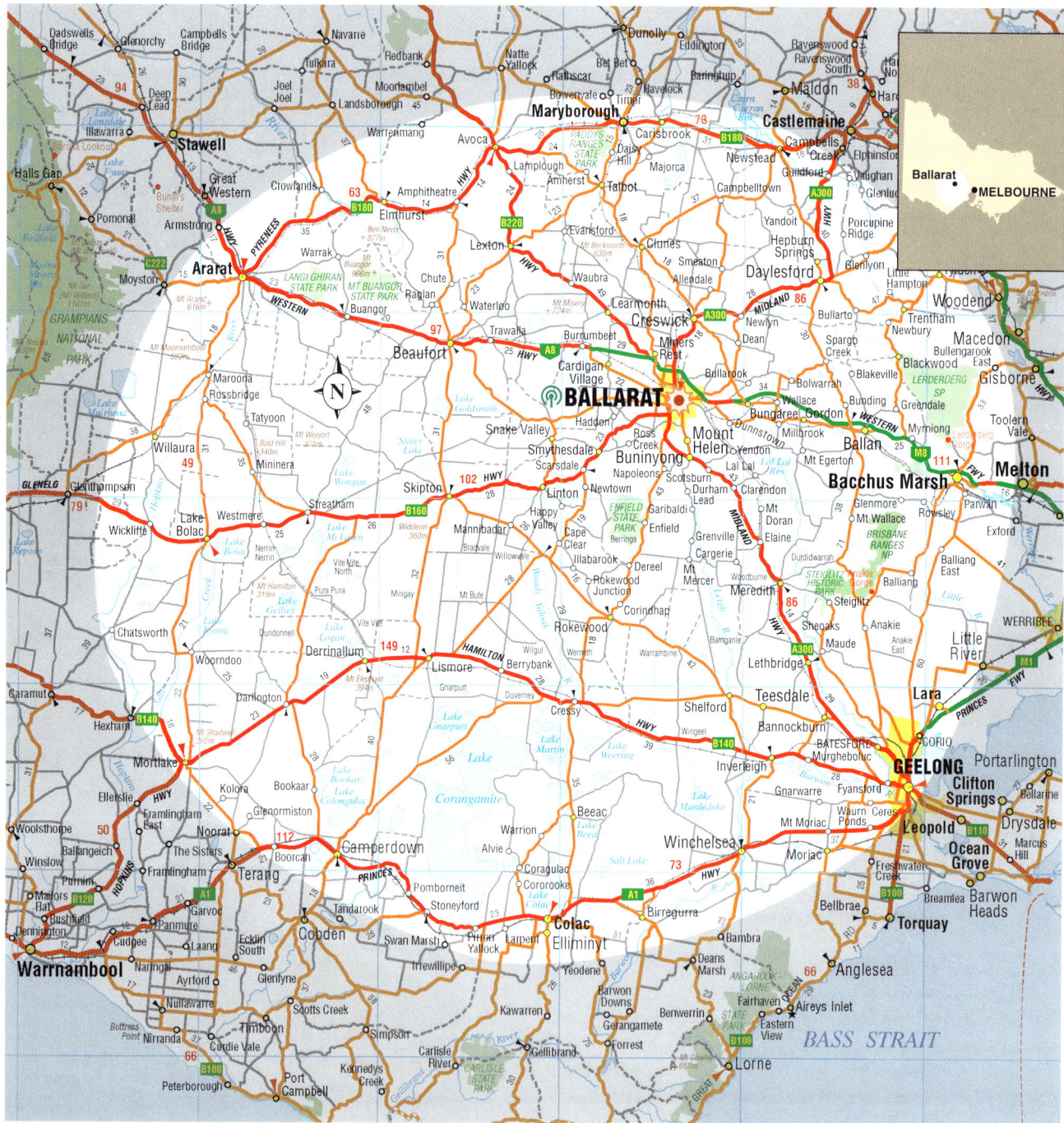

Location of ABC Local Radio studio

Ararat	107.9 FM	594 AM ABC Western Victoria
Ballan	107.9 FM	
Ballarat	107.9 FM	
Beaufort	107.9 FM	
Camperdown	107.9 FM	
Colac	107.9 FM	594 AM ABC Western Victoria
Creswick	107.9 FM	
Daylesford	107.9 FM	91.1 FM ABC Central Victoria
Lake Bolac	107.9 FM	
Lismore	107.9 FM	
Maryborough	107.9 FM	91.1 FM ABC Central Victoria
Meredith	107.9 FM	
Skipton	107.9 FM	

Ballarat has the only transmitter (FM) in the region

A s Victoria's largest inland city, Ballarat is steeped in history dating back to 1838, when a squatter called William Yuille camped on the shores of the Black Swamp, now known as Lake Wendouree. The words 'Balla Arat' were derived from the local Aboriginal dialect, meaning resting or camping place. The town is considered by some to be the birthplace of Australian republicanism, with the Eureka Stockade in Ballarat commemorating the miners' rebellion led by Peter Lalor on 3 December 1854. The remnants of the miners' blue and white flag can be seen in the Ballarat Fine Art Gallery.

Ballarat is a city of major industry, with well-known food and confectionery companies and building-industry suppliers, as well as an increasing number of local and multinational IT companies based here. Some of the area's primary industries include gold, clay, potatoes, wool and meat.

TOURISM AUSTRALIA

Sovereign Hill

ABC Local Radio's 107.9 ABC Ballarat is one of the ABC's newest stations, beginning its on-air existence one chilly winter morning on 30 June 2003. It's the largest ABC regional station for Victoria, primarily serving Ballarat, Ararat and Daylesford, as well as the greater south-west region including Hamilton, Portland, Port Fairy and Warrnambool.

NOT TO BE MISSED

- In **Maryborough** see the ornate Old Railway Station, described as 'a railway station with a town attached' by Mark Twain
- Visit the renowned **Sovereign Hill** in Ballarat, a superb reconstruction of a nineteenth-century mining settlement
- See the begonias (Ballarat's floral emblem) in bloom in March at the beautiful Botanic Gardens at **Lake Wendouree**
- Take the waters at the mineral springs in **Daylesford** and **Hepburn Springs**

Ballarat

Since the days of one of the biggest gold rushes Australia has ever seen, Ballarat has been a prosperous centre with a wealth of fascinating attractions, museums, galleries, parks and gardens. It was the scene of the famous Eureka Stockade, and today it is Victoria's largest inland city, with a population of 64 381. A short walk around the city centre will reveal that the city was built on the wealth of the region's goldfields. A drive will provide ample opportunity to enjoy a region of remarkable diversity.

SIGHTS AND ACTIVITIES • Visit the Fine Art Gallery in Lydiard Street, Australia's largest and oldest regional gallery • Try water sports, or a paddle-steamer tour with historical commentary, at Lake Wendouree • Take a relaxing stroll in Ballarat's Botanic Gardens, a showcase for begonias (the town's floral emblem) and site of the Robert Clarke Horticultural Centre • Visit the Tramway Museum, with its vintage trams, or ride the Vintage Tramway on weekends, and public and school holidays • Rush to Sovereign Hill, a renowned reconstruction of a goldmining settlement with re-enactments and displays; adjacent to Sovereign Hill is the Gold Museum with the history of goldmining and a large collection of gold coins • Step back into medieval times at Kryal Castle, just east of the city

VISITOR INFORMATION
Cnr Sturt and Albert streets (03) 5320 5741

Colac

Colac (population 9793), the centre of a prosperous agricultural region, was built by the shores of Lake Colac on the eastern side of the volcanic plain that extends over much of Victoria's Western District. The town is a popular destination for all kinds of water activities including fishing, boating and waterskiing.

SIGHTS AND ACTIVITIES • Hook a prized red-fin in Lake Colac • At Irrewarra Homestead, 10km north, taste delicious natural ice-creams • See 30 volcanic lakes from Red Rock Lookout, 22 kilometres north, including saltwater Lake Corangamite • Go platypus spotting at Lake Elizabeth, 32 kilometres south-east

VISITOR INFORMATION
Cnr Murray and Queen streets (03) 5231 3730

MEET THE LOCALS

The Tan Clan

The early bird may catch the worm, but he'll have to be quick to catch these Ballarat locals. Early risers may be lucky enough to catch the extraordinary sight of up to 70 joggers, called the Tan Clan, panting through the streets. They're named after their founder, Richard Tan, and they've been an informal jogging group for the last 25 years. They run about 10 kilometres four mornings a week, starting from their 'clubhouse' (the public toilets at the town's lake). They range in age and ability from teenagers to 60-year-olds, from social joggers to multiple-marathon runners.

Daylesford

The lovely town of Daylesford (population 3287) and adjacent Hepburn Springs are famous for their mineral springs. There are more than 60 springs in the area, but the town, which sits on the side of Wombat Hill, also boasts beautiful gardens and some excellent forest scenery and points of interest.

SIGHTS AND ACTIVITIES • Bathe, relax in a flotation tank or get a massage and sauna at Hepburn Springs Spa Complex • Stroll the Tipperary Walking Track and finish with lunch at Lake House, beside Lake Daylesford • Drive the 65-kilometre Wombat Forest Drive to see waterfalls and springs, and don't forget to pack a picnic • Admire the gardens at Convent Gallery, and in the Botanic Gardens take in the view from the lookout tower

VISITOR INFORMATION
Vincent Street (03) 5348 1339

TOURISM AUSTRALIA
Dining at Lake House

Maryborough

Like many of the towns in this region, Maryborough (population 7381) owes its existence to the gold rushes of the 1850s; today, sheep and secondary industry are the mainstays of its economy. The town retains much of the flavour of its prosperous past, making it a smaller-scale version of Ballarat, 70 kilometres to the south.

Yuulong Lavender Estate, Yendon

SIGHTS AND ACTIVITIES • Visit the historic museum in Worsley Cottage, Palmerston Street; the information centre, antique gallery and woodwork shop in the old Railway Station; or the Central Goldfields Art Gallery in the old fire station • Pick up a brochure and take a stroll through the streets to enjoy the magnificent buildings, such as the National Trust-listed courthouse, post office and town hall • Climb the Pioneer Memorial Tower at Bristol Hill

VISITOR INFORMATION
Cnr Alma and Nolan streets (03) 5460 4511

LOCAL TIPS

- There aren't many towns that can claim to have an eel factory, but in **Skipton** you'll find one that nets, processes and exports these slippery delicacies
- For fishing, boating and swimming, **Lake Bolac**, an hour west of Ballarat, covers 1460 hectares and boasts 20 kilometres of sandy shores
- See the large collection of parrots at **Buninyong**'s Flora and Bird Park
- Find some of the 61 species of orchids identified at **Enfield State Park**, 16 kilometres south of Ballarat

MEET THE LOCALS

Santa's little helper

What do you do if you find that raising sheep and growing vegetables is a lot of hard work for not much money? Ballarat farmer Peter Parry thought well outside the square some 20 years ago, when he decided to grow Christmas trees. These aren't just sad, stumpy things chopped out of the bush, they're nurtured and carefully shaped (a little like shearing sheep) and come in sizes from about 1.5 metres to 3 metres high.

MEET THE LOCALS

Club MUD

Club MUD (Mountain bikes Under Demolition) is a Ballarat-based group attracting competition and social cyclists who enjoy cross-country and downhill riding. Formed in 1996, the club ran for three years before disbanding – only to be reborn in 2002 after a huge response from local riders. It now hosts events such as the King of Ballarat downhill series, where MUD really meets mud.

JARROD WATT

ABC Mildura-Swan Hill

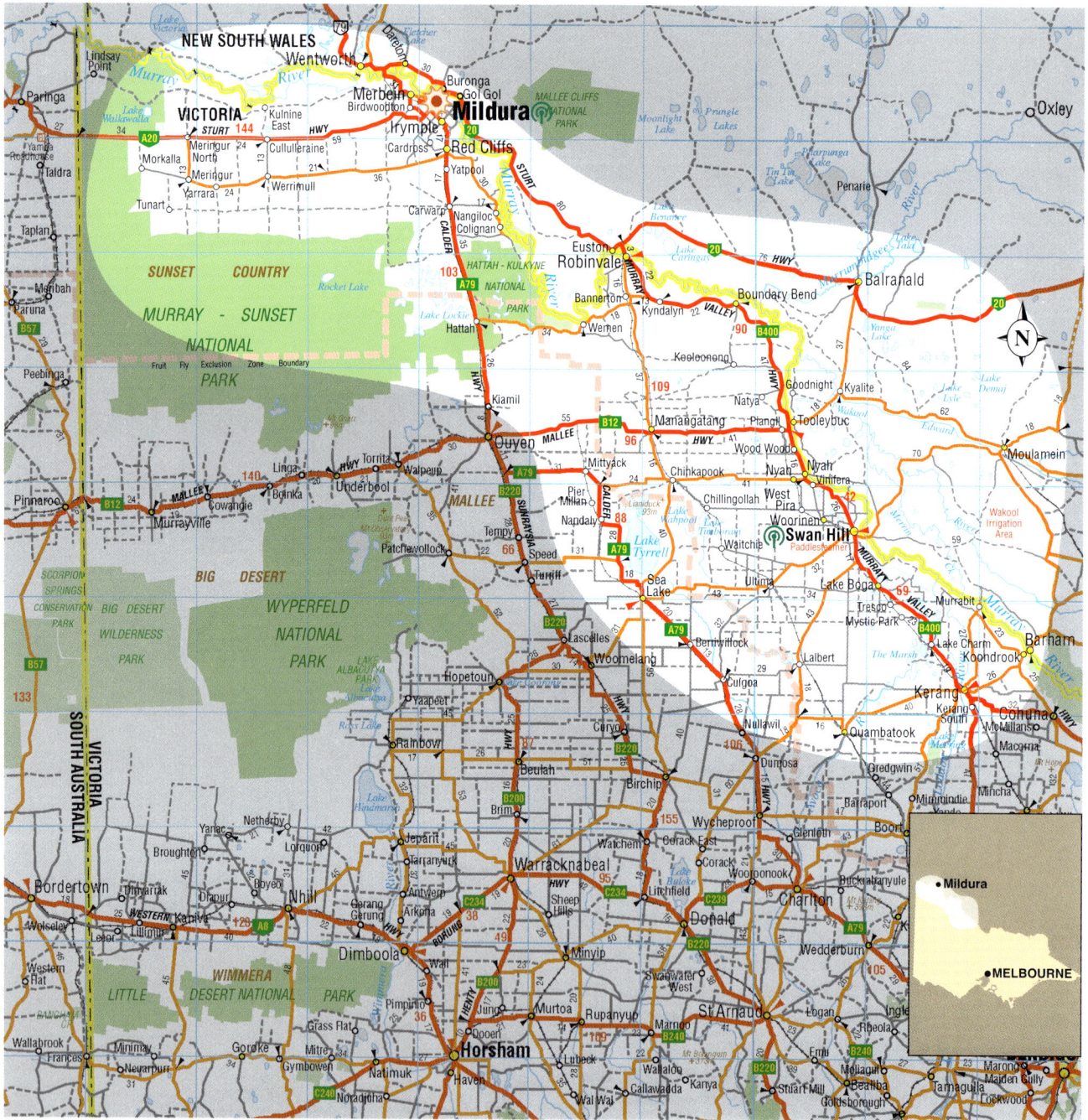

Location of ABC Local Radio studio

Local Radio Frequencies		
Balranald	102.1 FM	
Barham	102.1 FM	
Kerang	102.1 FM	
Mildura	104.3 FM	
Manangatang	102.1 FM	
Merbein	104.3 FM	
Red Cliffs	104.3 FM	
Robinvale	104.3 FM	
Swan Hill	102.1 FM	
Wentworth	104.3 FM	

Towns in green have their own FM transmitter

Grape vines near Mildura

The Mildura-Swan Hill region is renowned for having more days of sunshine than the Gold Coast and at one time was known as the 'Weather Resort'. Summer temperatures often exceed 40 degrees Celsius, but overnight winter temperatures can drop below zero. Spring and autumn in the region are close to divine.

Irrigation is the lifeblood of the region and, as Australians slowly come to terms with the finite nature of water, it's not surprising that water conservation is a major issue. Paddle-steamers still ply the waters of the Murray, but now take tourists, rather than grain, up and down the river. However, the region is not all rolling green vineyards. Many people live on broad-acre farms in what is considered 'outback' country. The amazing Mungo National Park, where the remains of Mungo Man and Mungo Woman have been found, is also in the region.

The Mildura office of the ABC was established in 1990 to service north-western Victoria and south-western New South Wales. It broadcasts from Kerang in the east through to the South Australian border in the west, and from north of Wentworth to Ouyen in the south.

NOT TO BE MISSED

- Cruise the Murray on one of the many **paddle-steamers** that hark back to an earlier era
- Go **bird-watching** along the Murray, especially to see the elusive black swans
- In **Mildura** enjoy a meal at the restaurant of television chef, Stefano di Pieri
- Watch the sun sink into the horizon on the vast plains north of the **Murray**

Mildura paddlesteamer

Ballooning, a popular activity in the region

TOURISM AUSTRALIA

LOCAL KNOWLEDGE

The world's tallest structure

Watch the space just outside Wentworth that is slated for an immense solar-power generation project that will include the world's tallest tower. At one kilometre high, it will be nearly twice the height of any other building on earth. Currently in the planning stage, the project will use solar power to heat air at ground level that will then rise by convection up the tower, turning turbines and generating enough energy to power 200 000 homes. (More details at www.enviromission.com.au.)

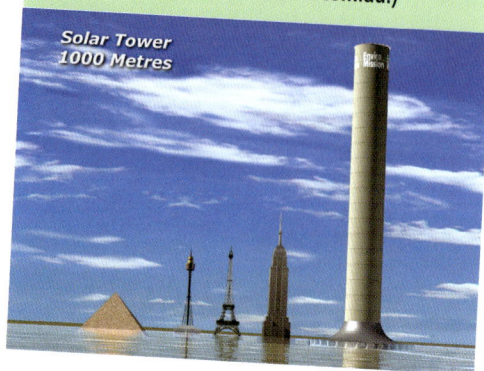

Solar Tower 1000 Metres

Mildura

This is the main town of an incredibly fertile, intensely irrigated area that was developed in the late nineteenth century. The city (population 24 142) owes much to Alfred Deakin, who encouraged the Canadian irrigators, the Chaffey Brothers, to investigate the possibilities. Today, the city is the centre of a premier fruit-growing region. Visitors are drawn to the area by the temperate year-round climate, the pleasant river scenery and water activities.

SIGHTS AND ACTIVITIES • Choose a paddle-steamer cruise of two hours to six days duration aboard a range of vessels that depart from Mildura Wharf at the end of Madden Avenue • Join a tour with an indigenous guide to nearby Mungo National Park • Visit the Alfred Deakin Centre for displays on the area, or the Mildura Arts Centre complex to see the original Chaffey home, the sculpture trail and more • Take the kids to Snakes and Ladders fun park, which also features a dunny collection • Tour the numerous wineries • See Australian native plant displays at the Australian Inland Botanic Gardens

VISITOR INFORMATION
Alfred Deakin Centre, 180–190 Deakin Avenue
(03) 5018 8380

Balranald

Not all of the towns in the region sit on the Murray. Balranald (population 1419) is a wool, cattle, wheat, fruit and timber town on the banks of the Murrumbidgee.

SIGHTS AND ACTIVITIES • Take a break in Heritage Park, with its Historical Museum (open Wednesday afternoons), gaol, pine school house, and picnic and barbecue facilities • Hop in your car to do the Memorial Drive or stroll the self-guide town walk (brochure available) • Fish or swim at nearby Yanga Lake

VISITOR INFORMATION
Heritage Park, Market Street (03) 5020 1599

Barham

Located on the north bank of the Murray, with its twin town of Koondrook on the opposite bank, this quiet rural town (population 1167) is renowned for its good water-sports facilities.

SIGHTS AND ACTIVITIES • Take the self-guide historic walk of both towns (brochure available) • Enjoy the recreational facilities at the artificial lakes of the Barham Lakes Complex • Visit the Kerang Ibis Rookery to see these and numerous other waterbirds

VISITOR INFORMATION
15 Murray Street (03) 5433 3100

Swan Hill

Named in 1836 by explorer Thomas Mitchell for the black swans in the area, Swan Hill (population 9385) was a busy river port. Today, the Murray and the pleasant climate attract visitors to enjoy the fishing, boating and other water sports.

SIGHTS AND ACTIVITIES • Experience what Swan Hill was like in its early days at the Pioneer Settlement, a 7-hectare park that includes aspects of Aboriginal and European culture • Cruise the Murray on the paddle-steamer PS *Pyap* • Picnic, fish and stroll along the riverside in Swan Hill or at Tooleybuc (46 kilometres north)

VISITOR INFORMATION
306 Campbell Street (03) 5032 3033

The Murray at Swan Hill

LOCAL TIPS

- See one of the world's largest ibis-breeding grounds in the wetlands near **Kerang**
- Keep an eye out for memorial markers around **Mildura**. During World War II the area was the country's largest pilot-training centre. Sadly, the price of mistakes was high and there are 45 sites where 52 pilots and crew died. The Mildura Royal Air Force Museum has identified and marked all of them
- Visit **Thegoa Lagoon**, near Wentworth, once the campsite of the notorious cattle duffer, Harry Redford (immortalised as Captain Starlight) who was subsequently arrested for a pub brawl in town and incarcerated in Wentworth Gaol for two days

MEET THE LOCALS

The pioneer puppeteer

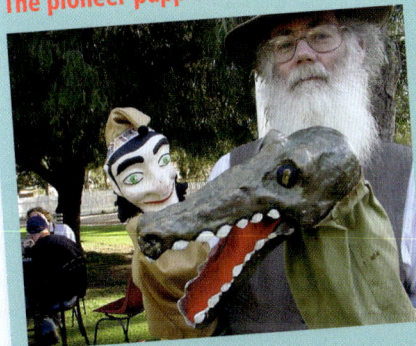

Step back in time at the Swan Hill Pioneer Settlement. You'll even find that the entertainment for children is true to the nineteenth century. In fact, the traditional Punch and Judy show put on by puppeteer Joe Blake uses donated antique puppets that date from the era, and keeps as close to the original script as possible. In an age of electronic games and sitcoms filled with snappy one-liners, the kids still love a tale with a snappy crocodile in it.

LOCAL KNOWLEDGE

Aboriginal burial grounds

It may be the largest Aboriginal cemetery in Australia, the final resting place for thousands of people built up over hundreds of years. The remains are to be found on Wallpolla Island, on Latje Latje Aboriginal land 50 kilometres west of Mildura. The site is of immense cultural significance, and a management plan to preserve it and educate people about it is being put in place by the North-West Aboriginal Cultural Heritage Board.

ABC Western Victoria

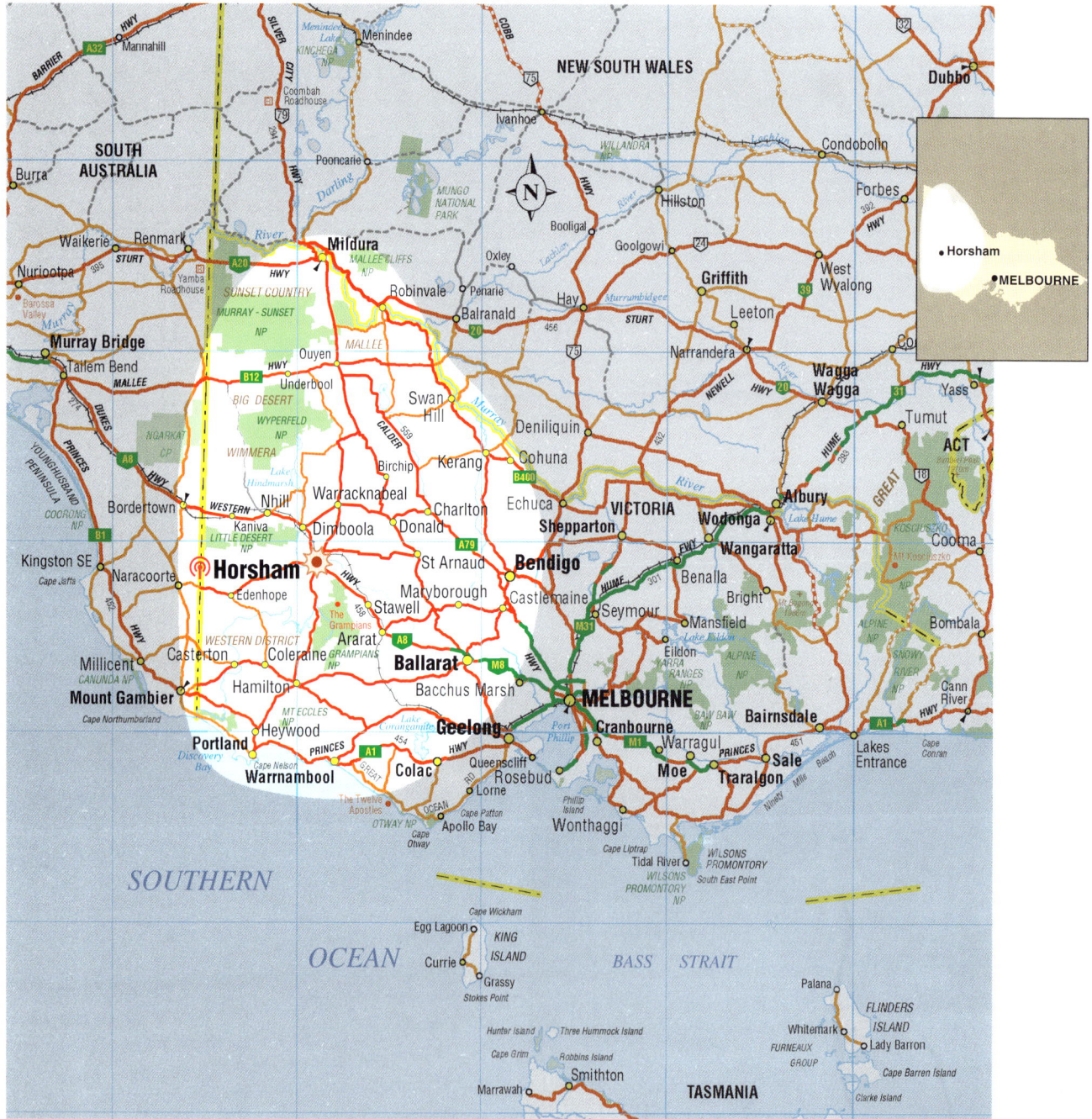

☼ Location of ABC Local Radio studio

Local Radio Frequencies

Ararat	594 AM	107.9 FM ABC Ballarat
Birchip	594 AM	
Casterton	594 AM	94.1 FM ABC South West Victoria
Charlton	594 AM	
Cohuna	594 AM	
Coleraine	594 AM	94.1 FM South West Victoria
Dimboola	594 AM	
Donald	594 AM	
Edenhope	594 AM	
Horsham	594 AM	
Kaniva	594 AM	
Nhill	594 AM	
Ouyen	594 AM	
St Arnaud	594 AM	91.1 FM ABC Central Victoria
Stawell	594 AM	
Warracknabeal	594 AM	
Underbool	594 AM	

Horsham has the only transmitter (AM) in the region

The vast region between the Murray and the Southern Ocean is a captivating area that combines big sky country and wide open spaces with spectacular mountain ranges and deep forests. Agriculture is the mainstay of the economy, especially wheat and fine wool, with many areas under irrigation. The area also enjoys a long history of grape growing and fine wine-making.

For visitors there are numerous attractions. In particular the Little Desert, Mount Arapiles and the Grampians are renowned for their sunsets, bird life, scenery, rock-climbing, walks and much more. Many of the towns have lively festivals, fascinating art galleries and museums, and beautiful buildings. And then there are the numerous lakes, famous for their fishing, swimming, boating and bird-watching possibilities.

It's no surprise that the local community is diverse in its interests and activities. The ABC has been a vital part of that community since the 1930s, when the first studios in Horsham were based in the post office. The studios moved to above the Commonwealth Bank in the early 1960s, and from then until the 1980s the staff included a rural officer, talks officer, two journalists, clerk-receptionist and part-time typist. Since 2003 ABC Local Radio has returned to its roots in the region, with the Wimmera and Southern Mallee local breakfast program.

TOURISM AUSTRALIA

Wheat, one of the mainstays of the region's economy

NOT TO BE MISSED

- Float over the sublime scenery on a balloon flight from **Stawell**
- Get a grip on one of Australia's best rock-climbing sites, **Mount Arapiles**
- Enjoy a short walk in the **Little Desert National Park**
- Take in the 360-degree views from One Tree Hill at **Ararat**
- Explore the fern-filled gullies, rocky escarpments, waterfalls and lakes of the **Grampians National Park**

Jan **Great Western:** Champagne Picnic Races

Feb **Halls Gap:** Grampians Jazz Festival

Mar **Ararat:** Jailhouse Rock Festival
Casterton: Vintage Car Rally

Easter **Stawell:** Gift (professional footrace)
Warracknabeal: Y-Fest

Apr **Dimboola:** Wimmera German Fest

May **Halls Gap:** Grampians Gourmet Weekend

June–July **Casterton:** Australian Kelpie Muster and Kelpie Working Dog Auction

Sept **Ararat:** Australian Orchid Festival

Oct **Ararat:** Golden Gateway Festival
Cavendish: Southern Grampians Open Gardens
Horsham: Spring Garden Festival

Nov **Horsham:** Kannamaroo Rock 'n' Roll Festival

Horsham

This is the major centre (population 12 591) of the Wimmera region. It is a good base for touring the Grampians, the Little Desert and Mount Arapiles, but the town itself has plenty of attractions as well. There are some excellent golf courses, a fine regional art gallery, and good shopping and dining opportunities.

SIGHTS AND ACTIVITIES • Picnic in the excellent Botanic Gardens, designed by Sir William Guilfoyle, curator of Melbourne's Royal Botanic Gardens • Watch a Wimmera

Scene in the Grampians

sunset from the Wimmera River (there's a historic river-walk as well) • Tour the Wool Factory, which produces extra-fine wool products from Saxon-Merino sheep • Go fishing, swimming or boating in the numerous lakes within a few kilometres of town • See an operating farm, Do See View, just out of town, with Clydesdale horses, native flowers and a blacksmith's shop

VISITOR INFORMATION
20 O'Callaghan Parade (03) 5382 1832

Ararat

The town (population 6890) was first settled by goldminers in the 1850s, but the rush soon gave way to sheep farming, and the town remains the centre of fine merino-wool production. There are numerous good quality wineries in the surrounding area.

SIGHTS AND ACTIVITIES • Pick up a brochure for a historic walk or drive; be sure to check out the landmark bluestone buildings in Barkly Street, including the post office, town hall, civic square and war memorial • Visit the Ararat Art Gallery, where local artists specialise in works using wool and fibre • See the orchid display, fernery and herb garden at the Botanical Gardens • Lock in a visit to the Old Ararat Gaol for a guided tour • Take the Great Grape Road tour (brochure available), visiting wineries through Ballarat and St Arnaud and back

VISITOR INFORMATION
Old Railway Station, 91 High Street (03) 5352 2096

MEET THE LOCALS

Working dogs

The kelpie is Australia's own working dog, and each year they're celebrated at the home of the cattle dog, Casterton. The Kelpie Muster is held over the Queen's birthday weekend and features displays of kelpie skills and special events, such as kelpie pinball and kelpie high jump. Breeders come from far and wide to auction their pups, and there's no shortage of willing buyers.

Nhill

One of the many charming country towns of the Wimmera, Nhill, population 1890, claims to have the largest single-bin wheat silo in the Southern Hemisphere. However, the main attraction in the area is the Little Desert National Park, renowned for its wildflowers, bird-watching, and scenic walks and drives.

SIGHTS AND ACTIVITIES • Take a historic walk or drive around town (brochure available), or ride the miniature railway, taking in such sights as the memorial to the Clydesdale horses that helped open up the area, and the cottage of lyric poet John Shaw Neilson • Bird-watch from the bird hide on the boardwalk from Jaypex Park to Nhill Lake • Visit Little Desert Lodge, the base for day tours and an October wildflower exhibition

VISITOR INFORMATION
Victoria Street (03) 5391 3086

Stawell

Best known for Australia's famous professional footrace, the Stawell Gift (held at Easter), this prosperous town (population 6272) has numerous other fascinating attractions. It is also another good base for daytrips to the Grampians and local wineries.

SIGHTS AND ACTIVITIES • Return to the days of goldmining with a city tour taking in strike sites, gold-processing operation sites and buildings built with the subsequent wealth (map available) • See working models of famous buildings and scenes from around the world at Casper's Mini World • Take your mark at the Stawell Gift Hall of Fame Museum • In spring, see wildflowers and rare orchids at Stawell Ironbark Forest • In the nearby village of Halls Gap, watch long-billed corellas return to roost each night • Go climbing, walking and camping in the Grampians National Park

VISITOR INFORMATION
50–52 Western Highway (03) 5358 2314

LOCAL TIPS

- For all things olive, visit Mount Zero Olives at **Laharum**, 30 kilometres south of Horsham
- One of the region's best known and oldest wineries is Seppelt's **Great Western**, between Stawell and Ararat; grapes were first planted here in 1865
- View Aboriginal rock art at **Bunjil's Rock Shelter**, just south of Stawell
- In the **Grampians**, a popular day trip from Halls Gap takes in Boroka Lookout, Reed Lookout and Mackenzie Falls, lunch at Zumstein's historic site and picnic area, then back to town via Silverband Falls and the forest and ferns of Delleys Dell

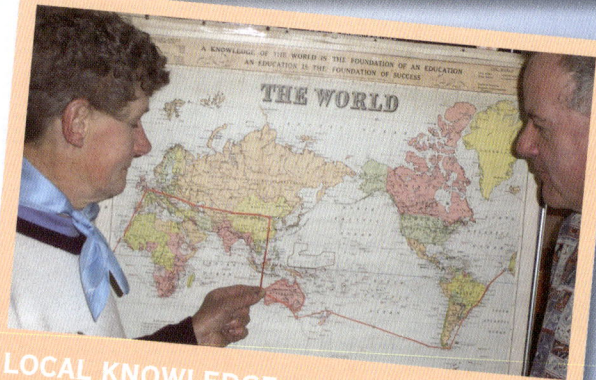

LOCAL KNOWLEDGE
Walking around the world

When you're visiting Dimboola, you might like to find out how far the locals have got as they attempt to walk around the world. In order to promote healthier lifestyles, the locals are encouraged to record how far they walk. The distances are then tallied, and displayed on a noticeboard in town. Thus a journey of 20 000 kilometres can start with a stroll to the shops.

LOCAL KNOWLEDGE
The arts have no limits

One of the best things about art is that disability is not an obstacle – the human spirit can always find a way to express itself. Horsham's annual Awakenings Festival, Australia's only regional disability arts festival, is a celebration of this. Held in October and supported by ABC Western Victoria, it has been getting bigger every year. For more details see www.awakenings.horsham.net.au

ABC South West Victoria

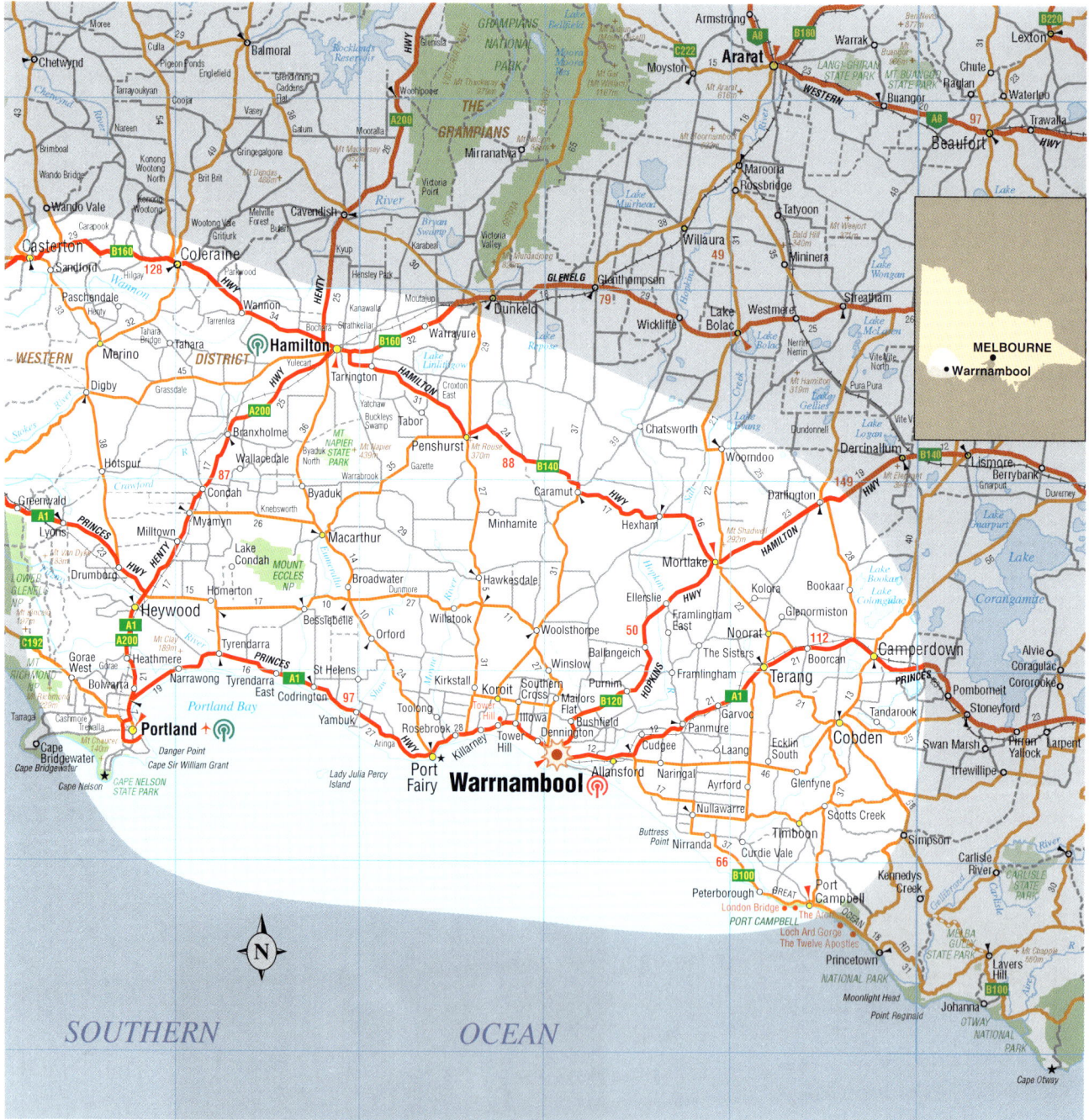

Location of ABC Local Radio studio

Local Radio Frequencies	
Cobden	1602 AM
Mortlake	1602 AM
Peterborough	1602 AM
Port Fairy	1602 AM
Terang	1602 AM
Warrnambool	1602 AM
Apollo Bay	89.5 FM
Casterton	94.1 FM
Coleraine	94.1 FM
Hamilton	94.1 FM
Portland	96.9 FM

Towns in red have their own AM transmitter
Towns in green have their own FM transmitter

ABC South West Victoria's coverage includes towns along the Great Ocean Road. However, due to the mountainous terrain of this region, some areas may not be able to receive a good-quality local signal. Apollo Bay, for example, is a networked Victorian Local Radio service fed by satellite. In other towns 774 ABC Melbourne may provide a clearer alternative.

The Twelve Apostles, Port Campbell National Park

Three words define this region: Great Ocean Road. It's one of the world's great drives and draws people from all over the world to enjoy the superb coastal scenery. However, there's much more to the south-west than driving. There are coastal trails and walks in subtropical rainforest. The Shipwreck Coast has left a legacy of maritime history that can be explored at several sites in the area. And the many coastal and rural towns in this quiet corner of Victoria offer a pace of life that many have almost forgotten.

ABC South West Victoria's programs are centred around the ABC Warrnambool studios. The station is a vital element in addressing issues that affect the local community, and it's also a great way for visitors to stay informed about everything that's going on in the area (and the rest of the world). The region has a thriving music community and plenty of year-round entertainment.

NOT TO BE MISSED

- Go whale-spotting from June to September at the beaches near **Warrnambool**

- Visit the spectacular coastal scenery of the **Shipwreck Coast**

- Drive the **Great Ocean Road**, one of the greatest scenic experiences in the world

- Surf at some of Australia's most famous beaches, including **Bells Beach**

TOURISM AUSTRALIA

- Hike in the stunning forest of the **Otway Ranges**, **Lorne State Park**, or along the Alan Marshall Walking Track near **Terang**

LOCAL EVENTS

Jan **Lorne:** Pier to Pub Swim; Mountain to Surf Footrace

Feb **Heywood:** Wood, Wine and Roses Festival
Mortlake: Buskers' Festival
Portland: Go Kart Street Grand Prix; Yachting Regatta
Warrnambool: Wunta Fiesta (family entertainment); Tarerer Festival (indigenous culture and music)

Mar **Port Fairy:** Folk Festival

Easter **Bells Beach:** Rip Curl Pro Surfing Championship

May **Warrnambool:** Grand Annual Steeplechase

July **Warrnambool:** Fun 4 Kids
Hamilton: Sheepvention

Aug **Casterton:** Kelpie Festival

Sept **Anglesea:** Angair Wildflower Festival

Oct **Warrnambool:** Spring Orchid Show

Nov **Portland:** Three Bays Marathon

Dec **Lorne:** Falls Festival

TOURISM AUSTRALIA

LOCAL KNOWLEDGE
Fun for kids

If you don't know what to do with the kids during the winter school holidays, you can always take them to their very own festival. Each year Warrnambool's annual Fun 4 Kids Festival attracts tens of thousands of youngsters and their parents from all over Victoria, as well as from around Australia and overseas. With musicians, more than 50 workshops, games, toys, and some of the biggest names in children's literature, all roads lead to fun.

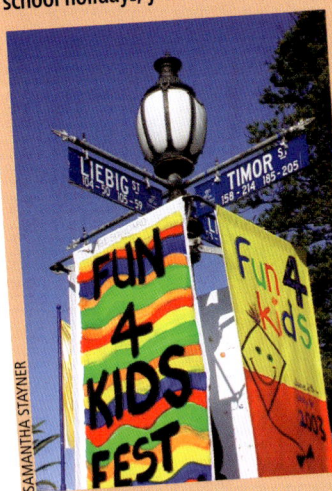
SAMANTHA STAYNER

Warrnambool

The major city in south-west Victoria, Warrnambool (population 26 052) is at the centre of a thriving agricultural, fishing and tourism region. The city itself has many attractive buildings and beautiful waterways. It is also the gateway to the famed Shipwreck Coast, where more than 150 vessels have met with disaster. Relics of some of the wrecks are to be found in the town's museum.

SIGHTS AND ACTIVITIES ● Step back in time at the reconstructed nineteenth-century maritime village at Flagstaff Hill Maritime Museum, where you'll also find relics from shipwrecks, such as the exquisite *Loch Ard Peacock* ● Take a heritage walk around the city's many historic buildings (brochure available) ● Pick up the Kid's Country Treasure Map and use it to explore the surrounding area ● Cruise or fish on the Hopkins River, or at Blue Hole at the river mouth ● Ride on the beaches as part of a horse trail-ride ● Explore the nearby Shipwreck Coast, with scenic points including the Twelve Apostles, Loch Ard Gorge and Port Campbell ● View rare southern right whales from June to September from the viewing platform just east of town ● Catch a trout at the Warrnambool Trout Farm ● Search for the mysterious Mahogany Ship on the 22-kilometre beach between Warrnambool and Port Fairy

VISITOR INFORMATION
Flagstaff Hill Maritime Museum, Merri Street (03) 5564 7837

Apollo Bay

Situated astride the spectacular Great Ocean Road, Apollo Bay (population 979) is a pretty seaside village that enjoys the best of all worlds. On one side are beaches, fishing and some of the best coastal scenery to be found anywhere. On the other are the shadowy forests of the Otways, laced with walking trails and dotted with waterfalls.

SIGHTS AND ACTIVITIES ● Take a historic or scenic tour, guided or self-guide, by car or mountain bike (brochures available) ● Enjoy the views around Carisbrook Falls, Turtons Track, Marriners Lookout, Crows Nest Lookout and Paradise Scenic Reserve ● See the 300-year-old native beech in Otway National Park, and the 150-year-old Cape Otway Lighthouse

VISITOR INFORMATION
100 Great Ocean Road (03) 5237 6529

Port Fairy

An utterly charming seaport that started as a whaling station, this beautifully preserved fishing village of 2625 people has some 50 National Trust-classified buildings. Another remarkable aspect of the town is the wild surf on the beaches facing the exposed south-west and the sheltered stretch of water south-east of Griffiths Island.

SIGHTS AND ACTIVITIES • Stroll along the docks of the Moyne River and remind yourself that you're not back in the nineteenth century • Take a tour of the many significant buildings around the town (brochure available) and visit the History Centre in the old courthouse • Pick up some fish and crayfish from the wharf, in season • Wait patiently at Griffiths Island at dusk (or maybe later) for the spectacular return of short-tailed shearwaters (mutton birds) to their rookery

VISITOR INFORMATION
22 Bank Street (03) 5568 268

Whale watching is popular in the region

TOURISM AUSTRALIA

Portland

Victoria's most westerly coastal town, with a population of 9664, is the gateway to a dazzling range of things to see and do. The town is the oldest in the State, settled by the Hentys in 1834.

SIGHTS AND ACTIVITIES • Marvel at the skeleton of a 13-metre sperm whale and the lifeboat used to save survivors of the shipwreck *Admella* at the Portland Maritime Discovery Centre; the wreck of the *Regia* is nearby • Take a tour to see some of the town's 200 historic buildings, including the Steam Packet Inn and Edward Henty's homestead • Keep a lookout for whales from Water Tower Lookout or Portland Battery • Hike to see a petrified forest, blowholes and wildlife including fur seals at Cape Bridgewater • View the spectacular gorge, wildflowers, bird life and Princess Margaret Rose Caves at Lower Glenelg National Park

VISITOR INFORMATION
Lee Breakwater Road (03) 5523 2671

LOCAL TIPS

- While driving through the south-west, stay tuned to ABC Local Radio for the latest on what's happening in the music scene. The south-west is host to one of the country's biggest folk festivals at **Port Fairy**. It's also home to plenty of home-grown talent, including local indigenous artists, and gets plenty of visits from numerous international acts as well. You can hear them year-round, performing live in the **Warrnambool** studio

- Take a boat trip at **Cape Bridgewater** to see Australian fur seals at play

- Head to **Torquay** for great bargains on surf gear, and visit the Surfworld Museum which celebrates the wonders of the wave

- Play golf among the kangaroos at the **Anglesea Golf Club**; non-players can witness the spectacle from Golf Links Road

- Walk all or a stage of the **Surf Coast Walk** which runs from Jan Juc to Moggs Creek and enjoy the magnificent coastal scenery

MEET THE LOCALS

The Friends of the Great South West Walk

It's a job that never ends, but the Friends of the 250-kilometre Great South West Walk are devoted to maintaining the trail that takes in superb coastal scenery, wonderful forest, stretches of river and sweeps of beach. Erosion is one of their biggest challenges, especially on the cliff tops. Friend Bill Golding (pictured) has worked on the track in 100 kilometre-per-hour gales, but he says, 'The greatest favour anyone can do it is to use it, because it was put there for that purpose'. Of course, you don't have to do it all at once. Like maintaining it, you can take it one step at a time.

SAMANTHA STAYNER

MEET THE LOCALS

Upstanding citizens

If the idea of being laid to rest isn't a thing of the gravest importance, check out the proposal being considered in Derrinallum, 100 kilometres north-east of Warrnambool. The small country town is considering offering to bury people standing up, saving both money and space. The proposal means it'll be standing tomb only, and means that you can continue to be an upstanding member of the community long after you've gone.

SAMANTHA STAYNER

ABC Central Victoria

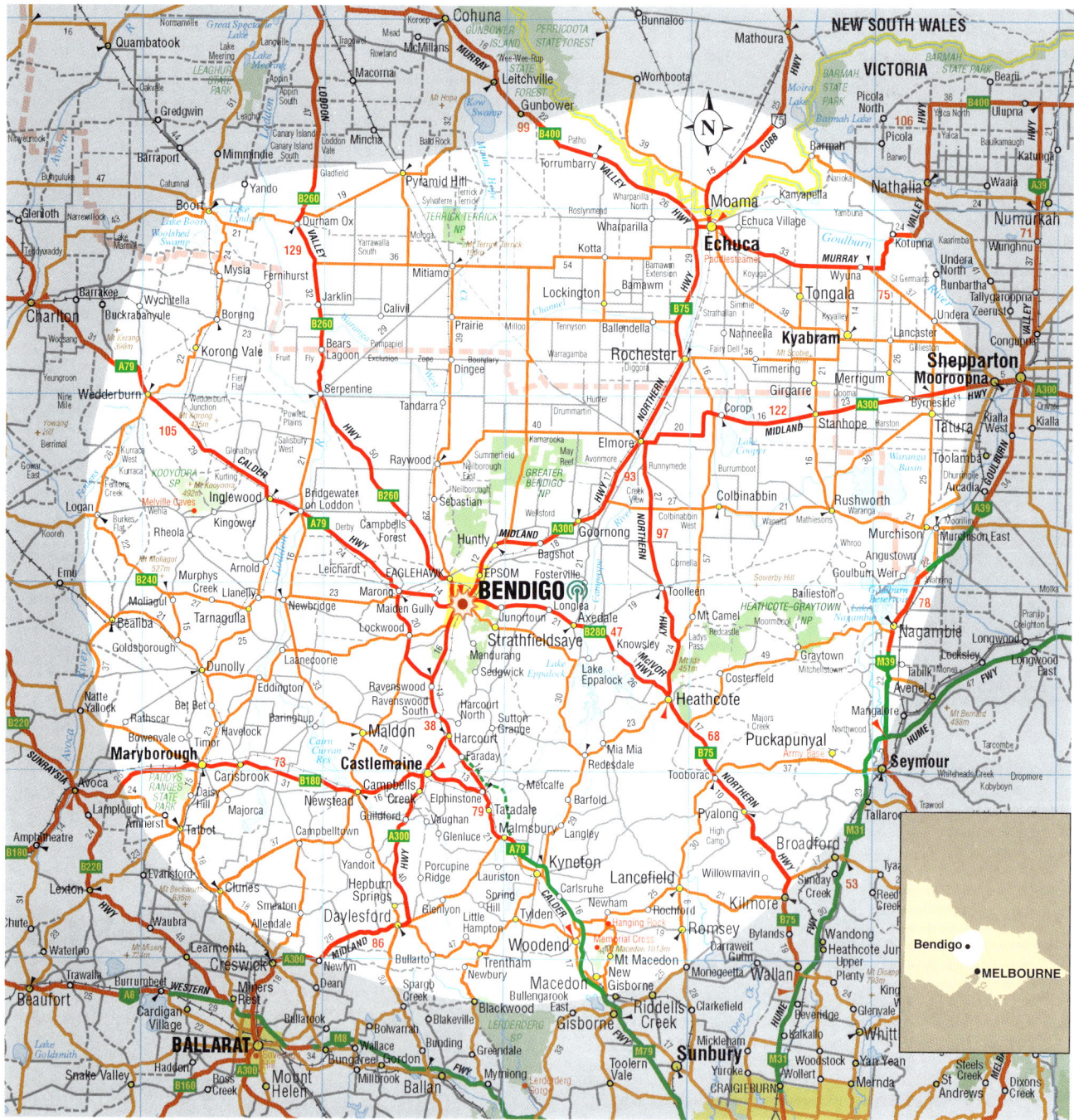

Location of ABC Local Radio studio

Local Radio Frequencies

Bendigo	91.1 FM	
Bridgewater on Loddon	91.1 FM	
Castlemaine	91.1 FM	
Dunolly	91.1 FM	
Echuca-Moama	91.1 FM	97.7FM ABC North-East Victoria
Elmore	91.1 FM	
Heathcote	91.1 FM	
Kyabram	91.1 FM	
Kyneton	91.1 FM	
Maldon	91.1 FM	
Rochester	91.1 FM	
Wedderburn	91.1 FM	
Woodend	91.1 FM	

Bendigo has the only transmitter (FM) in the region

Echuca's historic wharf

Central Victoria has a strong sense of history which is reflected in the magnificent gold-rush Victorian architecture in many of the region's towns, such as the extraordinary latticework on the Rochester Hotel. And a new gold rush is happening in the region, with a massive tunnel being driven under the city of Bendigo, and hundreds of people trying their luck on the goldfields each weekend with detectors and gold pans.

There are many fine art galleries throughout the region. For example, Bendigo Art Gallery now attracts 70 000 visitors a year, and is the largest and most popular gallery outside Melbourne. The region is also economically diverse with broad-acre farming, horticulture, viticulture, tourism and many other types of industry.

ABC Central Victoria began broadcasting in January 1993. The purpose-built studios overlook Bendigo's picturesque Lake Weeroona, which attracts thousands of visitors each year.

NOT TO BE MISSED

- Take a **Murray River** cruise on a paddle-steamer, or simply enjoy the sights of the boats in the Port of **Echuca**
- Learn about Australia's native dog at **Castlemaine**'s Dingo Farm
- See what is considered country Australia's most impressive street, Pall Mall in **Bendigo**
- Discover the history of Chinese miners on the goldfields at the Golden Dragon Museum in **Bendigo**

TOURISM AUSTRALIA

- Explore **Castlemaine**, a historic gold-mining town with a community of potters, painters, instrument makers and other traditional craftspeople

MEET THE LOCALS

The bush nurse

Head 50 kilometres up the road from Bendigo and, if you're in need of a little medical attention, you may be lucky enough to meet Dingee's bush nurse, Viv Fazzula. When she got the job, she thought she'd last two years. Recently the people of Dingee helped Viv celebrate 25 years. Her strangest case: a small boy with a piece of Lego stuck in his nose. She got the Lego out and kept it, presenting it to the patient on his 21st birthday.

LOCAL KNOWLEDGE

Dragons on the loose

If you go down to the Bendigo Easter Parade, be sure of a big surprise. If you go down to the street procession, you'll meet dragons of every shape and size. They're the dragons from the Golden Dragon Museum, and they've participated in the parade since 1892. The longest, Sun Loong (pictured), is 100 metres and requires 50 people to carry him. Another 50 carriers stand by for when the first 50 need a rest. Five of the Museum's seven dragons usually take part.

Bendigo

Big and prosperous, the evidence of the wealth generated in the goldfields around Bendigo (population 59 936) is abundantly clear in its many beautiful buildings, parks and gardens. And for visitors there's also a wealth of things to see and do in this delightful city and the surrounding region. Gold tours abound, and there are also wineries, heritage trails and much more.

SIGHTS AND ACTIVITIES • Take an 8-kilometre Vintage Tram Ride or a bus tour or a heritage walk around the many superb historic buildings, especially in Pall Mall • See Sun Loong, the world's oldest imperial dragon, in the Golden Dragon Museum (Chinese mining exhibits), and next door you can relax in the Chinese Garden of Joy • Have a hands-on experience at the Discovery Science and Technology Centre • Take a guided or self-guide prospecting trip on the Goldfields Tourist Route • See potters at work at the highly regarded Bendigo Pottery • Pick up a guide to the many excellent wineries in the area, and take a picnic to scenic viewpoints like One Tree Hill

VISITOR INFORMATION
Old Post Office, 51–67 Pall Mall (03) 5444 4445

Castlemaine

As with many of the towns in this region, Castlemaine (population 6690) was built on gold and it shows in the superb gold-era Victorian buildings. More recently, the town has become a haven for artists and craftspeople, and the centre of a highly regarded wine district.

SIGHTS AND ACTIVITIES • Check out the exhibitions at the Regional Art Gallery (Lyttleton Street) and the Castlemaine Market Building in Mostyn Street • Follow the Alexander Diggers Trail to several gold-rush sites (brochure available) • Visit the local wineries such as Harcourt Valley, Blackjack and Mount Alexander

VISITOR INFORMATION:
Old Market, Mostyn Street
(03) 5470 6200

Echuca-Moama

Echuca (population 10 014) and its twin town Moama (across the river in New South Wales) are on the junction of the Murray, Campaspe and Goulburn rivers. Once Australia's largest inland port, the town is now famous for its historic paddle-steamers which still cruise the Murray.

SIGHTS AND ACTIVITIES • Discover the early history of the region at the Port of Echuca, restored to the period of its heyday • Hire a houseboat and cruise, or take a self-guide camping canoe trip along the mighty Murray • Board one of the majestic paddle-steamers for a cruise of one to several days, or for a memorable dinner • Relax with a beer at the Star Hotel, with its underground bar and escape tunnel • Play rare penny-arcade machines at the award-winning Sharp's Magic Movie House and Penny Arcade

VISITOR INFORMATION
2 Heygarth Street (03) 5480 7555

Kyabram

Not all the towns in Central Victoria were built on gold. Kyabram (population 5738) is one of those that missed out on the yellow metal, but did very well supplying the needs of the hungry miners. Today it's the centre of a prosperous dairying and fruit-growing district.

SIGHTS AND ACTIVITIES • Visit the community-owned waterfowl and fauna park on Lake Road, the pride of the town • Shop for local pottery and other crafts at The Stables, adjacent to the fauna park

VISITOR INFORMATION
Kyabram Fauna Park, 75 Lake Road (03) 5852 2883

Maldon

The little town of Maldon (population 1255) has the big distinction of being the first in Australia to be declared a 'notable town' by the National Trust. It's a popular location for visitors, due to its well-preserved old-world charm, its Easter fair and spring wildflowers. Gold fossickers are still active in the area as well.

SIGHTS AND ACTIVITIES • Strike it rich while fossicking at locations such as the Tarrangower diggings • Take a walking tour of the town to see its many historic buildings (brochure available) • See Porcupine Township, the reconstructed goldmining town just outside Maldon

VISITOR INFORMATION
High Street (03) 5475 2569

LOCAL TIPS

- The little town of **Dunolly** is near where the Welcome Stranger, possibly the largest nugget ever discovered in the world, was found. Replicas of this and other spectacular nuggets can be seen in the Goldfields Historical and Arts Society collection

- In **Maldon**, take a steam-train ride on the Goldfields Railway (Sunday, Wednesday and public and school holidays)

- Fossick for gold in the vicinity of **Wedderburn**, which was once one of Victoria's richest towns, and still has yields of the precious metal

- **Woodend** is a pleasant stop on the way to the goldfields, with numerous attractions including the famed Hanging Rock nearby

MEET THE LOCALS

The gunzels

If you don't know what they are, then you're obviously not a railway or tram enthusiast. In Bendigo, you'll find tram gunzels aplenty, especially around the Tramways Depot, responsible for restoring, maintaining and driving the trams that operate, among other things, the town's Talking Tram tours. Many of the gunzels are volunteers, and several of the Tramway Trust's trams (such as the beautiful Tram No 19) have been restored by them at their own cost.

MEET THE LOCALS

The FireKings

They're big, they're yellow and they're one of Bendigo's local specialities. Built for Forestry South Australia, the FireKings are just one of the many off-road and special-purpose vehicles built at the Australia Defence Industries facility in Bendigo. Many of its orders have a military application, but the FireKings are ready to battle the worst nature can throw at them, able to withstand temperatures of more than 1000 degrees Celsius for short periods, while protecting its occupants. So these yellow nuggets may not be made of precious metal, but when it comes to saving life and property, the FireKings are worth their weight in gold.

ABC Goulburn-Murray

⊙ Location of ABC Local Radio studio

Towns in green have their own FM transmitter

Victorian Alps

ABC Goulburn-Murray is a major part of the ABC's regional services. The broadcast area reaches more than 350 000 people, making it the third-largest regional station in the ABC network, in terms of population. The station is instrumental in profiling the characters, music and history of the region, achieved through both local programs and through direct, live links to other ABC networks. The area covered stretches from the rich agricultural land in the east, west along the New South Wales-Victoria border to the snow-capped peaks of the Australian Alps.

The Goulburn River is the backbone of this central northern region, and provides irrigation for the abundant orchard harvests of the Goulburn Valley – the 'fruit bowl' of Victoria. The region is also dotted with farms producing venison, poultry, smoked trout, berries, organic vegetables, honey, jams, fruit juices, mustards, pickles, liqueur, truffles and wine.

To the west lie the Victorian Alps, including Mount Hotham and Falls Creek, offering some of Australia's best skiing. Fast-flowing trout streams originate in the mountains and feed into the upper reaches of the Murray River.

NOT TO BE MISSED

- Ride the High Country on horseback through the beautiful mountain town of **Corryong**
- Drive through the snow-capped mountains on **The Great Alpine Road**, and down to the Gippsland lakes
- Come face to face with Ned Kelly, Australia's most infamous bushranger, at the Ned Kelly Memorial Museum and Homestead in **Glenrowan**
- Shop for some gourmet cheeses in **Milawa**, and then head to the Rutherglen vineyards, renowned for their fortified wines
- Slalom (or snow-plough!) down some of Australia's best **ski runs** – Mount Buller, Mount Hotham, Falls Creek
- Take a bite into the juiciest peaches, nectarines and pears from the orchards around the lovely fruit-growing town of **Cobram**
- Sample some of the award-winning **wines** produced at the beautiful National Trust-classified Tahbilk winery (1860), south of Nagambie on the Goulburn River

LOCAL KNOWLEDGE
Morse code

In an age of modern communications, the old ways of telecommunication have become something of a lost art. But visit the Beechworth Historic Precinct and you'll find that not only have they not been forgotten, they're still being practised. There, telegraphist Leo Nette will send a telegram for you using Morse Code. Other volunteer operators receive the messages, decode them and then post them on. The fun, of course, is getting to see how messages were tapped out at a time when the Internet wasn't even imagined.

Historic bridge, Yackandandah

Shepparton

Shepparton (population 31 945), the capital of the rich Goulburn Valley, is a thriving city with more than 4000 hectares of orchards within a 10-kilometre radius, and a further 4000 hectares of market gardens along the nearby river flats. The area's canneries process much of the harvest grown on the land irrigated by the Goulburn Irrigation Scheme.

SIGHTS AND ACTIVITIES • Wander through the art gallery on Welsford Street • Experience farming life in the 1930s at the Emerald Bank Heritage Farm • Take a guided tour of the historic SPC cannery, one of the world's largest fruit canneries • Pack a picnic and relax in the Parkside Gardens and Aboriginal Keeping Place on Parkside Drive • Pick your own berries at the Belstack Strawberry Farm, then take a farm tour, a river walk or dine in the restaurant (open daily from September to May or by appointment) • Take a drive to Nagambie to the Mitchelton Winery, known for its Marsanne and Riesling grown on the sandy, riverine soils

VISITOR INFORMATION
534 Wyndham Street (03) 5831 4400

Albury-Wodonga

Wodonga (population 25 825), and its twin town Albury, sit astride the Murray River in north-east Victoria and south-east New South Wales. It's another great base for exploring the surrounding regions with the alps, goldfields, heritage towns, river valley and wineries all within easy reach.

SIGHTS AND ACTIVITIES • Take the self-guide Wiradjuri Walkabout river walk and learn about the area's Aboriginal heritage (brochure available) • Get a bird's eye view of this stunning region on a day-break hot-air-balloon ride • Pick up some fresh local produce at the Country Fair, Gateway Village, every second Sunday • Fulfil your adventurous spirit with white-water rafting, mountain horseback riding, trout fishing, gold panning and mountain-bike riding • Drive south to the attractive little town of Yackandandah (population 592), with its avenues of English trees and traditional verandas • Get a taste for the region's world-class fortified wines in the dozen or so wineries around Rutherglen

VISITOR INFORMATION
Lincoln Causeway (02) 6051 3650

Bright

Nestled in the beautiful Ovens Valley at the foothills of the Victorian Alps, Bright (population 1898) provides access to the ski resorts of Mount Hotham, Mount Buffalo and Falls Creek. The area is also excellent for bushwalking, mountain-bike riding, canoeing and trout fishing.

Autumn leaves, Bright

SIGHTS AND ACTIVITIES • Stroll down the avenues of deciduous trees – a photographer's dream in autumn • Take in the Canyon Walk along the Ovens River where remains of the early goldmining industry can be seen • Explore the Mount Buffalo National Park along the walking tracks set among the streams, waterfalls and snow gum and mountain ash forests • Challenge yourself at Mount Hotham, Australia's 'powder capital'

VISITOR INFORMATION
119 Gavan Street (03) 5755 2275

Wangaratta

Wangaratta's proximity to the High Country, the Murray and the winery regions makes it an ideal base for exploring north-eastern Victoria. With a population of 15 527, the centre provides services to an area producing wool, wheat, tobacco, kiwifruit, walnuts, chestnuts, hops and wine grapes.

SIGHTS AND ACTIVITIES • Take the 'Walk Through History' (brochure available) and discover the town's historic buildings • Visit the grave of the bushranger Daniel 'Mad Dog' Morgan, where his body was buried after his head was sent to Melbourne for examination • Take a scenic drive south to the beautiful King Valley and Paradise Falls • Explore the interesting old gold township of Beechworth, one of the State's best preserved and most beautiful • Head north to Chiltern to see the Famous Grapevine, Australia's longest grapevine, planted in 1867

VISITOR INFORMATION
Cnr Tone Road and Handley Street (03) 5721 5711

LOCAL TIPS

- The drive from **Corryong** to **Thredbo** is one of the most scenic in the country. Chains may be required in winter, when the road may be closed
- White-water rafting down the Murray from **Tom Groggin** takes you between giant mountains known as the Murray Gates
- Another great drive is the **Alpine Way**, 300 kilometres from Wangaratta through to Omeo
- Take a microlight flight over the **Mount Buffalo** area from the airstrip near Bright
- Several of the towns in the region are postcard-perfect, including **Yackandandah**, **Myrtleford**, **Bright** and **Mount Beauty**
- In summer, mountain resorts like **Mount Buller** become a major drawcard for mountain biking, with lifts operating (to save you pedalling) and tracks of varying degrees of challenge

MEET THE LOCALS

Ned Kelly

Come face to face with Australia's most infamous bushranger…well, a giant effigy of Ned Kelly anyway, which greets visitors to Glenrowan. After killing three local policemen in 1878, the Kelly gang hid out for two years in the Warby Range, near Wangaratta. Ned was captured in 1880 after a shootout in Siege Street, Glenrowan.

MEET THE LOCALS

The Man from Snowy River

The grave of Jack Riley, the man who inspired A. B. 'Banjo' Paterson's famous poem *The Man from Snowy River* is located in Corryong Cemetery. The upper reaches of the Murray River remain almost the same as when the poem was written in 1890. A festival is held every April in Corryong, and features The Man from Snowy River Challenge.

ABC Gippsland

Location of ABC Local Radio studio

Local Radio Frequencies		
Bairnsdale	828 AM	
Bemm River	828 AM	97.1 FM
Buchan	828 AM	100.7 FM
Lakes Entrance	828 AM	100.7 FM
Loch Sport	828 AM	100.7 FM
Maffra	828 AM	100.7 FM
Marlo	828 AM	106.1 FM
Omeo	720 AM	
Paynesville	828 AM	100.7 FM
Swifts Creek	720 AM	
Cann River	106.1 FM	
Latrobe Valley (Traralgon)	100.7 FM	
Mallacoota	104.9 FM	
Moe	100.7 FM	828 AM
Morwell	100.7 FM	828 AM
Orbost	97.1 FM	828 AM
Sale	100.7 FM	828 AM
Traralgon	100.7 FM	828 AM
Yarram	100.7 FM	828 AM

Towns in red have their own AM transmitter
Towns in green have their own FM transmitter

Fishing boats at Port Albert, near Yarram

This diverse region includes the wild beaches and calm inlets on the coast at Wonthaggi; historic fishing, mining and farming towns; and spectacular stretches of bushland. Throughout much of the district, well-watered fields and rolling hills support one of Australia's biggest dairy industries, as well as wine and gourmet-food produce. To the north, this region borders the high country of the Great Dividing Range. Travelling further east along the coast takes you past the remote beauty of Ninety Mile Beach and provides access to the Gippsland Lakes.

Victoria's first ABC regional radio station was opened in October 1935. Being the tallest and most powerful transmitter mast in Victoria at the time, it soon became a landmark for both locals and visitors.

Today, ABC Gippsland's programs display creativity, invention and novelty. This is achieved through outdoor broadcasts, creative use of production technology and regular departures from standard program formats – and always keeping listeners up to date with the latest breaking news.

NOT TO BE MISSED

- Jump aboard the three-hour tourist train and ride along an historic Gippsland route, beginning at **Leongatha**
- Go fishing at **Anderson Inlet** near Inverloch, one of the many great coastal fishing spots
- Stop to smell the roses in spring at the Rose Garden in **Morwell**
- See the cutest, and world's smallest, fairy penguins on **Phillip Island** at sunset
- Explore more than 150 kilometres of walking tracks on the remote and beautiful **Wilsons Promontory**
- Tour for trout, venison, fine cheeses, wines and more on the **Gourmet Deli Trail** (brochure available)

TOURISM AUSTRALIA

Norman Bay, Wilsons Promontory.

Daffodil display at Leongatha

MEET THE LOCALS

Lulu the kangaroo

Lulu is an international hero, and she's also a local kangaroo. From humble beginnings as a family pet with a love for Teddy Bear biscuits on the Richards' Gippsland farm, she was one day able to return the favour. As Len Richards lay unconscious in a paddock after a branch had fallen on him, Lulu found him, nudged him onto his side and started barking (well, a gruff barky sort of sound) to alert the family. Since then news crews and journalists worldwide have covered the story and she has received the RSPCA's highest honour. Lulu is now using her fame for a campaign that promotes awareness and consideration of local wildlife, all from her own website: www.luluthekangaroo.com.au

Sale

Sale, with a population of 13 366, is the main administrative centre in Gippsland, with the nearby Bass Strait oilfields making up a large component of the local industry. Sale is a convenient base for exploring the Gippsland Lakes area.

SIGHTS AND ACTIVITIES • Visit the Ramahyuck Aboriginal Corporation for locally produced art and craft; it is part of the Bataluk Cultural Trail • Take in Sale's impressive swing bridge • Explore miles of unspoilt remote coastal beach on Ninety Mile Beach • Cruise the beautiful Gippsland Lakes to The Lakes National Park which offers bird-watching, swimming and camping

VISITOR INFORMATION
Princes Highway (03) 5144 1108

Bairnsdale

Bairnsdale (population 10 890) lies on the Mitchell River flats at the junction of the Princes Highway and the Great Alpine Road, making it another ideal base for touring the region. Both a commercial centre and a tourist destination, this is a beautiful, relaxed and friendly country town.

SIGHTS AND ACTIVITIES • Take a self-guide heritage walk, which passes the Historical Museum and St Mary's Church (brochure available) • Shop for antiques in the quaint local stores, or visit the Hillmay House Antique • See the Canoe Tree, a 170-year-old tree with a 4-metre-long scar where the local Aborigines stripped the bark to make canoes • Go four-wheel driving and explore this diverse region's rivers, mountains and forests • Go bushwalking in the Mitchell River National Park and discover the Den of Nargun, an Aboriginal cultural site set in a gorge

VISITOR INFORMATION
240 Main Street (03) 5152 3444

Latrobe Valley

At the centre of the Latrobe Valley lies one of the world's largest brown coal deposits, which is mined and turned into electricity, supplying 85 per cent of the State's power. 'The Valley' is made up of three major cities: Morwell (population 13 823), Moe (population 15 558) and Traralgon (18 993). Nearby are some magnificent national parks and mountain ranges.

Sunset in the Latrobe Valley

ROSS IPENBURG

SIGHTS AND ACTIVITIES • Visit Morwell's Powerworks for dynamic displays of the power industry • Step back in time at the Old Gippsland Pioneer Township in Moe • Drive along the Walhalla Mountain River Trail to the picturesque old mining township of Walhalla (population 15), set in a steep and narrow valley • Join the Grand Ridge Road at the tiny town of Seaview and travel the 132 kilometres (mostly gravel) along the spine of the Strzelecki Ranges and through to the Tarra-Bulga National Park

VISITOR INFORMATION
Moe: Gippsland Heritage Park, Lloyd Street (03) 5127 3082
Morwell: Powerworks Visitor Centre, Ridge Road (03) 5135 3415
Traralgon: The Old Church, Princes Highway (03) 5174 3199

Lakes Entrance

This popular holiday destination is at the northern end of the vast waterways of the Gippsland Lakes, and is an ideal base for fishing and boating tours. A bridge across Cunningham Arm gives access to pristine surf beaches, while the town (population 5248) also caters for travellers to the mountain country to the north.

SIGHTS AND ACTIVITIES • Buy the freshest seafood straight from the port's large fishing fleet • Get away from it all – hire a boat and sail through the largest inland waterways in Australia, or take the Wyanga Park Winery cruise, offering a lakes cruise from town to the cellar door • Visit the Seashell Museum on The Esplanade, which offers more than just a collection of 100 000-odd shells

VISITOR INFORMATION
Cnr Esplanade and Marine Parade (03) 5155 1966

LOCAL TIPS

- Hire a yacht or cruiser from **Metung** for a relaxing getaway on the Gippsland Lakes
- Take a tour of the State Coal Mine at **Wonthaggi** with an old-time miner as a guide
- Cool off in the rock pools of the Mitchell River Gorge, in the **Mitchell River National Park**
- Drop in for a coffee or a meal at the **Koonwarra** Store; the village also has a thriving art and crafts industry
- Visit the remote Point Hicks Lighthouse in **Croajingolong National Park**
- Go underground – discover the Royal and Fairy caves in the **Buchan Caves Reserve**
- Check out the pottery at Gooseneck Pottery near **Ruby**

MEET THE LOCALS

Fresh and fabulous produce

The Culinaire Cooking School, nestled in the hills of East Gippsland and overlooking the Tambo River, gives you the know-how to bring the freshest local produce to the table. Chris and John Phillip believe in a hands-on approach to cooking, offering small groups the opportunity to get their hands dirty, test their senses, learn the basics or pick up a speciality. As well as running cookery classes, they also take groups for a tour around the on-site garden and teach people how to identify and use the fresh herbs collected.

MEET THE LOCALS

Fishing expert

With so many top fishing spots throughout the region – from trout fishing in the mountains, to bream, trevally and flathead in the lakes, and salmon and tailor off the coast – you are spoilt for choice. So you may need an expert like Peter Coulton, the ABC Gippland's fishing reporter for more than 15 years, to give you the tips and tricks for the best fishing in his 'backyard'. Catch Peter's show every Friday morning at 7.20.

In Tune with the Locals

Inter-city tuning guide

To help you stay tuned as you travel between the major capital cities, use the guide on the right for each leg of your journey to ensure excellent reception. This is just what you need if you're trying to follow anything from sport to your favourite Statewide or national programs. Good drivers know that it's important to take a break at least every two hours. So why not use the guide to work out when to take a break, stretch your legs, have a meal and take a moment to tune to the next ABC Local Radio station?

Of course, in a country as vast as Australia, there are some areas, particularly in Western Australia, the Northern Territory and South Australia, where you may find the only coverage is near major towns or on short-wave. Detailed information on the coverage available in these areas is provided in the descriptions of the individual regions. If all else fails, there's a good chance of picking up one of the five very large transmitters that cover much of inland Queensland, New South Wales, Victoria and Western Australia. See the feature article (page 44) on these transmitters for more details.

TUNING GUIDE FOR THE MAJOR INTER-CAPITAL ROAD ROUTES

Sydney ▶ Melbourne via Hume Highway (881 km)

Sydney ▶ Goulburn ▶ Gundagai ▶ Holbrook ▶ Wangaratta ▶ **Melbourne**
702 AM   549 AM   89.9 FM   675 AM   774 AM

Sydney ▶ Melbourne via Princes Highway (1040 km)

Sydney ▶ Wollongong ▶ Termeil ▶ Narooma ▶ NSW/VIC Border ▶ Orbost ▶ Moe ▶ **Melbourne**
702 AM   97.3 FM 107.3 FM   810 AM   104.9 FM/106.1 FM/97.1 FM   828 AM   774 AM

Sydney ▶ Brisbane via New England Highway (1001 km)

Sydney ▶ Muswellbrook ▶ Armidale ▶ Tenterfield ▶ Warwick ▶ **Brisbane**
702 AM   648 AM   819 AM   104.9 FM   612 AM

Sydney ▶ Brisbane via Pacific Highway (969 km)

Sydney ▶ Newcastle ▶ Bulahdelah ▶ Kempsey ▶ Tweed Heads ▶ **Brisbane**
702 AM   1233 AM   95.5 FM/756 AM   738 AM   612 AM

Sydney ▶ Adelaide via Sturt and Hume highways (1417 km)

Sydney ▶ Goulburn ▶ Wagga Wagga ▶ Balranald ▶ Renmark ▶ **Adelaide**
702 AM   549 AM   675 AM   594 AM   891 AM

Sydney ▶ Canberra (292 km)

Sydney ▶ Goulburn ▶ **Canberra**
702 AM   666 AM

Melbourne ▶ Adelaide via Western and Dukes highways (733 km)

Melbourne ▶ Ararat ▶ Bordertown ▶ **Adelaide**
774 AM   594 AM   891 AM

Melbourne ▶ Adelaide via Princes Highway (906 km)

Melbourne ▶ Warrnambool ▶ Kingston S.E. ▶ **Adelaide**
774 AM   594 AM   891 AM

Adelaide ▶ Darwin (3026 km)

Adelaide ▶ Port Augusta ✳ Woomera ✳ Coober Pedy ✳ Alice Springs ✳ Tennant Creek ✳ Katherine ✳ Batchelor ▶ **Darwin**
891 AM   639 AM   1584 AM   106.1 FM   783 AM   106.1 FM   106.1 FM   105.7 FM

✳ *Large areas have no medium-wave coverage. Short-wave is available in the Northern Territory, see individual regions for details.*

Adelaide ▶ Perth (2700 km)

Adelaide ▶ Streaky Bay ▶ Yalata ✳ Belladonia ▶ Southern Cross ▶ **Perth**
891 AM   693 AM   105.9 FM   648 AM   558 AM / 531 AM   720 AM

✳ *Note: Yalata to Belladonia has no coverage.*

Brisbane ▶ Darwin (3406 km)

Brisbane ▶ Dalby ▶ Roma ▶ Augathella ▶ Cloncurry ▶ Mount Isa ✳ Tennant Creek ✳ Katherine ✳ Batchelor ▶ **Darwin**
612 AM 747 AM 603 AM   540 AM   567 AM 106.5 FM   106.1 FM   106.1 FM   105.7 FM

✳ *Large areas have no medium-wave coverage. Short-wave is available in Northern Territory, see regions for details.*

The frequencies in the guide aim to minimise the amount of station changing during your trip. Along the way, you can also tune to individual town frequencies for many towns you pass through. Check the appropriate region in this book for additional frequencies you may prefer to use in a town, particularly if you plan to spend some time there. For journeys in the opposite direction to that given in the guide, simply reverse the instructions and order of frequencies.

Tasmania

The island State of Tasmania is also one of the most beautiful places on earth – some of the first mariners to set eyes on it thought they'd found paradise. It's a place whose small size can be deceptive. There's an extraordinary amount to see and do, from the sheer beauty of the harbour city of Hobart to the spectacular gorges of the south-west to the stunning lakes of the interior and the beautiful townships, inlets and waterways of the north and east coasts. Tasmania is full of history, scenery and some of the finest food and wine in the country.

Burnie

Launceston

ABC Northern Tasmania

HOBART

ABC Hobart and Southern Tasmania

See inside back cover for a list of ABC Local Radio stations and their frequencies.

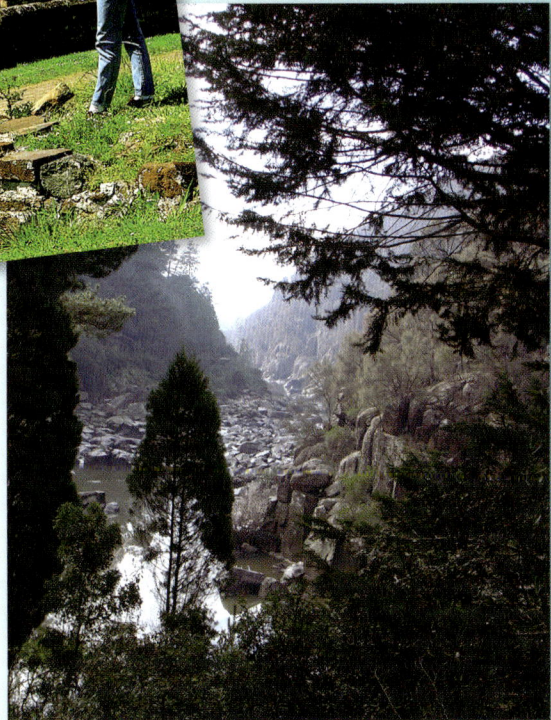

ABC Hobart and Southern Tasmania

☼ Location of ABC Local Radio studio

Hobart, jewel of the south

Local Radio Frequencies		
Bridgewater	936 AM	
Bothwell	936 AM	
Bushy Park	936 AM	
Cygnet	936 AM	
Dunalley	936 AM	
Eaglehawk Neck	936 AM	
Glenora	936 AM	
Hamilton	936 AM	
Hastings	936 AM	
Hobart	936 AM	
Huonville	936 AM	
Kettering	936 AM	
Kingston	936 AM	
New Norfolk	936 AM	
Pontville	936 AM	
Port Arthur	936 AM	
Richmond	936 AM	
Sorell	936 AM	
Orford	90.5 FM	936 AM

(**⦿**) Hobart has the only AM transmitter in the region
(**⦿**) Orford has the only FM transmitter in the region

I n the south, the coastline fronting the Tasman Sea is a long, ragged and spectacular strip of peninsulas, islands, inlets and channels. Imposing mountains shadow the coast, and the two major rivers, the Huon and Derwent, meander through verdant valley pastures. The slow-paced development of the area has resulted in the preservation of the natural landscape and maintained the rich colonial history, from the sandstone buildings to the elegant houses and small towns that dot the countryside.

To the south-west lies one of the planet's great wilderness areas, part of the Tasmanian Wilderness World Heritage Area. It is an almost uninhabited landscape of dolomite mountains, glacial lakes, majestic rivers, waterfalls, gorges, virgin temperate forests and 1000-year-old trees.

The Local Radio station, 936 ABC Hobart works 24 hours a day to provide a mix of information, fun and entertainment in the mornings, regular local news updates and national and international current affairs throughout the day, as well as the latest in rural and market news.

NOT TO BE MISSED

- Wander around the bustling local market at **Salamanca Place**
- Be drawn by the aroma of chocolate at the **Cadbury Schweppes Chocolate Factory** in Claremont
- Take a trip to **Richmond**, Australia's best-preserved Georgian colonial village
- Follow the **Southern Tasmanian Wine Route** with more than 18 boutique wineries
- Explore the historic **Port Arthur** penal settlement
- Drive through the **Derwent Valley**, where rows of poplars mark the old hop fields, and shingled barns and waterwheels recall the old farming life

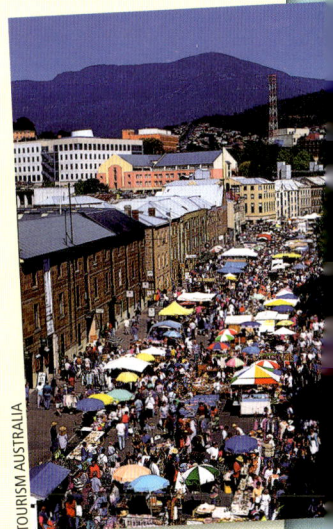
Salamanca Market, Hobart

LOCAL EVENTS

Jan	**Hobart:** Cup Carnival; Sailing South **Cygnet:** Folk Festival
Feb	**Hobart:** Royal Hobart Regatta; Australian Wooden Boat Festival
Mar	**New Norfolk:** Hop Harvest Festival **Bothwell:** International Highland Spin-in (wool-spinning competition, odd-numbered years)
Mar–Apr	**Hobart:** Ten Days on the Island Festival (arts music, dance, film and theatre)
Sept	**Hobart:** Tulip Festival of Tasmania
Oct	**Richmond:** Village Fair **New Norfolk:** Spring in the Valley **Kingston:** Olie Bollen (Dutch community festival)
Nov	**Hobart:** Point to Pinnacle Road, Run and Walk **Brighton:** Agricultural Show **Huonville:** Huon Agricultural Show
Dec	**Hobart:** Sydney and Melbourne to Hobart yacht races; Taste of Tasmania (food and wine festival); Antique Fair **Port Arthur:** Boxing Day Woodchop
Dec–Jan	**Hobart:** Summer Festival

Mount Wellington lookout

Hobart

Hobart (population 196 000), Australia's second-oldest city, extends along both sides of the River Derwent, reaching into the foothills of the majestic Mount Wellington. A strong maritime heritage and European feel define this well-preserved city, and many areas appear today as they would have when it was a seafaring town in the nineteenth century.

SIGHTS AND ACTIVITIES • Explore the city by foot, from the cottages and antique stores in Battery Point to the grandeur of Parliament House • Drive to the summit of Mount Wellington for panoramic views • Cruise along the Derwent or sail to Port Arthur aboard one of the many vessels departing from the city's lively waterfront • Pack a picnic and head to the State's horticultural jewel, the beautifully landscaped Royal Tasmanian Botanical Gardens • Eat out and discover why this city is attracting gourmet travellers worldwide for its innovative menus, fine seasonal produce, excellent seafood and distinctive local wines • Take a break in St David's Park, Hobart's first colonial burial ground (the pioneer gravestones dating from 1804 make for fascinating reading) • After dark settle in to one of the cosy historic pubs bearing a seafaring name or bet on black at the Wrest Point Casino

VISITOR INFORMATION
Cnr Elizabeth and Davey streets (03) 6230 8233

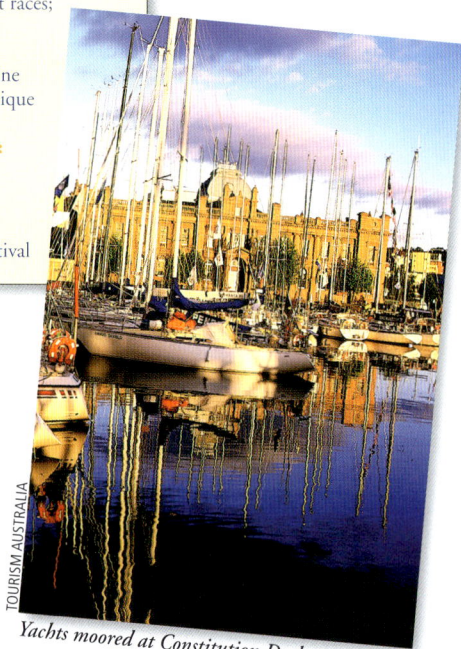

Yachts moored at Constitution Dock

Bothwell

The peaceful town of Bothwell (population 356) in the beautiful Clyde Valley was settled by Scottish immigrants in the 1820s. Now proclaimed an historic village by the National Trust, it is in the centre of sheep and cattle country.

SIGHTS AND ACTIVITIES ● Play a round of golf at Ratho Golf Course, where Australia's first game of golf was played (the course is open to visitors with golf membership elsewhere) ● Visit the home of Tasmanian tartan at the Lamont Weaving Studio ● Wet a line in one of the nearby lakes, rivers or streams for some of the best freshwater trout fishing in Australia ● Explore Mount Field National Park, a wilderness for beginners, featuring the 40-metre Russell Falls and winding trails around lakes, mountains, moorland and forests

VISITOR INFORMATION
Australasian Golf Museum, Market Place (03) 6259 4033

Buckland

Situated on the Tasman Highway north-east of Hobart, Buckland (population 228) has a history that is now some seven centuries old. In the seventeenth century Oliver Cromwell sacked England's Battle Abbey, but before he did, the Abbey's stained-glass window depicting the life of John the Baptist was removed for its protection and hidden from Cromwell's men. The window itself dates from the fourteenth century, and in the nineteenth century the Marquis of Salisbury gave it to Buckland's rector, the Reverend T.H. Fox. Now, in the twenty-first century, it can still be seen in the east window of Buckland's church.

SIGHTS AND ACTIVITIES ● Soak up the history of the fourteenth-century stained-glass window on the east wall of the Church of St John the Baptist ● Enjoy a meal at Ye Olde Buckland Inn, a nineteenth-century tavern and restaurant

VISITOR INFORMATION
Ye Olde Buckland Inn, Kent Street (03) 6257 5114

LOCAL TIPS

● Visit **Bruny Island**, home to Tasmania's most famous Aboriginal, Truganini (died 1876), and take the eco-cruise, one of the State's top attractions

● See Tasmania's massive hydro-electricity industry at **Strathgordon**

● Take a dip in the thermal pools at **Hastings** or explore the spectacular dolomite caves nearby

● Don't miss the Folk Festival in **Cygnet** in January

MEET THE LOCALS

Homes for penguins

When is an igloo not an igloo? Well the answer is easy: when it is constructed to house penguins. Swansea Primary School students assisted in assembling miniature igloos for the local penguin population, as part of an ongoing long-term project to rehabilitate the beach area at Masons Bluff on the State's east coast. The igloos were created using pine bark and mortar, and are a form of protection from domestic animals.

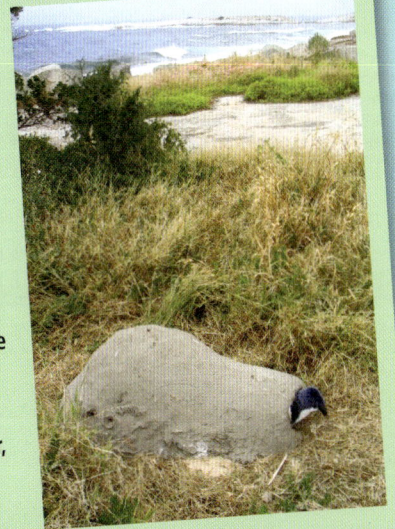

MEET THE LOCALS

The Hansens

The Hansen family has had a long association with apple-growing in Tasmania, mostly in the Huon Valley. Howard Hansen, one of Tasmania's main orchardists, supplies Australia's major supermarkets with much of their fruit. Animals, vegetables and minerals have been Tasmania's main exports for eons, and not too much has changed since the State was first called the Apple Isle. Apples, potatoes and opium poppies are today's big crops.

TOURISM AUSTRALIA

Port Arthur

This historic site (population 190) on the Tasman Peninsula was one of Australia's most infamous penal settlements from the 1830s to the 1870s, and it is said that visitors still sense the hardship endured by the early convict population. The stunning setting and beauty of the imposing sandstone prison buildings belie the site's tragic history.

SIGHTS AND ACTIVITIES • Depart at dusk for a lantern-lit ghost tour of Port Arthur Historic Site or just wander the restored ruins of the convict settlement, period houses and historic museum • In summer, take a boat trip to the Isle of the Dead, the final resting place for both convicts and prison personnel • Fly above the Tasman Peninsula on a scenic flight • Jump aboard a steam train at the Bush Mill Steam Railway and Settlement just north of town • Spot the Tasmanian Devil, among other native creatures, at the Tasmanian Devil Park • Stop off at Eaglehawk Neck, now a quaint fishing village, once heavily guarded by a line of ferocious dogs • Explore Tasman National Park with its magnificent coastal scenery, unique rock formations and wildlife

VISITOR INFORMATION
Port Arthur Historic Site, Arthur Highway (03) 6251 2310

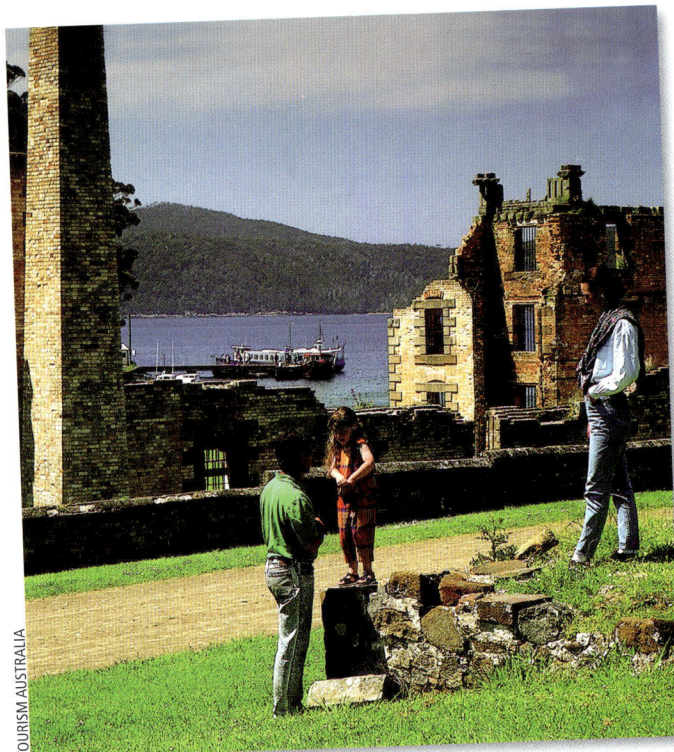
TOURISM AUSTRALIA
Port Arthur Historic Site

Richmond

One of the most important historic towns in Australia, and one of the most charming, Richmond (population 768) is located among the attractive farms and vineyards of the Coal River valley.

SIGHTS AND ACTIVITIES • See Richmond's premier attraction, the Richmond Bridge, Australia's oldest surviving freestone bridge (built 1823–1825) • Take a stroll to see the Gaol (1825), St John's (1837, the oldest Catholic church in Australia still in use), St Luke's (1834–36), general store and former post office (1832) and many more buildings from the mid to late nineteenth century (brochure available) • Visit other attractions such as Old Hobart Town (a model of the settlement in the early 1820s), the Toy Museum and The Maze • Tour the Southern Tasmania Wine Route (brochure available) • Enjoy a scenic drive north through Campania and Colebrook

VISITOR INFORMATION
Old Hobart Town Model Village, 21a Bridge Street (03) 6260 2502

TOURISM AUSTRALIA
Richmond Bridge

Painted Cliffs, Maria Island

Triabunna

This former garrison town and whaling station is now a scallop and abalone centre (population 766). It is also the gateway to some of the south-east's finest scenery.

SIGHTS AND ACTIVITIES • See the Tasmanian Seafarers' Memorial on the Esplanade, honouring all those who have lost their lives in Tasmanian waters • Relax at the Girraween Gardens and nearby tearooms • Take the ferry to Maria Island (departs just south of town) and admire the extensive fossil deposits of the Painted Cliffs, go bushwalking (maps essential) and explore the historic penal settlement of Darlington • At Orford, enjoy a pleasant walk along Old Convict Road which follows the Prosser River • Picnic, swim, waterski or fish at beaches along this stretch of relatively sheltered coast • Go north to Coles Bay and the world-renowned Freycinet National Park with its superb coastal scenery, flora and fauna, and the Peninsula Walking Track to Wineglass Bay which offers spectacular views

VISITOR INFORMATION
Cnr Charles Street and Esplanade West
(03) 6257 4090

MEET THE LOCALS

Cricket legends

Charles Eady (a pioneer of Tasmanian cricket) made his Test debut at Lords in 1896 and holds the record for the highest score by an adult in cricket: 566! During this time Australia's captain was Joe Darling, Eady's contemporary. The men were great friends. They toured England together in 1896 and had careers in the Tasmanian Parliament and in cricket administration. In a nice coincidence, Eady and Darling are buried very close to each other at the Cornelian Bay cemetery in Hobart.

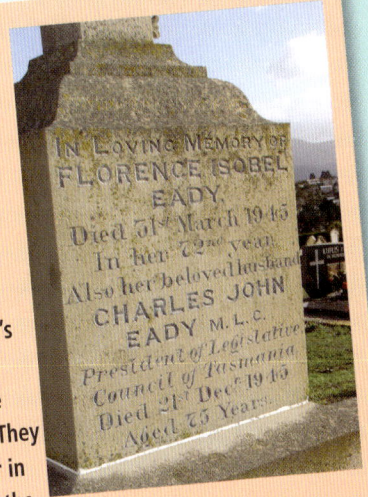

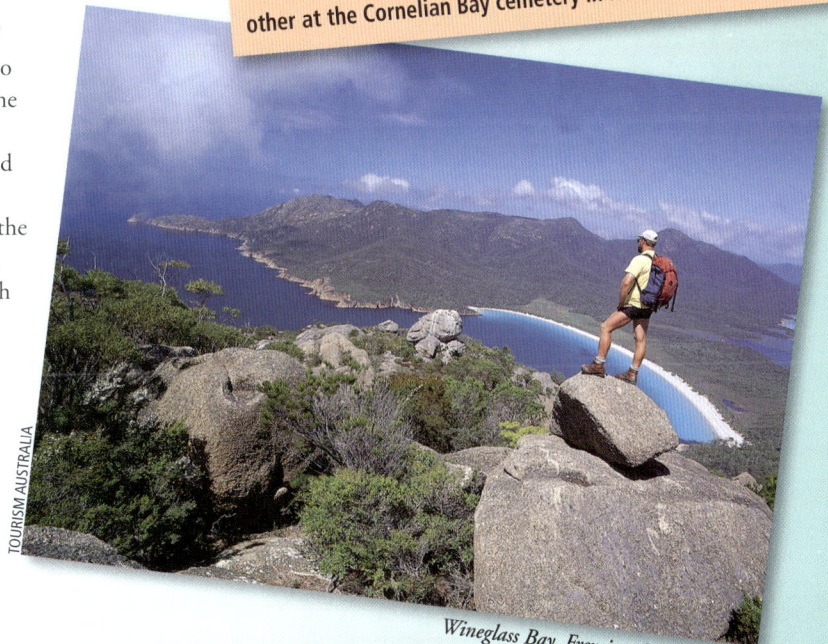
Wineglass Bay, Freycinet National Park

ABC Northern Tasmania

Location of ABC Local Radio studio

TOURISM AUSTRALIA

Cradle Mountain

Local Radio Frequencies

Fingal	1161 AM
Flinders Island	711 AM
Launceston	711 AM
St Helens	1584 AM
Bicheno	89.7 FM
Burnie	102.5 FM
Devonport	100.5 FM
King Island	88.5 FM
Latrobe	100.5 FM
Lileah	91.3 FM
Queenstown	90.5 FM
Rosebery	106.3 FM
Savage River	104.1 FM
Somerset	102.5 FM
St Marys	102.7 FM
Stanley	91.3 FM
Strahan	107.5 FM
Swansea	106.1 FM
Ulverstone	102.5 FM
Waratah	103.3 FM
Weldborough	97.3 FM
Wynyard	102.5 FM
Zeehan	90.5 FM

(◉) Towns in red have their own AM transmitter
(◉) Towns in green have their own FM transmitter

ABC Northern Tasmania's broadcast area stretches from a coastline of rolling breakers and dangerous headlands in the west, through the undulating country of the Arthur and Pieman rivers, and south to the dolomite peaks and still lakes of Cradle Mountain-Lake St Clair National Park. The fertile midland plains run from Launceston south along the island's spine, and the area is famous for its gourmet produce and wines. As well, the natural landscapes and extensive national parks offer some of the best walking, skiing and trout fishing in Australia.

The east coast has a mild climate, exquisite coastal scenery and breathtaking peaks, gorges, waterfalls and forests in the surrounding region. Off the north coast lie the Bass Strait Islands, including Flinders and King islands, renowned for their high-quality produce, their fauna and their windswept beauty. All this is covered by ABC Northern Tasmania, from breakfast through to afternoon 'Drive' programs, with rural reports, local news and plenty of information on what's happening – for both locals and visitors.

NOT TO BE MISSED

- See Aboriginal middens in the **Bay of Fires Conservation Area**
- Catch the chairlift for impressive views at the top of The Nut in **Stanley**
- Explore the glaciated landscape of the **Cradle Mountain-Lake St Clair National Park**
- Take on the challenge of the 85-kilometre **Overland Track** through Tasmanian alpine wilderness
- Breathe in the world's freshest air at the spectacular **Cape Grim**
- Go trout fishing in the lakes of the **Central Highlands**, world-renowned for their stocks of brown trout
- Visit the Wybalenna Historic Site on **Flinders Island**
- See the blowhole, go diving or explore the magic of the underwater world by glass-bottom boat offshore from **Bicheno**

MEET THE LOCALS

The Tasmanian devil

There's only one place in the world where you'll see a Tasmanian devil in a restaurant: at Marrawah on Tasmania's north-west coast. Five times a fortnight, Marrawah farmer Geoff King feeds the local devils on animals that have unfortunately been killed on the roads nearby. When the devils come in to feed, tourists come to view the spectacle.

Launceston

Although a busy city centre, Launceston (population 67 701) retains a relaxed and friendly atmosphere, nestled in the hilly countryside where the Tamar, North Esk and South Esk rivers meet.

SIGHTS AND ACTIVITIES • Take a stroll through town starting at Princes Square, then head north to the Town Hall and the elegant Customs House • Go for a cruise along the Tamar River or go white-water rafting and rock-climbing at nearby Cataract Gorge • See the nineteenth century spring to life at Penny Royal World • Pack a picnic and relax at Trevallyn Dam, and if you are feeling adventurous, experience Australia's only hang-gliding simulator • Drive south to Woolmers Estate, regarded as Australia's most significant colonial property and home to Australia's National Rose Garden

VISITOR INFORMATION
Cornwall Square, 12–16 St John Street (03) 6336 3133

Burnie

Lying on the banks of Emu Bay in the north-west, Burnie (population 16 007) is the State's fourth-largest city and has grown with the rapid expansion of the paper industry. The deepwater port serves the west-coast mining centres, and the town itself serves as a great base for exploring the lush rolling countryside and the stunning national parks to the south.

SIGHTS AND ACTIVITIES • Admire the native flora in Burnie Park • Call in to the Lactos Cheese Tasting Centre on Old Surry Road • Admire the truly spectacular coastal scenery of the Ulverstone to Stanley section of the Bass Highway • Explore the clear water and rocky points of the quaint village of Boat Harbour, ideal for diving and fishing • Head to Devonport and take the Tasmanian Trail, a 477-kilometre Devonport–Dover trail for walkers, horse riders and mountain bikers • Take the chairlift to the top of The Nut at Stanley

VISITOR INFORMATION
Civic Centre Plaza, off Little Alexander Street
(03) 6434 6111

LOCAL KNOWLEDGE

Mural town

Most Australian towns have a claim to fame, but not many are as artistic as Sheffield. It's the home of the annual Mural Fest, held every April, and it's so highly regarded that the town is hoping to hold the World Mural Conference in 2008. Meanwhile, the visual feast doesn't end with the festival. The murals remain on display in Mural Park throughout the ensuing year, with visitors able to vote for their favourite. The winner is announced at the following year's festival.

King Island

The name King Island is synonymous with rich cheeses and creams, succulent beef and excellent seafood. As well, the island has long isolated beaches and abundant wildlife, and offers everything from beach strolls to game fishing, diving and fossicking. Its population of 1700 enjoys a laid-back lifestyle that others only dream about.

SIGHTS AND ACTIVITIES • Enjoy the view across to Victoria from Wickham Lighthouse (1861) • Scuba dive the reefs and some of the many shipwrecks • Fish for salmon, flathead and whiting from the beaches along the coast • See the Australian fur seals at Reid Rocks, a short boat ride away • Taste the stand-out double brie and camembert at the King Island Dairy • Browse the local galleries and shops for craft made of kelp • Visit the significant wetland bird habitat at the Lavinia Nature Reserve

VISITOR INFORMATION
Currie (03) 6462 1355

St Helens

This seaside resort (population 1280) on the shores of Georges Bay is renowned for its crayfish and scale fish, and is a base for the local tuna, marlin and shark-fishing industries. The coastal scenery is stunning and the surrounding region boasts gourmet produce.

SIGHTS AND ACTIVITIES • Discover the history of the east coast in the St Helens History Room • Dine at one of the many seafood restaurants specialising in the freshest local catches • Charter a deep-sea fishing boat • Hit the East Coast Gourmet Trail • Explore the coast at a leisurely pace, stopping off at the lovely fishing villages dotted up and down the coast

VISITOR INFORMATION
St Helens History Room, 61 Cecilia St (03) 6376 1744

Strahan

This pretty little port (population 701) on Macquarie Harbour on the forbidding west coast is a popular holiday town, home to many artists and craftspeople, and a base for the crayfish, abalone and fishing industries.

SIGHTS AND ACTIVITIES • Take morning or afternoon tea at Ormiston House, one of Strahan's first houses • Ride the Strahan–Queenstown Wilderness Railway through wild rivers and pristine forest • Cruise along the Gordon River and explore the Franklin-Gordon Wild Rivers National Park • Drop into Strahan Visitors Centre for an excellent historical display of Tasmania's south-west

VISITOR INFORMATION
The Esplanade (03) 6471 7622

LOCAL TIPS

- Taste leatherwood honey, unique to Tasmania, at Stephen's Honey Factory at **Mole Creek**

- From December to January take a stroll through lavender fields at Bridestowe Estate Lavender Farm near **Nabowla**

- Sample some of the local **wine** at one of northern Tasmania's 13 wineries

- Kate's Berry Farm near **Swansea** is a gourmet institution – stop in for a taste sensation

- It's not quite the Melbourne Cup, but it's the next best thing; the **Launceston** Cup has been luring keen punters, mug punters, fashion victims and those simply out for a good time to the Mowbray Racecourse on the last Wednesday of February

- The State's best skiing is in **Ben Lomond National Park**; in summer the park is ablaze with wildflowers and perfect for bushwalking

MEET THE LOCALS

The Tasmanian tiger

Though believed to be extinct, nearly 5000 sightings of the Tasmanian tiger have been reported since 1936 – and this is just from the mainland! Some of the sightings are from as far away as the Northern Territory. When it comes to investigating the sightings, Dorothy Williams from the Australian Rare Fauna Research Association says it's very rare to find any evidence, although there have been paw prints in the past, which have only deepened the mystery further. Keep an eye out – this mystery is not yet solved.

NATIONAL ARCHIVES OF AUSTRALIA

South Australia

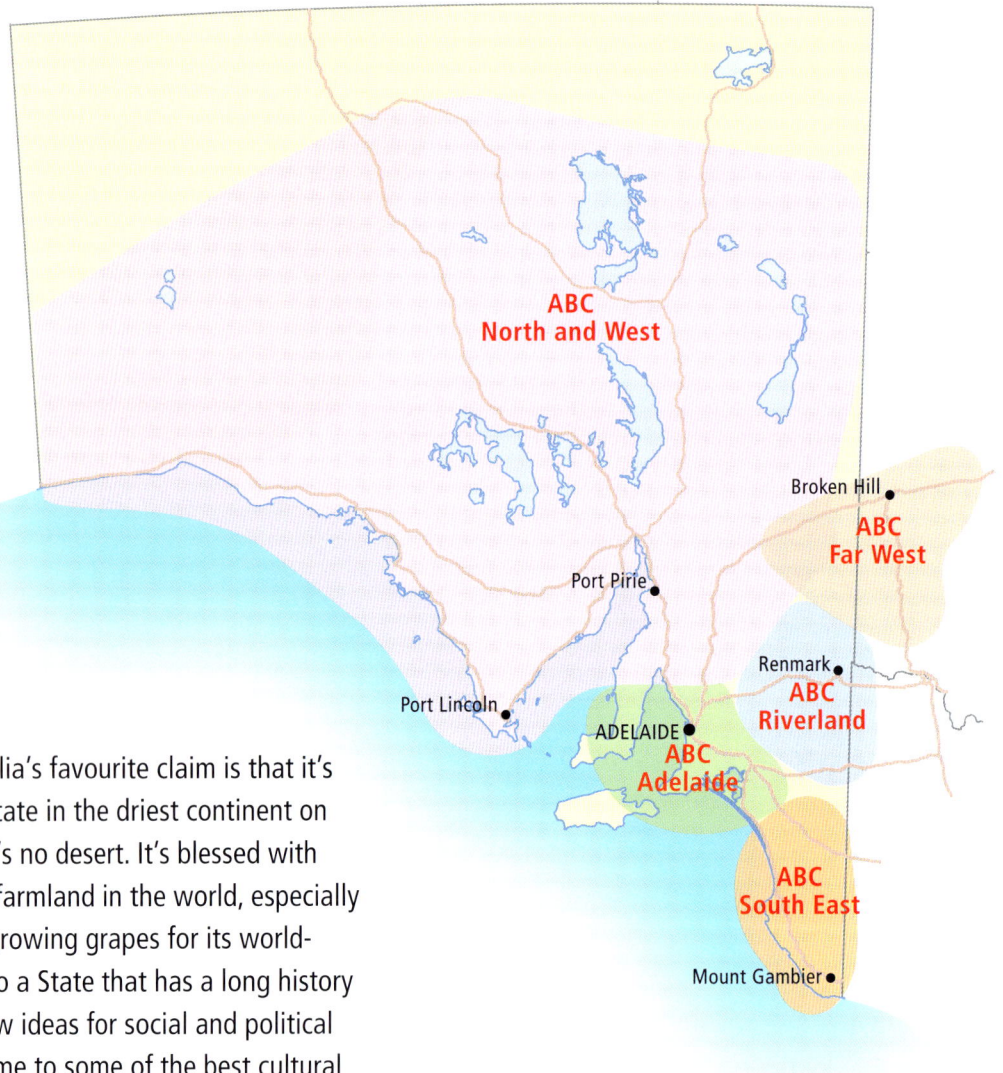

ABC North and West

Broken Hill •

ABC Far West

Port Pirie •

Renmark •
ABC Riverland

Port Lincoln •

ADELAIDE •
ABC Adelaide

ABC South East

Mount Gambier •

South Australia's favourite claim is that it's the driest State in the driest continent on earth. Yet it's no desert. It's blessed with some of the finest farmland in the world, especially when it comes to growing grapes for its world-class wines. It's also a State that has a long history of leadership in new ideas for social and political reform. And it's home to some of the best cultural festivals in the world. It's a place of surprises, of stark landscapes that give way to superb scenery, of deserts that give way to fertile valleys and of remote outposts that are home to some of the most civilised communities anywhere.

(◉) See inside back cover for a list of ABC Local Radio stations and their frequencies.

ABC Adelaide

Location of ABC Local Radio studio

Local Radio Frequencies

Adelaide	891 AM
Angaston	891 AM
Gawler	891 AM
Kingscote	891 AM
Mount Barker	891 AM
Murray Bridge	891 AM
Yorketown	891 AM

Adelaide has the only transmitter (AM) in the region

The State of South Australia was established as a settlement that would allow people from around the world to establish themselves in farming communities. However, it has since become one of the most urbanised societies in the world, and its main industries include mining and heavy industry.

ABC Adelaide broadcasts to more than 70 per cent of the State's 1.5 million population, as much of the rural and industrial activity, hence population, is concentrated in the south-east corner of the State. Yet, while there's a city focus, the regional coverage reflects the many townships and walks of life of an extremely diverse listening audience.

TOURISM AUSTRALIA

Adelaide and the Torrens

There's a down-to-earth honesty about Adelaide and its surrounds. Locals enjoy a high standard of living, measured not just in financial terms but as a result of a superb climate, great regional produce and abundant natural wonders. History, culture and commerce rub shoulders in a community that has pioneered many of the reforms the rest of the country later took for granted. Adelaide is known as the city of churches, but there's a lot more to it than that. It's a place where you can set your own pace, from a quiet stroll in one of the many beautiful parks and gardens, to a world-class premiere in the arts.

NOT TO BE MISSED

- Catch a performance at the renowned **Adelaide Festival Centre**
- Get an excellent overview of Australian art at the **Art Gallery of South Australia**
- Stroll in Adelaide's **Botanic Gardens**, among the finest in the country
- Catch the tram to the beachside suburb of **Glenelg**
- Let your tastebuds do the walking with a tour of the region's wines at the **National Wine Centre of Australia**
- Marvel at the beauty of **St Peter's Cathedral**, backdrop to the lovely Pennington Gardens
- Don't miss the **steam train** from Mount Barker to Victor Harbor
- Enjoy the superb scenery of the **Barossa Valley** on a drive from Angaston to Tanunda on Menglers Hill Scenic Drive
- Hike the bush tracks or canoe the calm water of Antechamber Bay, on **Kangaroo Island**

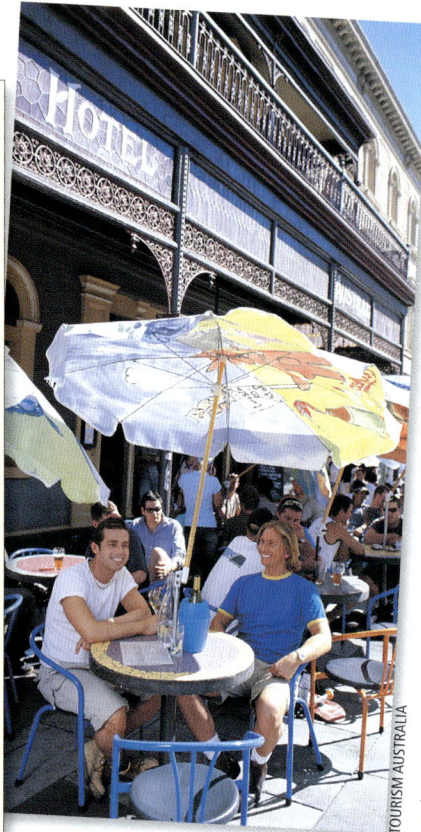

LOCAL EVENTS

Jan   **Adelaide:** Schützenfest (German festival); Jacobs Creek Tour Down Under (cycling)

Feb   **Rowland Flat:** Barossa Under The Stars
Kingscote: Racing Carnival; Street Fair
Mount Barker: Highland Gathering

Feb–Mar   **Adelaide:** Festival of the Arts; Fringe festival (even-numbered years)

Mar   **Adelaide:** WOMADelaide (world music and dance festival); Glendi Festival (Greek culture)

Easter   **Oakbank:** Easter Racing Carnival
Parndana: Easter Fair
Penneshaw: Art Exhibition

Apr   **Adelaide:** Clipsal 500 (V8 Supercars)
Barossa Valley: Barossa Vintage Festival (odd-numbered years)

May   **Aldgate:** Autumn Leaves Festival
Mount Barker: Highland Gathering and Heritage Festival

Aug   **Tanunda:** Jazz Weekend

Sept   **Adelaide:** Bay to Birdwood Run (vintage vehicles)

Sept–Oct   **Hahndorf:** Heysen Festival

Oct   **Adelaide:** Tasting Australia (odd-numbered years)
Barossa Valley: International Music Festival
Kingscote: Agricultural Show
Tanunda: Brass Band Contest

Nov   **Birdwood:** Rock and Roll Rendezvous
Emu Bay: Floraison (vineyard flowering)

Adelaide

Adelaide is one of the few Australian cities whose foundations lie in an idea rather than a convict prison system. It was established as an experiment in free settlement in 1836, and it retains a reputation as a socio-political laboratory and bastion of enlightened democracy. This finds expression in an inspired city plan, the only one in the world that sees the commercial centre surrounded by parkland. Combine that with a Mediterranean climate, great food and wine, excellent museums and a world-famous festival, and you've got a city that locals are justifiably passionate about. The city centre is incredibly compact and well laid out, making getting around on foot remarkably easy.

SIGHTS AND ACTIVITIES • Take a cruise boat along the Torrens, and combine it with a visit to the Adelaide Zoo • Do some dolphin spotting while cruising on the MV *Port Princess* • Capture the relaxed city atmosphere in the main pedestrian thoroughfare, Rundle Mall • Shop in Victorian-era style at the Adelaide Arcade • Tour the classic architecture of Edmund Wright House, the Town Hall, the Botanic Gardens' Palm House, the Post Office, the Treasury Building and St Francis Xavier Cathedral, and the city's iconic rotunda in Elder Park • For lively nightlife and restaurants visit the West End's Hindley Street; for Mediterranean-style cafe culture, head for the East End • Pore over amazing exhibits at the Museum of Classical Archaeology, the Art Gallery of South Australia and the South Australian Museum

VISITOR INFORMATION
18 King William Street (08) 8303 2220

Adelaide Festival

North Adelaide

North Adelaide provides plenty of opportunity to experience more of the city's elegant architecture and beautiful parks and gardens. It is rich in history with a mix of stately Georgian mansions, old pubs bedecked with Victorian iron lace and humble workers' cottages. The area also boasts a restaurant strip that is well worth a visit.

SIGHTS AND ACTIVITIES • Visit one of the most beautiful sports grounds in the world, Adelaide Oval, and its Cricket Museum in one of the grandstands • Stroll around one of the architectural gems of this area, St Peter's Cathedral, and adjacent Pennington Gardens • Climb Montefiore Hill (it's not too difficult) for a great view of the city, then cool off afterwards at the Adelaide Aquatic Centre • Savour the best of local cuisine and wines in the dining strips of King William Road and O'Connell Street and surrounds

TOURISM AUSTRALIA

Glenelg tram

Seaside

The relatively sheltered waters of Gulf St Vincent make waterside recreation a particular attraction in Adelaide. There are boat-hire facilities, jetties to fish from, places to bathe, picnic and stroll, plus some great dining spots.

SIGHTS AND ACTIVITIES • Take the tram to Glenelg, a popular beachside suburb with great restaurants, cafes and pubs. There's a replica of HMS *Buffalo* here, the vessel that brought the first European settlers to found the colony of South Australia. The Magic Mountain Amusement centre is a great diversion for the kids • Head for Semaphore for a more relaxed seaside-village atmosphere, and take the Semaphore Railway, which runs 2 kilometres along the coast between Semaphore and historic Fort Glanville • Discover South Australia's maritime history at the Maritime Museum in Port Adelaide • Learn about the delicate coastal ecology, or just get some exercise, on St Kilda's Mangrove Boardwalk

LOCAL TIPS

- Adelaide's **casino** is also a piece of history, located in the beautifully restored railway station
- See the city from **Light's Vision**, the lookout from which Colonel Light planned the city
- Hit the ski slopes at the world's first artificial ski slope at **Thebarton Snow and Ice**
- Step back in time on the guided trail at **Jupiter Creek Goldfields**, near Echunga
- Experience the historic roots of the Barossa Valley with a tour of **Tanunda**'s Lutheran churches
- Fish for King George whiting off the jetty in **Kingscote**
- Ride the biggest rocking horse in the world at the Toy Factory, Gumeracha, in the **Adelaide Hills**

MEET THE LOCALS

The banksia men and women

Among the many points of interest in the Adelaide Hills is the State Flora Nursery in Belair National Park. It's South Australia's oldest national park (established 1891), and also features the governor's residence (1859) and gardens. At the Flora Nursery you can discover South Australian and other native plants, and learn about their uses and maintenance. Pictured is Birthday Candles (*Banksia spinulosa*).

Koala, Cleland Wildlife Park

MEET THE LOCALS

The first local railway

South Australians have many reasons for puffing up with pride, not least their local railway's status as the first public railway in Australia. It first ran in 1854 from the Murray River port of Goolwa across to Port Elliott, when horse-drawn carriages moved freight between waiting ships and riverboats. Now the line is part of the Steamranger Tourist Railway, which features mighty engines like SA Railways steam loco 621 (pictured).

Adelaide Hills

This getaway destination on Adelaide's doorstep offers a wonderful selection of things to see and do, with its quaint villages and towns, scenic points of interest, fine dining experiences, wineries and B&Bs that specialise in pampering.

SIGHTS AND ACTIVITIES • Sample some of the region's best wines at Petaluma, which also boasts a great restaurant • At Hahndorf, dine German-style, sample cheeses and berries, grab a slice of heaven at one of several excellent local bakeries, visit artist Hans Heysen's home and view local art at the Hahndorf Academy • Gaze in awe as the city of Adelaide is spread out below you at Mount Lofty Lookout • See your favourite marsupials at Cleland Wildlife Park • Admire more than 300 vintage exhibits in the superb collection of vehicles at Birdwood National Motor Museum

VISITOR INFORMATION
41 Main Street, Hahndorf (08) 8388 1185

Barossa Valley

Arguably Australia's most famous wine-growing region, the Barossa Valley is only just over an hour from the city, and is certainly one of the great attractions for most visitors to Adelaide. The Barossa isn't just grapevines, though. It's got plenty of superb scenery and activities for a wide range of interests. The many attractive towns reflect their original establishment by German settlers, both in their architecture and the cafes and restaurants.

SIGHTS AND ACTIVITIES • Take a cellar-door tour (one of the most popular activities) or pick up some great local produce and combine your favourite drop with a picnic in the vines • Walk off lunch on the trails at the Kaiser Stuhl Conservation Park, which supports wildlife and vegetation that existed before European development • Tour the stylish bluestone buildings of Seppelts Estate at Seppeltsfield, established in 1850 • Break your journey with a stop in heritage-listed Gawler, renowned for its many fine buildings and impressive city plan of squares, wide streets and reserves

VISITOR INFORMATION
Murray Street, Tanunda (08) 8563 0600

Wine-tasting in the Barossa

Kangaroo Island

One of Australia's largest islands, its isolation from the mainland has enabled much of the indigenous wildlife on Kangaroo Island to thrive almost undisturbed. Wildlife watching is a major activity, although the relaxed pace of life and the emerging gourmet produce are attracting more and more visitors. Access is by car ferry from the Fleurieu Peninsula (16 kilometres away) and a visit can be combined with a tour of the wineries of McLaren Vale, and the attractions of the Peninsula itself.

SIGHTS AND ACTIVITIES • See the fairy penguin colony, Hope Cottage Gold Museum and the State's oldest cemetery – all in and around the main town of Kingscote • Visit Flinders Chase National Park for its springtime wildflowers, fur seal colony and remarkable rock formations such as Admirals Arch • See Australian sea lions at Seal Bay Conservation Park, either from the boardwalk or up close on a ranger-guided tour • Tour the unusually shaped Cape Borda lighthouse; you can stay in the lighthouse-keeper's residence

MEET THE LOCALS
The new listeners
Every Tuesday at 9.30am, ABC Adelaide takes connecting with its audience very seriously by interviewing newborn babies and their proud parents. ABC reporters range all over the listening region in search of celebrity babies, who all get an ABC Adelaide T-shirt and their chance to be heard, even if it is only 'goo goo gaa gaa'.

MEET THE LOCALS
The tipster
You can get away with a lot of things on radio, but there's no escaping the fact that one of the strangest personalities on ABC Adelaide is small and furry, and the butt of off-colour jokes. However, Coco the guinea pig's claim to fame is her participation in the station's footy-tipping contest. And her skills aren't confined to footy. She also dabbles in the form guide, and tips runners in various prestige horse races. As with all gambling, you should always take a 'sure thing' with a grain of salt but, in this case, you might make that a stick of celery. Hear Coco's tips on 'Mornings' with Matthew Abraham and David Bevan.

LOCAL KNOWLEDGE
Anzac parade vehicles

For many, Anzac day is an opportunity to honour those who served Australia in war. However, in Adelaide it's also a chance to see exhibits from one of Australia's finest collections of military vehicles take to the street. The National Military Vehicle Museum in Port Adelaide provides several dozen vehicles for the annual parade, such as this amphibious US Army Gamagoat personnel carrier.

ABC South East

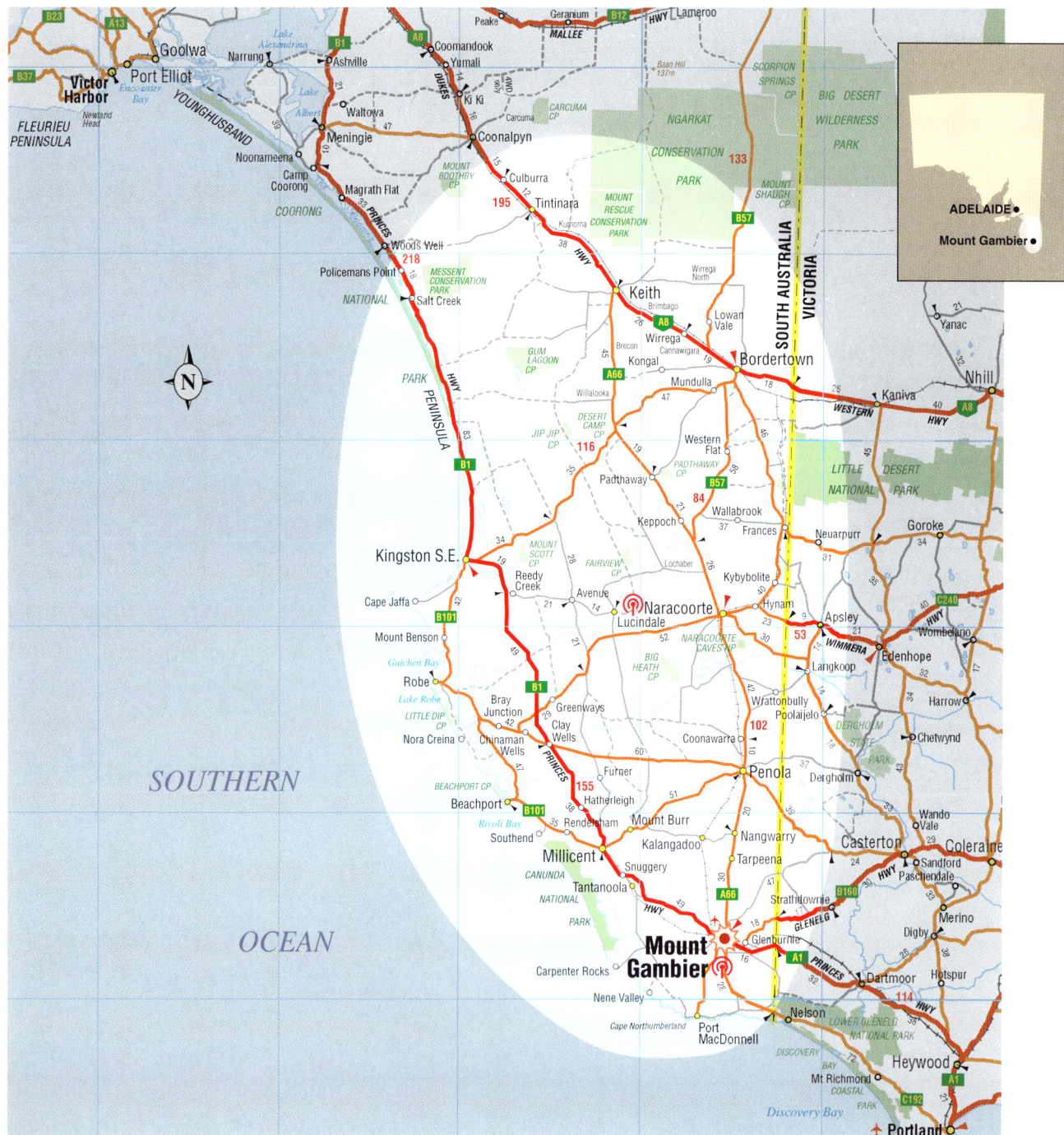

Location of ABC Local Radio studio

Local Radio Frequencies

Beachport	1161 AM
Bordertown	1161 AM
Keith	1161 AM
Kingston S.E.	1161 AM
Lucindale	1161 AM
Millicent	1161 AM
Mount Gambier	1476 AM
Naracoorte	1161 AM
Penola	1161 AM
Port MacDonnell	1476 AM
Robe	1161 AM

Towns in red have their own AM transmitter

Something of a getaway region for Adelaide people, the south-east of South Australia, known as the Limestone Coast, also has plenty of places of interest for visitors from further afield. There are attractive and historic coastal holiday towns for water sports and beautiful coastal scenery. Wildlife enthusiasts flock to the remarkable wetlands of the Coorong and wine enthusiasts make awed pilgrimages to the Coonawarra and Padthaway wine regions. And for extraordinary scenery, Mount Gambier is renowned for its stunning lake.

Tourism is understandably one of the mainstays of the local economy, but there are busy rural industries including wool and forestry, and fishing as well. This is one of those areas where it pays to relax and set yourself an easy-going pace. That way you'll enjoy the place as much as the locals do.

ABC South East is a proud part of this dynamic, diverse and delightful region. It is the best source of up-to-date information on the people, issues and events in the south-east.

Sunset at Robe

TOURISM AUSTRALIA

NOT TO BE MISSED

- Walking, fishing and watching the extraordinary bird life and wildlife in the renowned **Coorong**
- See the incredible colours of the Blue Lake at **Mount Gambier**
- Sample some of the finest wines in Australia in the famous **Coonawarra** area
- Enjoy the cafes, restaurants and sea-change lifestyle of the historic seaside villages, such as **Kingston S.E.**, **Robe** and **Beachport**

LOCAL EVENTS

Jan   **Cape Jaffa:** Seafood and Wine Festival
Kingston S.E.: Fishing Contest; Yachting Regatta
Port MacDonnell: Bayside Festival
Penola: Vigneron Cup

Feb   **Mount Gambier:** South-East Country Music Weekend
Naracoorte: Taste the Limestone Coast

May   **Mount Gambier:** Generations in Jazz
Naracoorte: Swap Meeting
Penola: Festival

Oct   **Bordertown:** Clayton Farm Vintage Field Day
Coonalpyn: Agricultural and Horticultural Show (includes Antique Tractor Pull)

Nov   **Coonawarra:** Cabernet Celebrations
Naracoorte: Limestone Coast Children's Expo
Robe: Village Fair

Mount Gambier

The major commercial centre (population 22 037) of the south-east is also a fascinating place for scenery and history. It's situated on an extinct volcano named in 1800, and is famed for its beautiful coloured crater lake. There is also an extensive system of limestone caves. The town is surrounded by Australia's largest pine plantations, as well as farms, vineyards and dairies.

Blue Lake

SIGHTS AND ACTIVITIES • Stroll around the town's many historic buildings, dating from the 1860s (brochure available) • Delve underground on a tour of the numerous caves • See Blue Lake turn a brilliant turquoise in November, reverting to a deeper blue at the end of summer • Find out about the local wildlife at Valley Lake's Wildlife Park and lake boardwalk (picnic and playground facilities available) • Enjoy great views of the district from Mount Schank's summit, 17 kilometres south

VISITOR INFORMATION
Jubilee Highway East (08) 8724 9750

Kingston S.E.

Situated at the southern end of the Coorong National Park, this pleasant farming and fishing town (population 1431) is also a seaside resort, and an excellent base for exploring the attractions of the surrounding area. These include numerous lakes and lagoons that are ideal for fishing and bird-watching.

SIGHTS AND ACTIVITIES • Get your photo taken with the giant Larry the Lobster, which greets visitors on the way into town • Dine on Larry's freshly caught cousins during the lobster season from October to April • Visit nearby Cape Jaffa, a small fishing village highly regarded for its fishing and diving • See the reconstructed Cape Jaffa Lighthouse in Kingston's Marine Parade, and the Pioneer Museum in Cooke Street

VISITOR INFORMATION
BP Roadhouse,1 Princes Highway (08) 8767 2404

MEET THE LOCALS

A gummy jumbuk

This is Henry, thought to be the oldest sheep in the south-east. He came to public attention when ABC Local Radio asked who had the oldest ovine candidate. Henry is 20 years old, blind and losing his teeth. He was originally a pet lamb for the daughter of Compton farmer, Hans Meinck. She's now grown up, and Henry is still going strong, running around with the lambs.

Naracoorte

The centre of major beef, sheep, grain and wine industries, Naracoorte (population 4674) is also famed for its World Heritage-listed limestone caves. The town dates from the 1840s and has several noteworthy historical buildings.

SIGHTS AND ACTIVITIES • Discover the history of the wool industry at The Sheep's Back Museum and Visitor Centre • In Naracoorte Caves National Park, view spectacular stalagmites and stalactites, see life-like representations of Australia's extinct megafauna, then find out all about bats at the Wonambi Fossil Centre • Ride the miniature railway at Tiny Train Park • Bird-watch at the Bool Lagoon Game Reserve, with its wetland boardwalks and bird hides

VISITOR INFORMATION
The Sheep's Back Museum and Visitor Centre, MacDonnell Street (08) 8762 1518

Penola

The gateway to the Coonawarra wine district, Penola (population 1189) is a fascinating place in its own right. It is one of the oldest towns in the State, and it was here in 1866 that Mary MacKillop (beatified in 1994) established the first school in Australia that catered for children regardless of income or social class.

SIGHTS AND ACTIVITIES • See the stone schoolroom where Mary MacKillop taught, and find out more about this saintly Australian at the adjacent interpretive centre • Discover local history at the Penola Coonawarra Information Centre • Taste the fruit of that history at some of the many wineries in the Coonawarra • Enjoy a picnic at Greenrise Reserve, just south of town

VISITOR INFORMATION
27 Arthur Street (08) 8737 2855

Robe

Arguably the most attractive of the State's coastal holiday and fishing villages, Robe has a relatively well-sheltered anchorage in Lake Butler. In the area you'll find many beautiful secluded beaches, lagoons and salt lakes, ideal for fishing, bird-watching or swimming.

SIGHTS AND ACTIVITIES • Take a heritage walk around town (brochure available) • Feast on freshly caught fish and crays (October to April); visit the yabby farm just outside town and catch your own • See sheep-shearing and sheepdog demonstrations at Narraburra Woolshed • Climb Beacon Hill south of town for panoramic views

VISITOR INFORMATION
Robe Institute and Library, Mundy Terrace (08) 8768 2465

LOCAL TIPS

- At the Lady Nelson Visitor and Discovery Centre in **Mount Gambier**, see a full-scale replica of the ship and learn about the region's history

- Capture the spirit of the seafaring past at **Port MacDonnell Maritime Museum**

- More than 240 bird species have been identified in the area around the **Coorong**

- In **Canunda National Park** you'll find massive dunes to explore

- See the Tantanoola Tiger, a Syrian Wolf shot in the district in the 1890s then stuffed, at the **Tantanoola Tiger Hotel**, between Millicent and Mount Gambier

MEET THE LOCALS

All the way back home
Travel broadens the mind, but absence makes the heart grow fonder. In Beachport, jeweller Tracey Chambers has seen the world but settled for the view of the water from her studio and cafe back in her home town. If you're there at the right time, you can also see her at work making pieces inspired by the crystal-clear water and clean sands of the Beachport beachfront.

LOCAL KNOWLEDGE

Mundulla pub
In rural Australia, the decline of small towns is all too common. But in tiny Mundulla, just south of Bordertown, things are looking up. In 2003 the historic Mundulla pub reopened for business, having last been licensed in 1912. It's now owned by locals Liz Goosens and George Tschaban, and follows the reopening of Maney's Drapery by new owners who recently settled there from Darwin. The pub is open seven days for a yarn and a chance to support a tiny town with a big future.

ABC Riverland

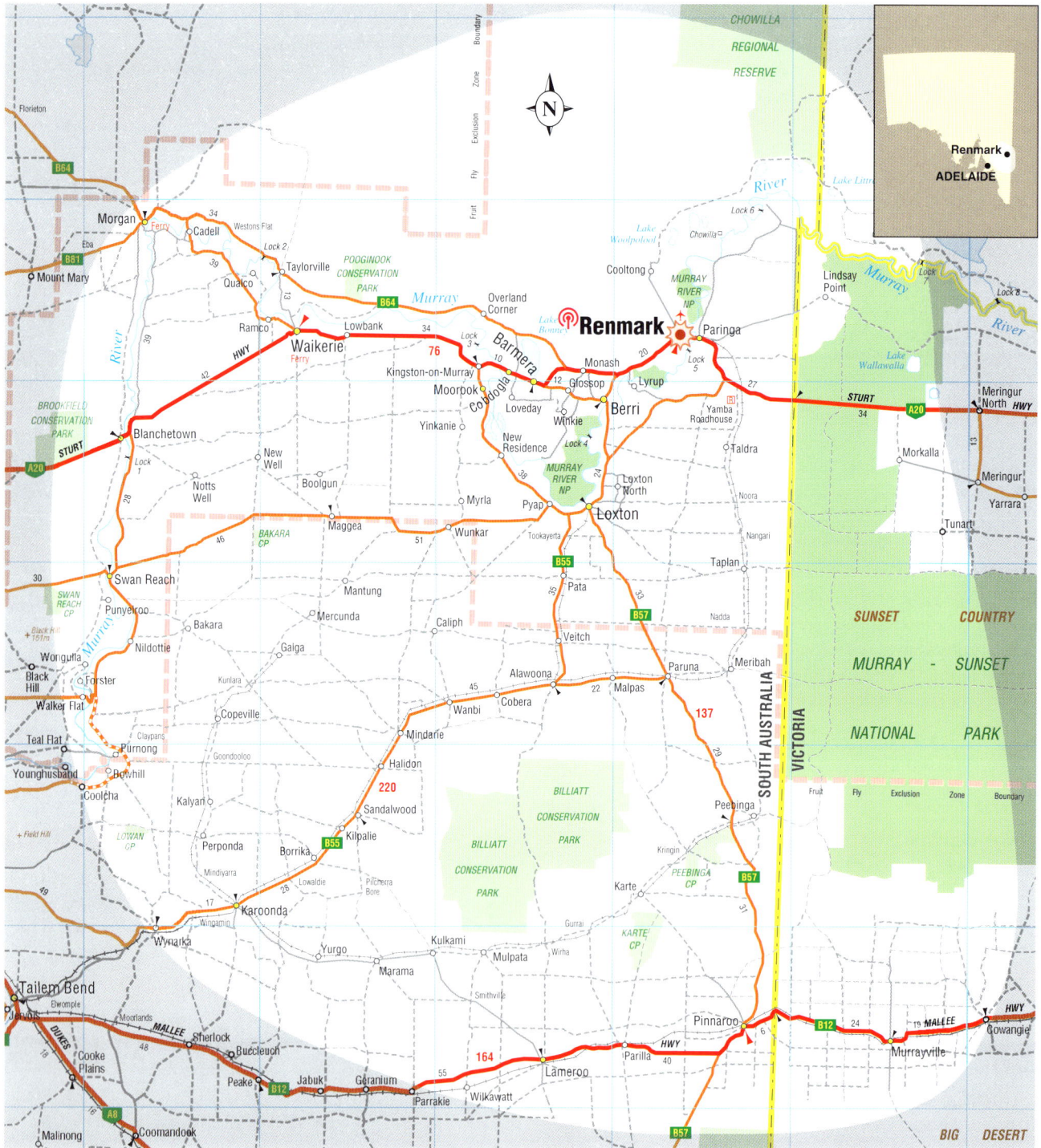

Location of ABC Local Radio studio

Local Radio Frequencies	
Berri	1062 AM
Barmera	1062 AM
Karoonda	1062 AM
Lameroo	1062 AM
Loxton	1062 AM
Morgan	1062 AM
Pinnaroo	1062 AM
Renmark	1062 AM
Swan Reach	1062 AM
Waikerie	1062 AM

Renmark has the only transmitter (AM) in this region

Murray River sunset

Fans of the television series *A River Somewhere* will understand perfectly the attractions of South Australia's Riverland region. Tranquil stretches of the mighty Murray lined with tall gums or stretches of cliffs – the calm only broken by passing vessels and paddle-steamers – create an idyll that is perfect for a relaxing getaway. The area traces the course of the Murray through South Australia from Swan Reach across the border into Victoria.

Not that the area is all sleepy river towns. It also produces citrus, wine grapes, olives, honey and almonds, while the cooler Mallee region produces wheat, barley, potatoes and onions, and hosts many sheep studs.

So you can enjoy camping, fishing, boating, skiing and houseboat holidays, and top it off by sampling the fine, fresh local produce and fruit of the vine. And you can keep abreast of local events and news, plus the world at large, simply by tuning to ABC Riverland.

NOT TO BE MISSED

- Discover the days of the paddle-steamers at the **Port of Morgan Museum**
- Take the helm of a houseboat for a relaxing cruise on the **Murray**, or board one of several paddle-steamers for a day cruise or longer

- For those who like their recreation in a park setting, visit the **Murray River National Park**, just near Renmark
- Visit some of the **wineries** of the region, such as Angoves and Berri Estates

MEET THE LOCALS

The kangaroo carers

In the town of Morgan, you may be fortunate to meet a remarkable local couple, Patricia and Bryan Patterson. Like many people around the country, they've volunteered to look after sick and injured wildlife. In the Patterson's case, they've turned their home into a kangaroo sanctuary, with more than 40 roos of different species keeping them on the hop with feeding and injury treatment. Hear their story at www.abc.net.au/riverland/stories/s867945.htm

MEET THE LOCALS

The princess

Capture all the charm and grace of a bygone era. The PS *Murray Princess* operates extended cruises out of the river town of Mannum, and is the largest paddle-steamer ever built in the Southern Hemisphere. Other vessels operating from there and other towns in the Riverland include the PS *Mayflower* and PS *Marion*, which operate day cruises, and the *Proud Mary*, which conducts longer cruises specialising in nature tours.

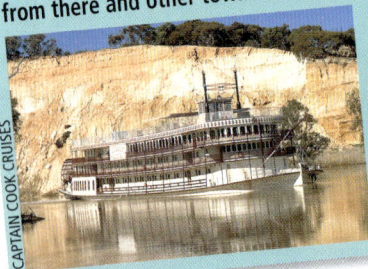

CAPTAIN COOK CRUISES

Oranges, a major product of the region

Renmark

Renmark (population 4366) is the major centre of the Riverland region, and is at the heart of the country's oldest irrigation scheme (set up by the Canadian Chaffey brothers in 1887). Today it's the focus of a wide range of agricultural activities, including food-processing industries. Being on the Murray, it's also a destination for those with water sports in mind.

SIGHTS AND ACTIVITIES • Board the PS *Industry* which is now a floating museum but also cruises on the first Sunday of the month • Visit the National Trust Museum, Olivewood, located in what was once the Chaffey homestead • Visit Bookmark Biosphere Reserve and historic Chowilla Station • Drive the self-guide tour of historic sites and wineries (brochure available) • Hire a houseboat and become the skipper of your own Murray cruise

VISITOR INFORMATION
84 Murray Avenue (08) 8586 6704

Berri

Once a refuelling stop for paddle-steamers, Berri is now a major commercial centre in the Riverland region, and has a population of 3912. It is surrounded by orchards and vineyards, while the river bank is dotted with great picnic and fishing spots.

SIGHTS AND ACTIVITIES • Head for the Lookout Tower for great views of the river and town • Visit the sculpture and cave memorial to Aboriginal tracker Jimmy James • Visit Angas Park Fruit Company and try their dried fruits and other products • Taste the wines at Berri Estates, the largest winemaking facility in the Southern Hemisphere, and other district wineries

VISITOR INFORMATION
Riverview Drive (08) 8582 5511

Loxton

Loxton (population 3310), regarded as the garden city of the Riverland region, has attractive parks and numerous historic sites and buildings. It was originally known as Loxton's Hut, after a boundary rider who was based in the locality. As with the rest of the region, the town is now surrounded by thriving agricultural activity, having been the focus of the largest post-World War II soldier-settler scheme in South Australia.

SIGHTS AND ACTIVITIES • Visit the numerous art galleries and craft shops dotted around town • Step into the past at Loxton Historical Village • See the pepper tree grown from a seed brought by Loxton over a century ago • Stroll the nature trail along the riverfront

VISITOR INFORMATION
Bookpurnong Terrace (08) 8584 7919

Swan Reach

A quiet little township with a population of just 255, Swan Reach is a popular holiday destination with picturesque river scenery and good fishing. In the area, fruit, grapes, almonds and flowers are grown.

SIGHTS AND ACTIVITIES • Make an appointment for a Murray River Nature Educational Tour • See wombats, emus and kangaroos at Swan Reach and Ridley conservation parks • Taste fresh yabbies at Murray Aquaculture Yabby Farm

VISITOR INFORMATION
General Store, 47 Anzac Avenue (08) 8570 2036

Waikerie

Press the locals for their town's claim to fame and you'll squeeze out of them the answer that it's considered the citrus centre of Australia. In fact, the area is a splash of irrigated orchards and vineyards in otherwise arid Mallee country. And like several other river towns, it has plenty of wonderful views of river gums and sandstone cliffs, and abundant bird life.

SIGHTS AND ACTIVITIES • Stay, dine or have a coffee at the unique floating motel, restaurant and cafe, Murray River Queen • Visit the Citrus-Packing House, the largest in Australia • Go bird-watching at Harts Lagoon, a wetland area with a permanent bird hide • Get great views of the river just north of town from the clifftop lookout and walk • Take a joy ride in a glider from the International Soaring Centre

VISITOR INFORMATION
Orange Tree Giftmania, Sturt Highway (08) 8541 2332

LOCAL TIPS

- Walk the Kia Kia Nature Trail in the **Murray River National Park**

- Enjoy great scenery and walks, a museum and a paddle-steamer ride at **Wilabalangaloo** homestead and flora and fauna reserve near Berri

- View the irrigated farmland and the impressive river cliffs at **Headings Lookout Tower**, 16 kilometres to the north-east of Renmark

- Visit the historic wharf (1877) in **Morgan**, once a busy river port that still preserves the feel of the day when the paddle-boats reigned supreme

- For a **relaxing time**, stay in one of the many caravan parks and camping areas dotted along the river, with access to swimming, fishing and boating

- Walk in the footsteps of the overlanders at **Barmera**, whose Lake Bonney is named after one of the first. It's also the site of Donald Campbell's water-speed record attempt in 1964 (there's a commemorative obelisk)

MEET THE LOCALS

The local transexuals

It's certainly not a delicate business – changing the sex of pistachio trees involves a chainsaw and grafting of new tree stock. It puts a whole new perspective on 'the unkindest cut of all'. It's one of the activities you may see being done in autumn around the Riverland, when the trees are dormant, to ensure the right ratio of unproductive males and productive females. And you might like to bear in mind, the next time you're enjoying pistachio nuts, that they may have come from a she who used to be a he. Bon appétit.

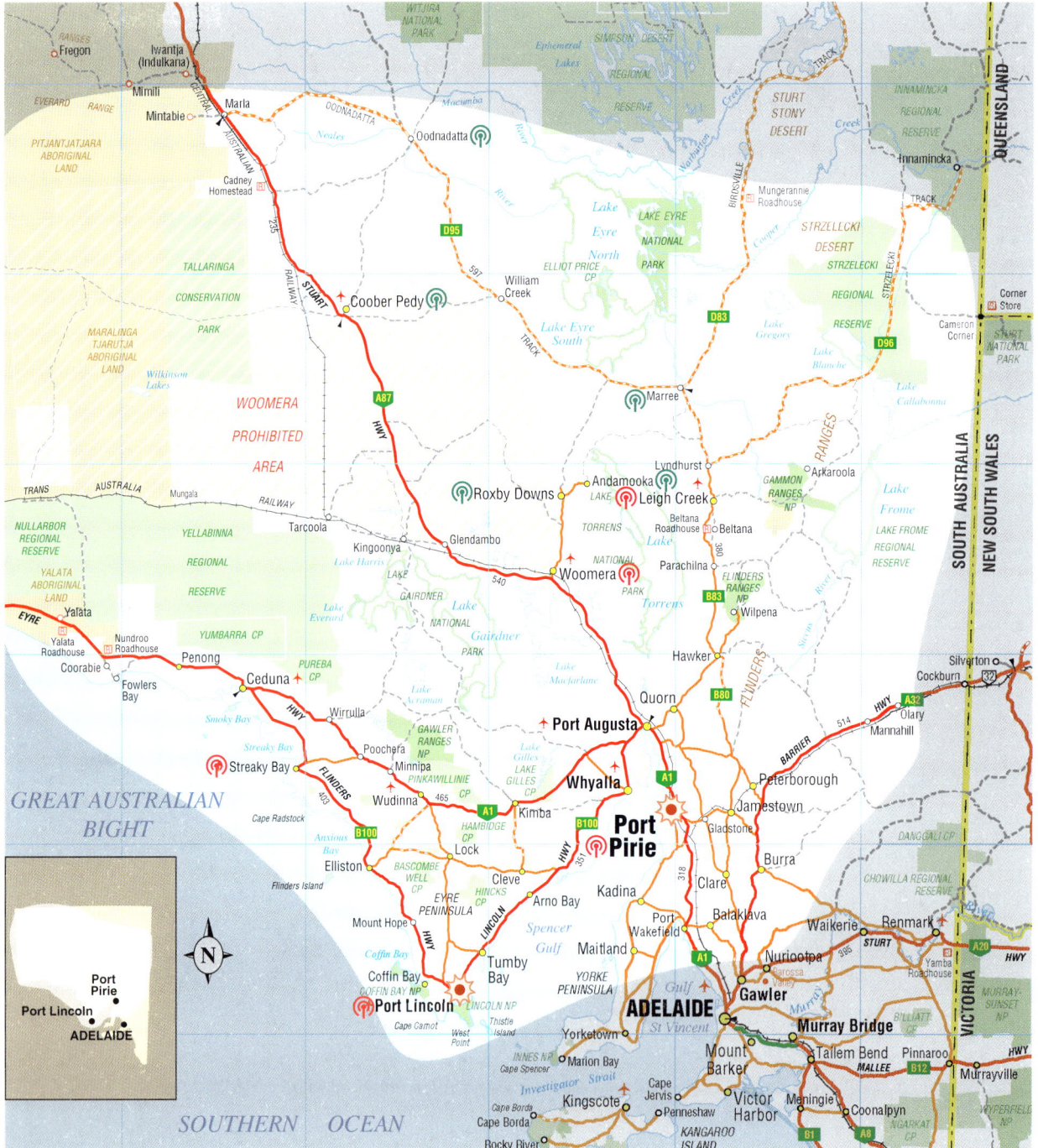

Location of ABC Local Radio studio

TOURISM AUSTRALIA

NULLARBOR PLÄIN·
EASTERN END OF TREELESS PLAIN

Local Radio Frequencies

Balaklava	639 AM	891 AM ABC Adelaide
Ceduna	693 AM	
Clare	639 AM	891 AM ABC Adelaide
Coorabie	693 AM	
Gladstone	639 AM	891 AM ABC Adelaide
Hawker	639 AM	891 AM ABC Adelaide
Jamestown	639 AM	891 AM ABC Adelaide
Leigh Creek	1602 AM	
Maitland	639 AM	891 AM ABC Adelaide
Olary	639 AM	891 AM ABC Adelaide
Penong	693 AM	
Peterborough	639 AM	891 AM
Port Augusta	639 AM	
Port Lincoln	1485 AM	891 AM ABC Adelaide
Port Pirie	639 AM	891 AM ABC Adelaide
Streaky Bay	693 AM	
Tumby Bay	1485 AM	
Whyalla	639 AM	891 AM ABC Adelaide
Woomera	1584 AM	
Wudinna	693 AM	
Andamooka	105.9 FM	
Coober Pedy	106.1 FM	
Marree	105.7 FM	
Oodnadatta	95.3 FM	
Roxby Downs	102.7 FM	639 AM

Towns in red have their own AM transmitter
Towns in green have their own FM transmitter

ABC Local Radio can also be heard in many remote localities to the west and north of the area shown on the map.

This is a region of vast distances and spectacular scenery, stretching from the Western Australian border to the Eyre Peninsula, from the Clare Valley south to the Yorke Peninsula and north through the Flinders Ranges and the outback.

The Clare Valley and mid-north region was settled in the 1840s as a major copper mining and agricultural district, though is now renowned for its vineyards, historic nineteenth-century buildings and scenic beauty. The Yorke Peninsula is a popular holiday destination a short drive from Adelaide, and is well known for its fishing, diving, surfing and spectacular coastal scenery. In the north lie the Flinders Ranges, abundant with flora and fauna, and magnificent scenery.

The Eyre Peninsula and Nullarbor stretch 1000 kilometres from Whyalla in the east to the Western Australian border. The fishing and surfing spots here are among the best in the world.

For the people of the remote north and west of the State, ABC Local Radio is a source of information, contact and community.

NOT TO BE MISSED

- Visit one (or more!) of the 30 wineries in the **Clare Valley**, renowned particularly for its Riesling
- Take a ridgetop tour via Arkaroola for a taste of the ancient peaks and valleys of the **Flinders Ranges**
- Go diving and follow the **Investigator Strait Maritime Heritage Trail** which takes in 26 dive sites
- Cycle or walk along the **Riesling Trail**, a 27-kilometre path between Clare and Auburn
- Take a surfing safari along the coast between **Ceduna** and **Penong**, boasting three world-famous surfing breaks

Scene near Clare

Port Pirie

This major industrial and commercial centre (population 13 633), located on Spencer Gulf, was established in 1845 to service the region's sheep industry. After winning BHP's smelting business, it now boasts the largest lead-zinc smelter in the world.

SIGHTS AND ACTIVITIES • Visit the Regional Tourism and Arts Centre • Take a walk on the waterfront to witness the town's thriving port • Drive to scenic Weeroona Island, north of town

VISITOR INFORMATION
3 Mary Elie Street (08) 8633 8700

Clare

This charming town (population 2815) was first settled in 1842. Famed for its wines, the first vines were planted by Jesuit priests at Sevenhill in the early 1850s to ensure a steady supply of alter wine.

SIGHTS AND ACTIVITIES • Tour the local wineries • Take a scenic drive south-west to Mintaro, an almost intact nineteenth-century village

VISITOR INFORMATION
Town Hall, 229 Main North Road (08) 8842 2131

Coober Pedy

This famous opal-mining town (population 2762), situated in the heart of the outback, is also famous for its unique 'underground buildings'. Today thousands of mines produce 70 per cent of the world's supply of opals.

SIGHTS AND ACTIVITIES • See demonstrations of opal cutting and polishing, or pop in and purchase these exquisite pieces of jewellery or stones • Play 18 holes at the Coober Pedy Opal Fields Golf Club, voted as one of the ten most unique courses in the world • Visit the Umoona Underground Mine and Museum • Say your prayers underground at one of the subterranean churches

VISITOR INFORMATION
Council Offices, Hutchison Street (08) 8672 5298

MEET THE LOCALS' LOCALS

The Warwick family

What makes a local a local? Well, since the 1880s generations of the Warwick family have been running the historic sheep station, Holowiliena, in the Flinders Ranges. The 330-square kilometre property's name translates to 'home of the stick nest rat'. Richard and Janne Warwick took over the station in 1981, but the history of the station hasn't been lost. It's kept alive through daily diary entries, and historical store, museum and school house. The station is well known throughout the community and has touched the lives of hundreds of people.

Port Augusta

A thriving industrial city at the head of the Spencer Gulf and in the shadows of the Flinders Ranges, Port Augusta (population 13 914) is a supply centre for the outback and is at the crossroads between Darwin and Alice Springs to the north, the Nullabor to the west and Adelaide to the east. The nearby Flinders Ranges are filled with spectacular scenery, amazing wildlife and steeped in the spellbinding power of the Aboriginal Dreamtime.

SIGHTS AND ACTIVITIES • Admire the desert flora at Port Augusta's Australian Arid Lands Botanic Gardens • Visit the multi-award-winning Wadlata Outback Centre in Port Augusta for an introduction to the sights and sounds of the Flinders Ranges • Drive to the Yourambulla Caves, one of several Aboriginal rock-art sites in the Flinders Ranges • Discover the outback and camp under the stars on a four-wheel-drive or camel-trek tour • Explore Arkaroola's 61 000 hectare wildlife sanctuary, featuring fascinating geological formations, hot springs, rare wildlife, historic mining areas and vast plains

VISITOR INFORMATION
Wadlata Outback Centre, 41 Flinders Terrace (08) 8641 0793

Port Lincoln

Nestled on beautiful Boston Bay, Port Lincoln (population 11 678) is renowned for its sheltered waters, Mediterranean climate, scenic coast roads, magnificent cliff faces and tuna fishing, making it one of the ultimate holiday destinations.

SIGHTS AND ACTIVITIES • Spend the day swimming, water-skiing, yachting and fishing • Stroll along the Parnkalla Walking Trail for superb coastal scenery • Jump aboard one of the many charter boats for underwater diving, game-fishing and dolphin, sea-lion and bird-life tours • Head down to Coffin Bay, famous for its oysters, and one of the most beautiful estuaries in Australia

VISITOR INFORMATION
3 Adelaide Place (08) 8683 3544

LOCAL TIPS

- Swim with sea-lions and dolphins at **Baird Bay**, near Streaky Bay
- Head to **Burra**, a former copper-mining centre where many of the quaint cottages have been turned into guesthouses and B&Bs
- Catch a flick at **The Coober Pedy Open Air Outback Cinema**
- Explore the **Nullarbor** where, during the day, you have an unbroken 360-degree view of the horizon of blue sky and, at night, you can see a canopy of stars brilliant in the clear southern sky

MEET THE LOCALS

The dog fence

You may have heard of the rabbit-proof fence in Western Australia, but what about the dog fence stretching from the cliffs overlooking the Great Australian Bight right through most of Queensland? This 5400-kilometre fence is two-and-a-half times longer than the Great Wall of China, and is the longest man-made structure, or fence, in the world. It not only protects the livestock, but also allows dingoes to be preserved as a legitimate wildlife species on the other side. The dog fence travels through most things in its path, including the salt lakes.

MEET THE LOCALS

The salt of the earth

One of the industries that has benefited from Australia's drought conditions is the Yorke Peninsula's salt industry, with the lack of rain aiding in the evaporation process. Local company, Cheetham Salt, is the largest food-salt producing company in Australia, and is experiencing its best harvest in a decade. The process involves sea water being pumped into the salt farm's ponds, and as the water evaporates it is moved around until it's at such a level that the salt 'falls' to the bottom. Once enough salt has gathered, the water is drained from the top of the pond, and the harvesters are sent out to 'scrape' it up, wash it and add it to the stockpiles. From here the salt is dried, crushed, packaged and finally ends up on our kitchen tables.

ABC Far West

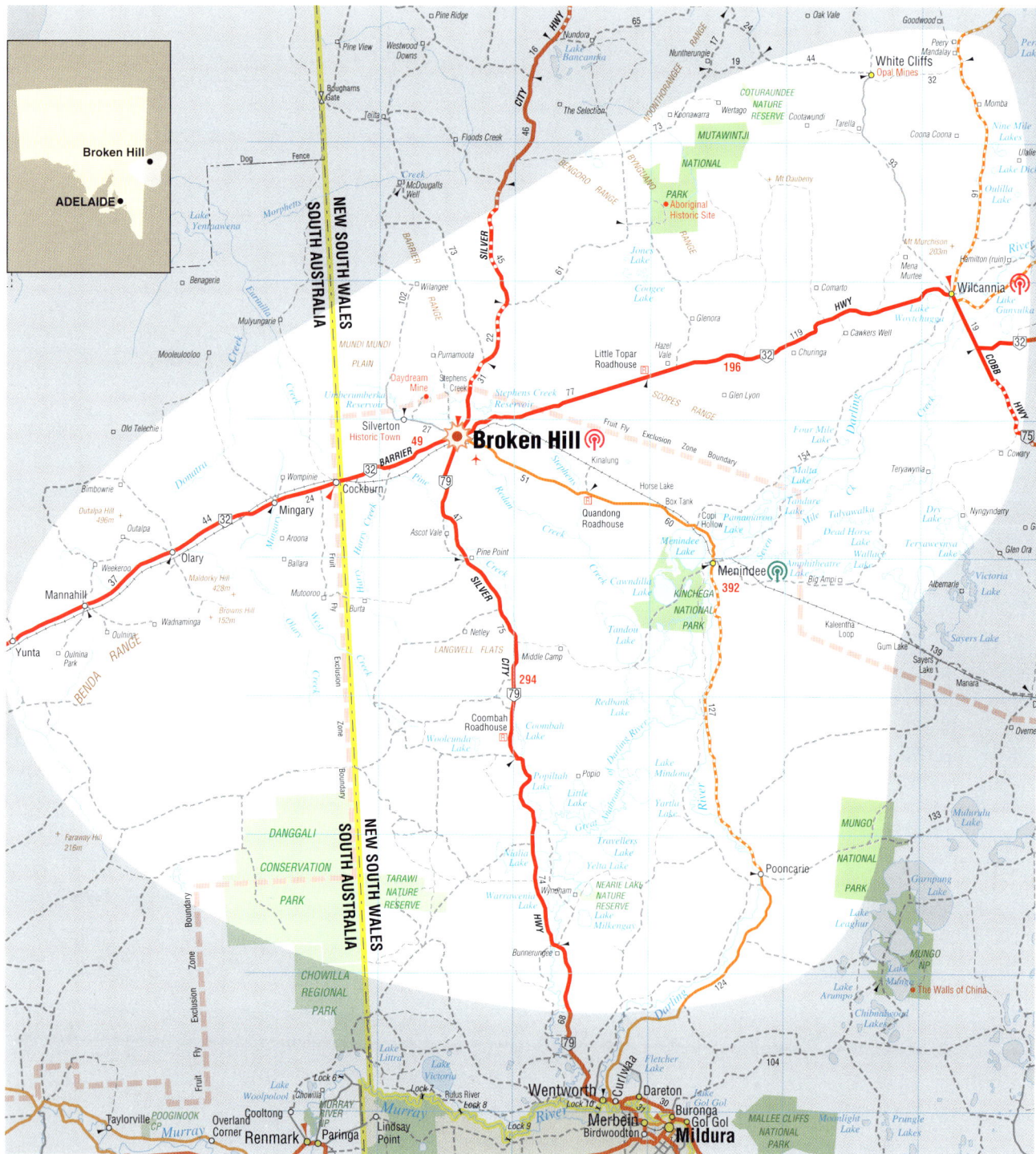

Location of ABC Local Radio studio

Local Radio Frequencies		
Broken Hill	999 AM	
Cockburn	999 AM	
Pooncarie	999 AM	
Silverton	999 AM	
Tibooburra	999 AM	1584 AM
Wilcannia	1584 AM	
Yunta	999 AM	
Ivanhoe	106.1 FM	
Menindee	97.3 FM	
White Cliffs	107.7 FM	

Towns in red have their own AM transmitter
Towns in green have their own FM transmitter

ABC Local Radio can also be heard in many remote localities to the north and east of the area shown on the map.

Broken Hill mine

This region is centred on Broken Hill, located in the far west of New South Wales and once the site for the world's richest deposit of silver, earning it the nickname 'the Silver City'. The vast, desolate, yet stunning landscape that surrounds Broken Hill has been the backdrop for many Australian films, including *Mad Max 2*, *Priscilla Queen Of The Desert* and *Mission Impossible 2*. It is also home to many internationally famous artists including Pro Hart and Jack Absalom.

Although it's physically part of New South Wales, the region identifies more closely with South Australia. It's only 500 kilometres to Adelaide, but 1200 kilometres to Sydney, and the local area operates on Central Standard Time. For the purposes of ABC broadcasting, it's the same story, which is why ABC Far West is in the South Australian section of *Meet the Locals*. It's easy to understand if you can come to terms with the Far West being in the north-east, and in another State. In any event, you can always just tune to ABC Local Radio to find out what's happening in one of the most fascinating regions in the country.

Visitors to this region should note that many areas are best visited in the cooler winter months.

NOT TO BE MISSED

- Go sailing in the outback, and fishing, swimming and camping, on the lakes near **Menindee**
- Fossick for opals in the dugout town of **White Cliffs**
- Head to **Sturt National Park**, in the State's corner country, for stunning landscapes, fascinating wildlife and remarkable wildflowers
- Explore the old mining towns dotted around the region – remnants of the frontier days
- Drive through the ancient wonders of **Mungo National Park**

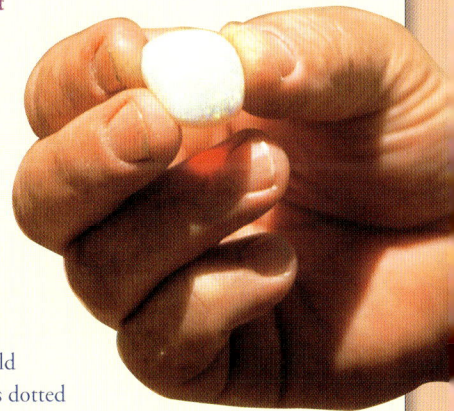

LOCAL EVENTS

Mar **Broken Hill:** Outback and All that Jazz

Mar–Apr **Broken Hill:** St Patrick's Race Day

May **Broken Hill:** National 4X4 Challenge (four-wheel-drive rally)
Menindee: Inland Speedboat Championships

July **Tibooburra:** Festival

Aug **Menindee:** Burke and Wills Fishing Challenge

Sep **Broken Hill:** Silver City Show

Oct **Broken Hill:** Country Music Festival
Tibooburra: Gymkhana and Rodeo

GAVIN SCHMIDT

Broken Hill

The phenomenally mineral-rich Barrier Ranges in the far west of New South Wales gave mining behemoth BHP its start. Broken Hill, one of Australia's most famous outback towns (population 20 963), is still a busy mining centre, but it has also become home to the Brushmen of the Bush, an artistic community drawn together by their love of the uncompromising landscapes of the area.

SIGHTS AND ACTIVITIES ● Take a self-guide historic town drive (booklet available), especially along National Trust-classified Argent Street ● See the Silver City Comet at the Sulphide Street Station Railway Museum ● Visit some of the galleries dotted around town, featuring works by the Brushmen of the Bush and indigenous artists ● Look out for the Living Desert, a superb collection of sculptures created by artists in 1993 on a hilltop along Nine Mile Road – the views from the site are also worth the trip ● Visit nearby Silverton, a frontier village of fascinating historic buildings, artists' galleries and a great pub that has featured internationally in television commercials and movies, as has the stunning scenery around the town

VISITOR INFORMATION
Cnr Blende and Bromide streets (08) 8087 6077

MEET THE LOCALS
The flying padre

You've heard of the Flying Nun? Well this is the Flying Priest. Pastor John Blair is based at Broken Hill (he's originally from Boston), and he's found that gathering in a flock that's spread over thousands of square kilometres means swapping God's plan for a flight plan. So while he carries out his ministry on a wing and a prayer, it's also a case of praise the Lord and pass the aviation fuel.

Silver City Comet

Menindee

The primary business of this remote town (population 385) is water. With the adjacent Menindee Lake providing a reliable source in an otherwise parched interior, it's a good business to be in. It still forms part of the water-storage scheme for Broken Hill.

SIGHTS AND ACTIVITIES • Visit Maiden's Hotel, where Burke and Wills stayed on their ill-fated journey north in 1860 • Sail, swim, fish and camp at Menindee Lake, just outside town • Get a good view of the area from the Menindee Lake Lookout, 10 kilometres north • Watch the abundant wildlife at the highly regarded Kinchega National Park, just west of town • See the wreck of the paddle-steamer *Providence*, on the Darling River 10 kilometres west

VISITOR INFORMATION
Railway Station, Maiden Street (08) 8091 4274

White Cliffs

The discovery of opal in the 1890s led to 4500 people descending on the opal fields – the population today is just 207. This is the only place where jewelled opal 'pineapples' are found.

SIGHTS AND ACTIVITIES • Take a guided tour of the town, visiting historic sites and learning about fossicking for opals • See the fascinating solar power station, just south of town (tours available) • Play a round of golf on an outback course that gives a whole new meaning to the term 'greens' • Stay in one of the area's underground accommodation places • Visit some of the several opal outlets and art galleries

VISITOR INFORMATION
Keraro Road (08) 8091 6611

Wilcannia

Once a thriving port on the Darling River, this town has declined somewhat in recent years (population 688), but remains the gateway to many fascinating areas nearby.

SIGHTS AND ACTIVITIES • Take a self-guide historical tour (brochure available) of several excellent sandstone buildings dating from the 1870s • Pick up a supply of water and other items for a visit to the Mutawintji National Park, with its stark gorges and rock outcrops, and Aboriginal art sites (access to sites by tours only) • Visit the Tilpa Pub, continually licensed since 1894 (140 kilometres north-east) • Take a four-wheel drive to Willandra National Park, 290 kilometres south-east – its scenery and archaeological history are fascinating

VISITOR INFORMATION
Council Offices, Reid Street (08) 8083 8910

LOCAL TIPS

- Check out the goat-dog trials at **Broken Hill**'s Silver City Show. They are like sheep-dog trials, but thought to be the only test of dog against goat in the country

- While you're in **Broken Hill**, you might get to see the School of the Air's Sports Carnival. No, the kids don't have mid-air races, it's actually one of the rare opportunities for the kids to get together. Tours of the school's facilities can be booked at other times

- Sunsets are spectacular throughout this region, particularly at **Silverton**, the Living Desert sculpture park, the Corner Country and **Mutawintji National Park**

- Keep an eye out for the travelling **Toy Library**. The Outback Mobile Resource Unit has four-wheel drives that provide remote stations with a range of resources including books, videos and toys

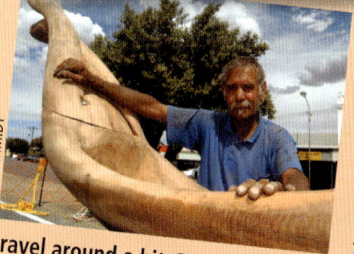

GAVIN SCHMIDT

MEET THE LOCALS

The artists
William 'Badger' Bates is one of the many Western and indigenous artists to be found in the Far West. But to get a feel for Badger's work, you'll need to travel around a bit. For example, he has one piece at the Living Desert sculpture park outside Broken Hill and the one pictured is on display in Wilcannia, 200 kilometres down the road. A 'canoe' carved from a single piece of local river red gum, it depicts a prehistoric plesiosaur discovered at White Cliffs and the Rainbow Serpent Nhatji, which represent the linking of the past, future and reconciliation.

GAVIN SCHMIDT

LOCAL KNOWLEDGE

Corner country
It obviously took some thought to decide that the north-west corner of New South Wales should be called 'Corner Country'. But while it's remote, it's also full of fascinating things to see and do. The scenery is extraordinary, the sunsets often spectacular and little towns like Milparinka and Tibooburra (which frequently boasts the State's highest temperatures) have several interesting buildings to explore. Then, there are places like Cameron's Corner, where three States meet, and nearby historic sites like the Explorer's Tree.

Emergency Broadcasting

ABC Local Radio – There when you need it most

Off the north-west of Western Australia, a tropical cyclone moves erratically towards the coast. It's already sending long streams of rain-laden clouds across the continent, raising the possibility of causing flood waters to rage down a dozen rivers. Meanwhile, in Tasmania, the people in a handful of small towns are watching the wind, to see if it will turn a fire-front towards their homes or away from them.

At times like these, people in hundreds of communities, often scattered over vast areas, tune to ABC Local Radio to get updates on the potential danger, and information on how to prepare for it. Of course, emergencies don't always occur in a predictable and orderly fashion. However, even when disaster strikes without warning, ABC Local Radio presenters and production staff have shown how readily they can grasp the situation and switch into emergency mode.

As the drama unfolds, such as during the devastating Canberra bushfires in 2003, normal programming is often suspended as ABC Local Radio becomes the primary source of information about what is going on. Homes without power or telephone contact can still keep abreast of developments if they have a battery-powered transistor radio. As information becomes available around the clock, it's not uncommon for reporters and presenters to stay on the job for extraordinary lengths of time, providing details on what is happening and how communities should respond, often not returning to their own homes until the crisis has passed.

'Local Radio's emergency role has been formalised in some areas, in order to facilitate closer working relationships between us and relevant authorities. In Victoria, for example, a Memorandum of Understanding has been signed with Emergency Services, in recognition of the vital role Local Radio played in regional Victoria during that State's 2003 bushfire crisis,' says Tony Rasmussen, Editor Networked Local Radio.

In that State, ABC Local Radio has a network that includes 774 ABC Melbourne and seven regional broadcasting centres, and is the only network that can broadcast immediately to any part of the State at any time. The use of the Remote Area Broadcasting Service (RABS) Satellite network enables listeners in isolated regions to access Local Radio (free) as well.

In the Northern Territory ABC Darwin keeps listeners in the Top End up to date on the movements of cyclones, while the

TOURISM AUSTRALIA

Backyard website provides comprehensive background on how to prepare for an approaching storm. 'In fact,' says Rasmussen, 'ABC Radio in every State has guidelines in place relevant to the types of emergencies likely to occur there, and detailing the procedures to be followed when they do.'

Even in the aftermath of a disaster, Local Radio is part of the healing process in affected communities. On the practical side, fundraising events are often organised and publicised on Local Radio. 'For many,' Rasmussen adds, 'ABC Local Radio is the obvious forum for the process of coming to terms with tragedy. And Local Radio also plays a role in reporting the investigations into what has occurred, and what can be done to prevent it happening again.'

Finally, Local Radio often becomes a primary source when historians examine major disaster events that have happened in the past. Interviews with those who were there, often recorded as events are unfolding, provide a unique insight and lasting record of the moments that have tested Australians, bringing them together to face whatever nature or the unpredictable throws at them. Added to these are memories of people as they rebuild their lives, either shared on air or now posted on the Backyard website. Their words, and the photographs that often accompany them, provide a potent reminder that no matter how bad things get, tomorrow is another day.

A lightning strike near Canberra prior to the 2003 bushfires.

Western Australia

By far the largest State in the Commonwealth, the Golden West is a mixture of vast deserts, spectacular natural wonders, stunning coastlines and rich farmland. It extends from the tropics in the far north to temperate coastal towns fronting the tempestuous seas of the Southern Ocean. The State is also blessed with an extraordinary amount of natural resources, its mineral wealth responsible for more than its share of the nation's wealth. Everything is big in Western Australia, and that's what the people who live there love about it.

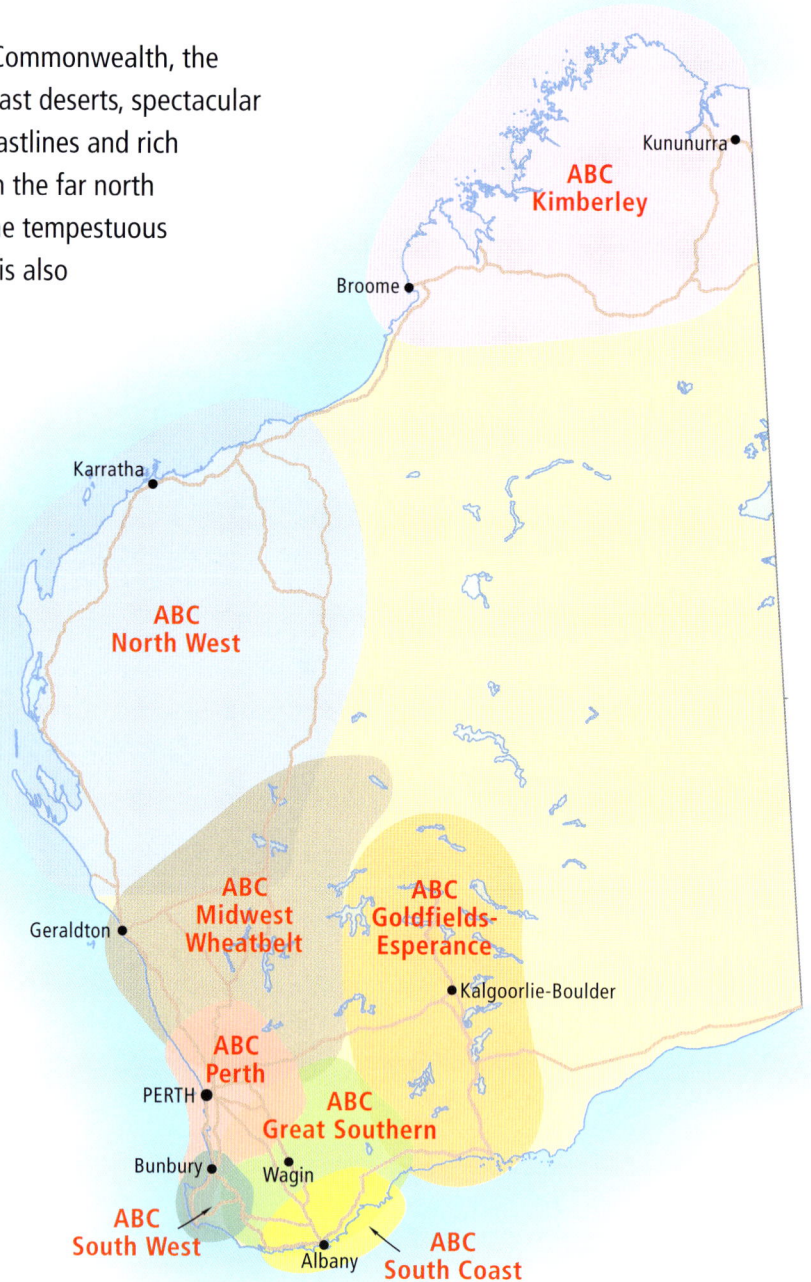

ABC Kimberley

Kununurra

Broome

Karratha

ABC North West

ABC Midwest Wheatbelt

ABC Goldfields-Esperance

Geraldton

Kalgoorlie-Boulder

ABC Perth

PERTH

ABC Great Southern

Bunbury

Wagin

ABC South West

Albany

ABC South Coast

(((•))) See inside back cover for a list of ABC Local Radio stations and their frequencies.

ABC Perth

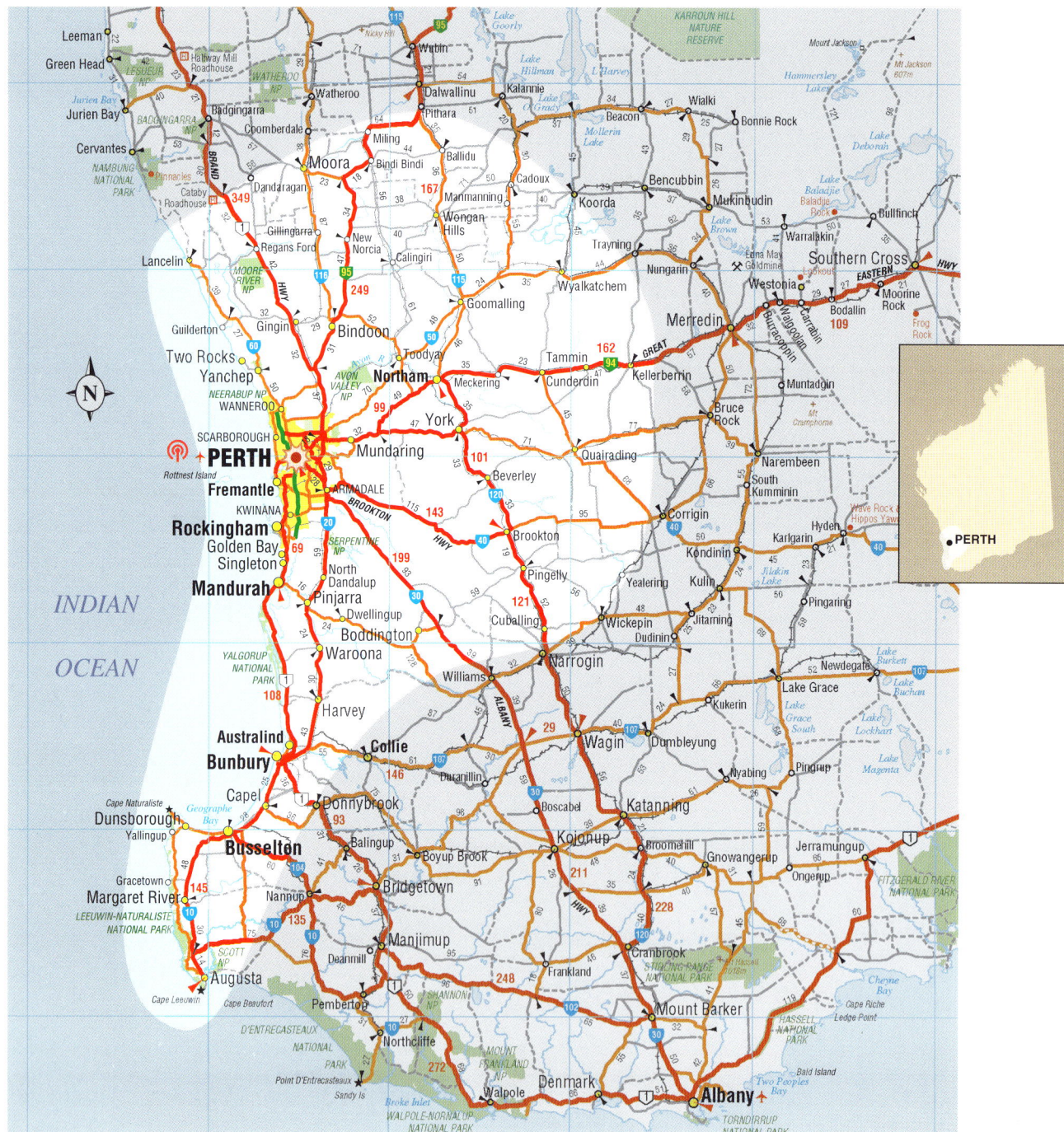

Location of ABC Local Radio studio

Local Radio Frequencies

Perth   720 AM

Perth has the only transmitter (AM) in the region

Despite being the world's most isolated capital city, Perth is one of the most welcoming places you could ever hope to visit. The people of this city of 1.4 million are remarkably friendly and the lifestyle they enjoy is one they're only too ready to share.

Navigating the city is a breeze with the free CAT (Central Area Transit) buses, while going further afield to places like Fremantle is easy with a fast and efficient public transport system. In the city itself everything is within walking distance or a short bus ride away. The arts precinct, for example, includes museums, art galleries and library all next door to each other, with the nightlife precinct of Northbridge on one side and the business district on the other.

The Swan River winds through the city and its suburbs and provides an enjoyable way to see many of its sights, say with a winery tour upstream or a ferry trip to Fremantle or Rottnest Island downstream. Along the coast are many safe swimming beaches, and beachside suburbs with attractive restaurant-and-cafe strips. Inland you'll find historic sights and beautiful national parks.

In this fascinating city, 720 ABC Perth broadcasts high-quality, relevant and entertaining radio programs to the Perth metro area, reflecting the issues, opinions and concerns of a well-informed West Australian audience. It also produces programming that is broadcast throughout the largest State in the nation.

TOURISM AUSTRALIA

NOT TO BE MISSED

- See displays of Western Australia's wildflowers in **Kings Park**
- Savour the cosmopolitan nightlife of **Northbridge**
- Dive into the crystal-clear waters of the city's beaches, such as **Scarborough** and **Cottesloe**
- See relics of Australia's oldest shipwrecks and the America's Cup-winning *Australia II* at the **Western Australian Maritime Museum**, Fremantle
- Stroll **Fremantle**'s picture-postcard streets, then watch the sunset over the Indian Ocean
- Take a day trip to **Rottnest Island** for swimming, fishing or a relaxing lunch

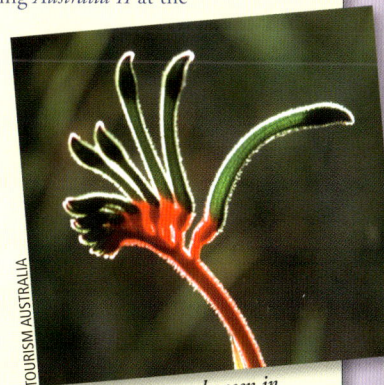

TOURISM AUSTRALIA

Kangaroo paws can be seen in Kings Park

MICHELLE HAVENSTEIN

MEET THE LOCALS

Floral beauties

Most people go wild for Western Australia's wildflowers, with good reason. They are spectacular, and abound throughout the central and southern parts of the State in season. But you don't have to go far to find them. In Kings Park, right next to the city, orchid-spotting is a popular activity, with 53 species identified so far. The one pictured is a spider orchid.

SARAH KNIGHT

City Centre

Sprinkled among the high-rises of Perth central business and cultural district are numerous reminders of the State's prosperous early days, including the buildings in the National Trust-classified Murray Street Precinct. Kings Park is on the western side of the city, the walking and cycling trails alongside the Swan River are on the southern side, and Northbridge's restaurants are on the northern side. To the east are sportsgrounds, parks and the casino.

SIGHTS AND ACTIVITIES • Head towards the Barrack Street Jetty and be entertained by the Swan Bells; from here you can also take a cruise up or down the Swan River, or a ferry to Rottnest • Ask directions to London Court, a shopping arcade modelled on the quaint streets of Elizabethan England • Wander around the Perth Cultural Complex, which includes the Art Gallery of Western Australia (with superb local and international works), the Perth Institute of Contemporary Arts and the Western Australian Museum • See the world's largest collection of natural gold specimens as well as gold being poured at the Perth Mint • Take a tour of the shrine to Western Australian cricket, the WACA ground

VISITOR INFORMATION
Cnr Forrest Place and Wellington Street (08) 9483 1111

Darling Range and Swan Valley

Heading east from the city centre, there's plenty more to see and do. North-east is the Swan Valley, renowned for its fine West Australian wines. Due east is the Darling Range with historic towns, jarrah forests, walking trails, lakes and scenic drives.

SIGHTS AND ACTIVITIES • Take a winery cruise along the Swan River to the many cellar doors dotted along the riverbank • Ride a camel, walk in the bush, watch whip-cracking and sheep shearing, hear Aboriginal music and see cultural displays at Whiteman Park • Learn about the remarkable engineer responsible for the water supply to the Kalgoorlie goldfields at the C. Y. O'Connor Museum, then picnic at nearby Mundaring Weir • Enjoy superb views of Perth from John Forrest National Park, then take the popular Heritage Trail along the park's western edge

VISITOR INFORMATION
Cnr Meadow and Swan streets, Guildford (08) 9379 9400

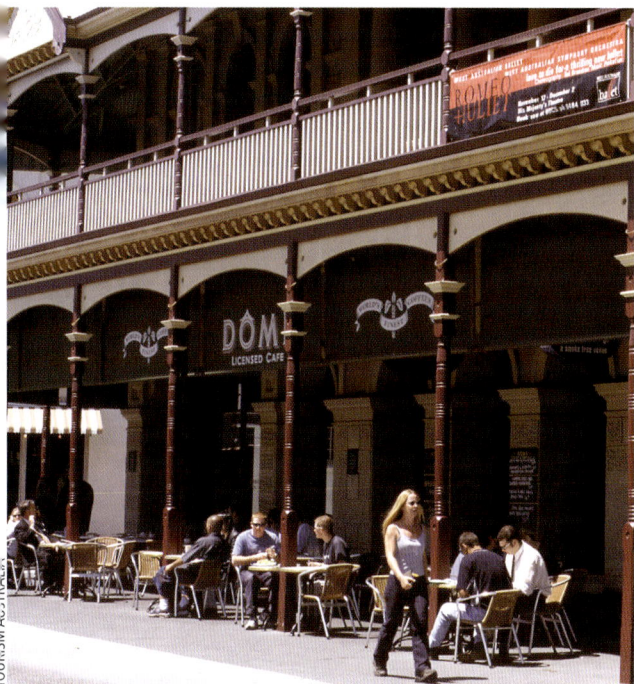
Cafe, Fremantle

Fremantle

The site of the original settlement in the Perth region and originally a penal colony, Freo (as it's affectionately known) has its own distinct charm and style. Historic buildings abound (walking tour information is available), and the town centre is also a lively spot for cafes, restaurants, pubs and nightclubs. Parts of the working port have been made accessible to the public, and provide a great spot for watching the boats come and go.

SIGHTS AND ACTIVITIES • Discover Western Australia's remarkable historic heritage at the Maritime Museum; note that there are two sites: the Shipwreck Galleries contain relics from Australia's oldest wrecks (dating from 1622) and the new museum houses contemporary items such as *Australia II* • Cruise the cappuccino strip of South Terrace, and stop in at the historic Fremantle Markets • Watch the sunset from the Round House, the State's oldest surviving building, dating from 1830 • Sample the boutique beers at Little Creatures, and enjoy great seafood there or at the other restaurants around Fishing Boat Harbour • While waiting for the ferry to Rottnest, grab some breakfast or shop at the markets in E Shed

VISITOR INFORMATION
Cnr William and Adelaide streets (08) 9431 7878

LOCAL TIPS

- For a very pleasant stroll, picnic or lunch, head for **Matilda Bay** on the Swan shore near the Royal Perth Yacht Club

MICHELLE HAVENSTEIN
Matilda Bay

- Delve into Western Australia's history at the monumental **Fremantle Prison**
- Enjoy the wildflowers from the **zigzag railway** in the Swan Valley
- Watch Lesmurdie Brook plunge 50 metres from the Darling Escarpment in the Swan Valley's **Lesmurdie Falls National Park**

MEET THE LOCALS

The swamp

What's the difference between a wetland and a swamp? Maybe it's just clever marketing, but that's not to say swamps don't have their merits. One of the fanciest is on the banks of the Swan River, right alongside Perth's city centre. It's hoped the area will provide habitat that will bring more life to the river in years to come.

SARAH KNIGHT

TOURISM AUSTRALIA

LOCAL KNOWLEDGE

Where the big rocks are

Every year in August thousands gather to watch, and hundreds more compete, in the third-biggest white-water event in the world. The 134-kilometre Avon Descent is a supreme test of boat-handling skills across a wide range of challenges. Pictured is ABC Perth presenter, Liam Bartlett going where the story is, and negotiating both rapids and foliage. At one stage he and fellow paddler, Liam Twigger led their age group, before being holed and forced to make frequent stops to bail.

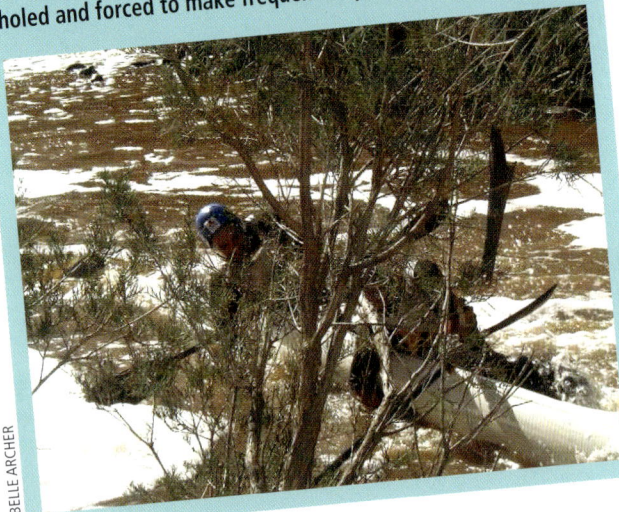

Rottnest Island

This charming car-free gem just off the coast from Fremantle is a perfect destination for a day trip, or a relaxing couple of days of sun, swimming, fishing and relaxation. At 11 kilometres long and 5 kilometres wide, it's quite easy to find quiet, secluded spots to while away the hours.

SIGHTS AND ACTIVITIES • Take a dive or snorkelling tour to some of the 15 shipwreck sites dotted around the island • Cycle or take a bus to Cape Vlamingh to see shearwaters, dolphins, terns and, of course, quokkas • Visit Rottnest Museum to find out about the cultural, environmental and maritime history of the island • Fish for flathead, tailor, moon wrasse, marlin and tuna, or take it easy and order them from the menu at the Rottnest Hotel

VISITOR INFORMATION
Settlement (08) 9372 9752

South of the Swan

Laced with walking and cycling trails, dotted with marinas and waterfront restaurants, and with its own upmarket suburbs, the area south of the Swan River is also quite lively.

SIGHTS AND ACTIVITIES • Enjoy the wildflowers in Wireless Hill Park, or the views of the Swan from its lookout towers • Find out why Perth Zoo is renowned for its gardens, butterflies and exhibits of Australian animals • At Bibra Lake, visit Adventure World, the State's biggest theme park • Have flutter at the Burswood Casino, or wander around the surrounding beautiful gardens

Western Suburbs

The suburbs between the city and the coast are among the city's finest, bounded by the calm waters of the Swan River and the beaches of the Indian Ocean. The architecture of the houses is also worth a look, with many fine stately homes set among very well-kept gardens. In areas like Subiaco, Claremont and Cottesloe, cafes and restaurants abound.

SIGHTS AND ACTIVITIES • Tour the Swan suburbs of Nedlands, Dalkeith, Claremont, Peppermint Grove and Mosman Park • Take a dip in the Indian Ocean at Cottesloe, Swanbourne (nude bathing), City, Floreat, Scarborough, Trigg and North beaches • See the world-class exhibits at Sorrento Quay's oceanarium, Aquarium of Western Australia (AQWA), a feature of Hillarys Boat Harbour • Dine or enjoy some refreshments in Cottesloe, at the tearooms or at the main street's cafes, restaurants and pubs

MEET THE LOCALS

Eat the locals

One of the signature trees of Western Australia is the remarkable boab, from the State's north-west. However, what most visitors don't realise is that it's also a great food source. The roots of young boabs taste like water chestnuts, and the leaves are also edible. They're grown commercially, and you can buy boab in one Cottesloe outlet, with others planned soon. And keep an eye out for it on local menus.

TOURISM AUSTRALIA

Cottesloe Beach and tearooms

ABC Kimberley

Location of ABC Local Radio studio

Local Radio Frequencies		
Broome	675 AM	
Derby	873 AM	
Kununurra	819 AM	
Warmun	819 AM	105.9 FM
Bidyadanga	106.9 FM	
Fitzroy Crossing	106.1 FM	
Halls Creek	106.1 FM	
Lake Argyle Tourist Village	105.9 FM	
Wyndham	1017 AM	

Towns in red have their own AM transmitter
Towns in green have their own FM transmitter

The Kimberley, one of the last great frontiers

The Kimberley is a vast, remote and mythical land of reddened landscapes, deep gorges, a wild uninhabited coastline and the signature beehive shapes of the Bungle Bungles. While the coastal town of Broome, with its wide beaches, turquoise water and warm, sunny climate is gaining a reputation as a world-class resort, there are large tracts of this region that are completely inaccessible by road.

Although the resident population of the region is less than 30 000, ABC Kimberley plays host to more than 300 000 tourists annually. The programming reflects the needs of these visitors, with weather reports and road-condition updates, tidal information, air services and more.

The Kimberley is renowned as one of Australia's most important regions for Aboriginal rock art and the ABC's proud association with indigenous radio groups has maintained close links throughout the community, especially during the NAIDOC and Stompem indigenous festivals.

NOT TO BE MISSED

- Take a scenic flight from **Derby** over the Buccaneer Archipelago to view around 1000 stunningly beautiful islands bathed in a bright turquoise tropical sea
- Study 130-million-year-old dinosaur footprints at **Gantheaume Point** near Broome
- Visit the historic town of **Wyndham**, the State's most northerly town and port
- Stay at **El Questro Station**, a huge cattle property also renowned as Australia's most luxurious outback resort
- Ride a camel at sunset along the magnificent **Cable Beach** in Broome

- Fly from Kununurra to the remote **Mitchell Plateau** – a significant Aboriginal heritage site boasting spectacular rainforest, waterfalls and bird life

Easter **Broome:** Dragon Boat Regatta

May **Kununurra:** Ord Valley Muster
Derby: King Tide Day (celebrating the highest tide in Australia)

June **Kununurra:** Dam to Dam Dinghy Race
Derby: Moonrise Rock Festival; Mowanjum Festival (indigenous art and culture festival)

June– July **Broome:** Race Round (horseracing week)

July **Derby:** Boab Festival (including rodeo, Mardi Gras and mud football)

Aug **Kununurra:** Rodeo
Broome: Opera Under the Stars

Aug– Sept **Broome:** Shinju Matsuri (Festival of the Pearl)

Sept **Wyndham:** Munumburra Music Festival
Kununurra: Night Rodeo

Oct **Broome:** National Indigenous Art Awards
Kununurra: Apex Barra Bash (fishing comp)

Nov **Broome:** Mango Festival

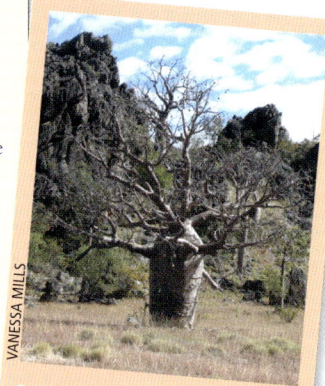

VANESSA MILLS

MEET THE LOCALS

Boab

The Australian boab is indigenous to the Kimberley region, and has large fragrant white flowers that start to bloom during the wet season. Local Aboriginal people use boab nuts as decorative ornaments by scratching pictorial scenes into the nut's surface. Boab trees tend to have their own personality and are as diverse in their appearance as humans. Keep an eye out for their unique beauty.

Broome

Broome (population of 11 368) is a lively and cosmopolitan town with a balmy winter climate, palm-fringed white-sand beaches and a multicultural heritage. Founded in the 1880s with the discovery of pearling grounds off the coast, by 1910 it had become the world's leading pearling centre and now is renowned as a popular tourist destination.

SIGHTS AND ACTIVITIES • Start with a self-guide heritage tour to familiarise yourself with the town's buildings and culture • Catch a movie at the Sun Theatre, opened in 1916 and believed to be the oldest operating outdoor theatre in the world • Relax on the beautiful Cable Beach, ideal for swimming, shell collecting and year-round fishing • Charter a boat for an expedition to coral reefs, Prince Regent River and the waterfalls at Kings Cascades

VISITOR INFORMATION
Cnr Bagot Street and Broome Road (08) 9192 2222

Kununurra

Located on the Ord River and adjacent to Mirima National Park, Kununurra (population 4884) is the starting point for tours to the Bungle Bungles, Mitchell Plateau and Kalumburu, and is close to the world's largest diamond mine, the Argyle.

SIGHTS AND ACTIVITIES • Purchase or peruse the perfect pink diamonds and other gems at various outlets and boutiques throughout town • Discover fine local artworks at the Diversion Gallery • Take a flight to the marvellously coloured and shaped Bungle Bungles in the Purnululu National Park

VISITOR INFORMATION
Coolibah Drive (08) 9168 1177

Derby

Derby (population 3236) is the administrative centre for several Aboriginal communities and an ideal base for exploring the outback regions of the Kimberley.

SIGHTS AND ACTIVITIES • Stroll along Derby Wharf to see the amazing tidal waters • Charter a flight over the Kimberley coast, the King Leopold Ranges and Cockatoo and Koolan islands • Visit the 'prison tree' – an early gaol cell in a boab tree • Take a tour to the spectacular Windjana Gorge

VISITOR INFORMATION
2 Clarendon Street (08) 9191 1426

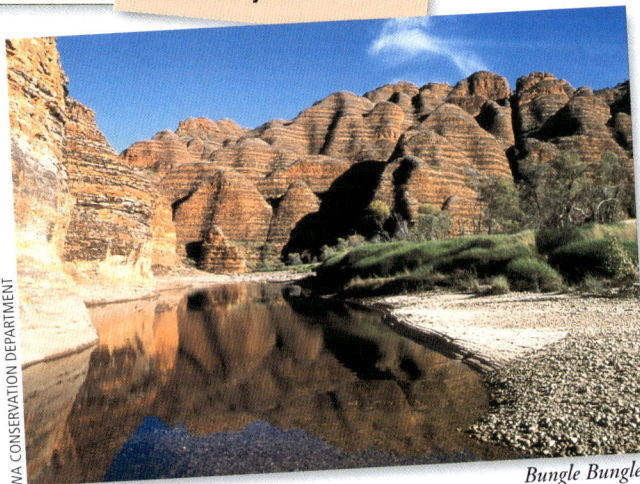

WA CONSERVATION DEPARTMENT

Bungle Bungles

Geikie Gorge

Fitzroy Crossing

Located where the Great Northern Highway crosses the Fitzroy River, the township (population 1147) has grown as a result of Aboriginal settlement, the mining industry and visitors to the nearby Geikie Gorge National Park.

SIGHTS AND ACTIVITIES • Visit the picturesque waterholes surrounding the town, home to an abundance of fish and bird life • Explore Tunnel Creek in the Tunnel Creek National Park, a unique creek tunnel through the mountain range • Don't miss the region's highlight: the magnificent Geikie Gorge, a 7-kilometre gorge, famous for its beauty and its wildlife • Take an Aboriginal Heritage Cruise to see Geikie Gorge, from May to November

VISITOR INFORMATION
Cnr Great Northern Highway and Flynn Drive (08) 9191 5355

Halls Creek

Located in the heart of the Kimberley at the edge of the Great Sandy Desert, Halls Creek (population 1263) was the site of the State's first gold find in 1885; today beef cattle is the main industry.

SIGHTS AND ACTIVITIES • Learn about the mystical Aboriginal Dreamtime with information from the Kimberley Language Resource Centre • Try your luck prospecting at Old Halls Creek • Pack a picnic and head to Palm Springs or Sawpit Gorge on the Black Elvire River for great fishing and swimming • Take a four-wheel drive south of town (two hours on unsealed roads) to Wolfe Creek – the world's second-largest meteorite crater, measuring 850 metres across and created one million years ago

VISITOR INFORMATION
Cnr Great Northern Highway and Hall Street (08) 9168 6262

LOCAL TIPS

- In **Broome** wander through Chinatown, where there are Chinese merchants, pearl dealers and a variety of places to eat
- Also in **Broome**, experience the Staircase to the Moon, a natural phenomenon of light reflecting off mudflats, visible during the full moon in the dry season
- Near **Kununurra**, take a dip at Twin Falls, a popular local swimming hole
- There are significant Aboriginal rock-art sites alongside the **Drysdale River**
- Humpback whales can sometimes be seen from the lighthouse at beautiful **Cape Leveque**

MEET THE LOCALS

The 'Rock Doctor'

The East Kimberley is a wonderful place to go fossicking. And collecting rocks has been a lifelong passion for Kununurra resident Jim Gardiner, known locally as the 'Rock Doctor'. He has collected a wonderful range of gems, rocks, fossils and a myriad of other interesting pieces from his expeditions into the bush, and believes that this region has some of the best fossicking in the world.

MEET THE LOCALS

Watching the weavers

An enriching way to pass a hot Kimberley afternoon is to sit beneath a shady mango tree and weave baskets from coloured wool and dried grass. All the while there's a continuous stream of conversation keeping things ticking over. Cackles of laughter frequently erupt from the circle of women, like those pictured here at the Wuggubun Community near Kununurra, during the Kimberley Land Council's 25th anniversary. Sit, watch, listen and learn ...

ABC North West

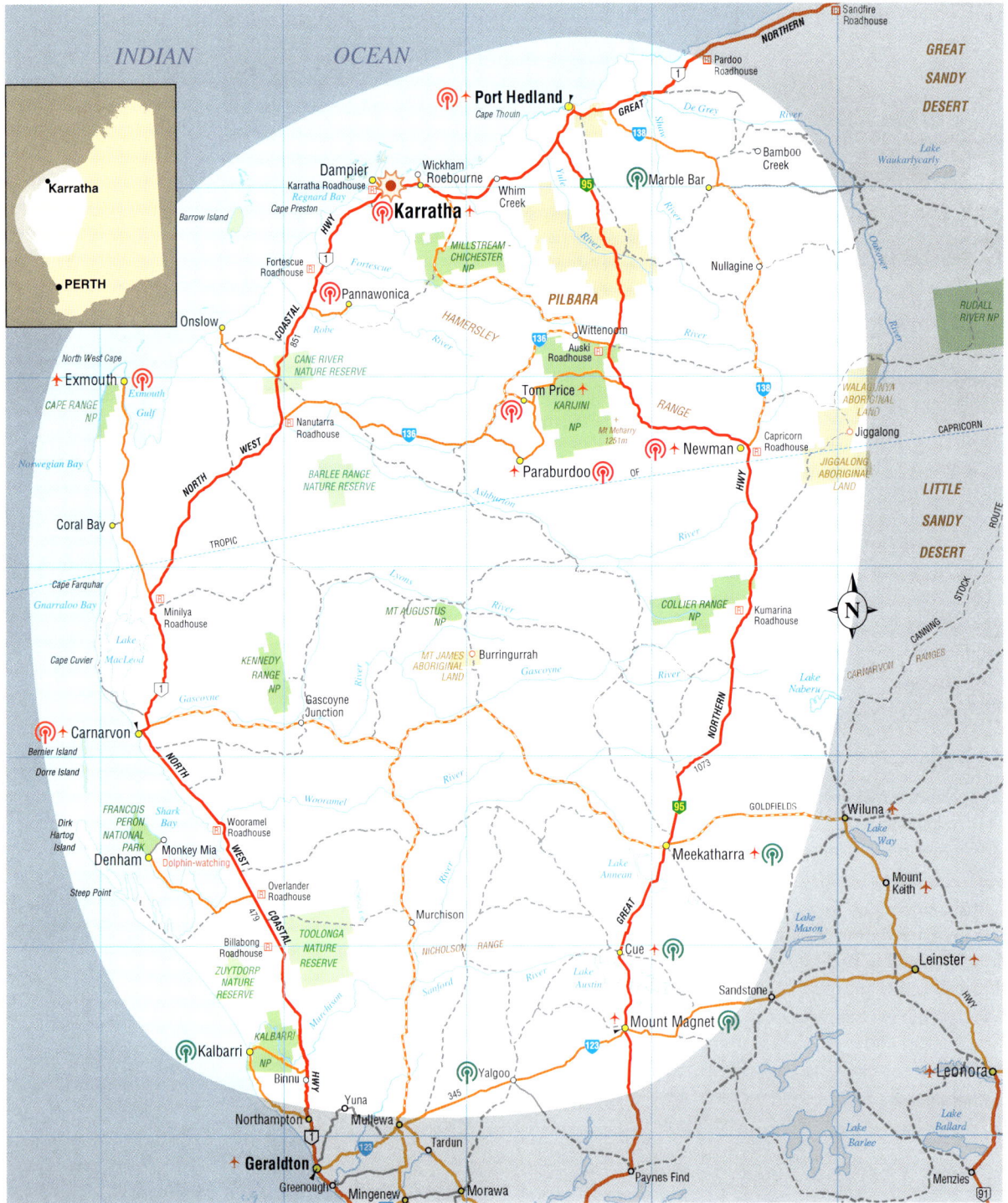

INDIAN OCEAN

GREAT SANDY DESERT

Sandfire Roadhouse

NORTHERN

Pardoo Roadhouse

Port Hedland
Cape Thouin

GREAT

De Grey River

Bamboo Creek

Lake Waukarlycarly

Dampier
Karratha Roadhouse
Wickham
Roebourne
Whim Creek
Marble Bar

Regnard Bay
Cape Preston
Karratha

Nullagine

Barrow Island

Fortescue Roadhouse

MILLSTREAM-CHICHESTER NP

PILBARA

Pannawonica

Onslow

CANE RIVER NATURE RESERVE

HAMERSLEY

Robe River

Wittenoom

Auski Roadhouse

RUDALL RIVER NP

North West Cape

Exmouth

CAPE RANGE NP

Exmouth Gulf

Nanutarra Roadhouse

Tom Price
KARIJINI NP
Mt Meharry 1251m

RANGE

Capricorn Roadhouse

WALALINYA ABORIGINAL LAND

Jiggalong

CAPRICORN

Norwegian Bay

BARLEE RANGE NATURE RESERVE

Paraburdoo

Newman

JIGGALONG ABORIGINAL LAND

LITTLE SANDY DESERT

Coral Bay

TROPIC

Ashburton River

STOCK ROUTE

Cape Farquhar

Gnarraloo Bay

Minilya Roadhouse

MT AUGUSTUS NP

Lyons River

COLLIER RANGE NP

Kumarina Roadhouse

CANNING RANGES

CARNARVON

Lake MacLeod

Cape Cuvier

KENNEDY RANGE NP

Gascoyne

MT JAMES ABORIGINAL LAND

Burringurrah

Gascoyne River

Lake Nabberu

Bernier Island

Carnarvon

Gascoyne Junction

Wooramel River

1073

Dorre Island

Dirk Hartog Island

FRANCOIS PERON NATIONAL PARK

Shark Bay

Wooramel Roadhouse

Wiluna

Lake Way

GOLDFIELDS

Monkey Mia
Dolphin-watching

Denham

Meekatharra

Mount Keith

Steep Point

Overlander Roadhouse

Murchison

Lake Annean

Lake Mason

479

COASTAL

TOOLONGA NATURE RESERVE

NICHOLSON RANGE

Lake Austin

Sandstone

Leinster

Billabong Roadhouse

ZUYTDORP NATURE RESERVE

Murchison River

Cue

Mount Magnet

Leonora

KALBARRI NP

Kalbarri

Binnu

Yalgoo

345

Paynes Find

Lake Ballard

Menzies

Northampton

Yuna

Mullewa

Tardun

Morawa

Geraldton

Greenough

Mingenew

N

⚹ Location of ABC Local Radio studio

Local Radio Frequencies

Carnarvon	846 AM	
Dampier	702 AM	
Denham	846 AM	531 AM ABC Midwest Wheatbelt
Exmouth	1188 AM	
Karratha	702 AM	
Newman	567 AM	
Pannawonica	567 AM	
Paraburdoo	567 AM	
Port Hedland	603 AM	
Roebourne	702 AM	
Tom Price	567 AM	
Cue	106.1 FM	
Kalbarri	106.1 FM	
Marble Bar	105.9 FM	
Meekatharra	106.3 FM	
Mount Magnet	105.7 FM	
Yalgoo	106.1 FM	

Towns in red have their own AM transmitter
Towns in green have their own FM transmitter

The southern towns of Nannup (98.1 FM) and Augusta
(98.3 FM) are also serviced by ABC North West.

Karijini National Park

A BC North West includes the Pilbara, Gascoyne and Murchison regions, and the offshore communities of Christmas and Cocos islands. The region's centrepiece is the vivid, ochre-hued Hamersley Range, which stretches for 300 kilometres on its south-easterly path to Newman. The mining towns of Tom Price and Newman are ideal bases for exploring the gorges and waterfalls of the Karijini National Park.

The station has a broad focus, ranging from the big business of the resource industry to stories about the region's amazing weather patterns and its unique plant and animal life. The ABC plays an important role in combating the isolation and vast distances in this north-western corner of the State.

The region prides itself on the people who make up the rich tapestry of the North West, where everyone has a wonderful tale to tell.

NOT TO BE MISSED

- Go bird-, turtle-, dolphin- and humpback whale-watching on the islands of the **Dampier Archipelago**, with its pristine beaches and serene bushwalking tracks

- Pitch a tent and explore the **Karijini National Park**, renowned for its extraordinary gorges, multicoloured walls and hidden pools and waterfalls

- Take the plunge into one of the many natural waterholes north-west of **Newman**, featuring spectacular gorges, waterfalls and river-gum scenery

- Take **Karratha**'s three-hour Jaburara Heritage Trail to Aboriginal rock carvings and artefact scatters

- Follow the 52-kilometre **Emma Withnell Heritage Trail** around the historic sites of Roebourne, Cossak and Point Samson

LOCAL EVENTS

May   **Carnarvon:** Fremantle
to Carnarvon Yacht Race
(even-numbered years)

June   **Karratha:** Pilbara Pursuit
Jet Boat Classic
Port Hedland:
Black Rock Stakes
(wheelbarrow race)

Aug   **Karratha:**
FeNaClNG Festival
(annual show)
Dampier: Game-
Fishing Classic
Newman:
Campdraft and
Rodeo
Port Hedland:
Spinifex Spree
(celebrates
community's
diversity)
Roebourne: Cup
and Ball (part of the
North West Jockey
Club Race Round)
Tom Price:
Nameless Festival

Dec   **Carnarvon:**
Mainstreet Party

LOCAL KNOWLEDGE

Meet at the local roadhouse

If you're travelling through the region, to or from the Kimberley by road, chances are you'll stop at the Sandfire Roadhouse, 290 kilometres from Port Hedland and 320 kilometres from Broome. Sandfire is the only fuel stop along 610 kilometres of road. Local owner Ken Norton has been at Sandfire since 1970 when it was set up by his parents. The roadhouse is nestled in between the last and the second-last sand dunes of the Sandy Desert, and is 55 kilometres from 80 Mile Beach. The roadhouse is famous for it's hamburgers.

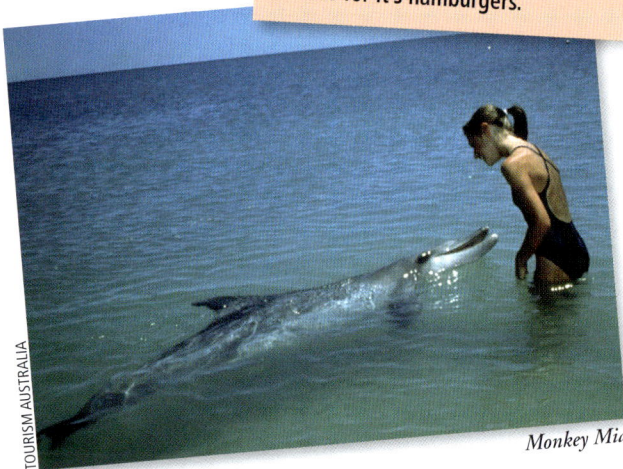

Monkey Mia

Karratha

This modern town (population 10 057) on Nickol Bay was established in 1968 to service the mining and petroleum industries. It now boasts the premiere tourist facilities in the Pilbara.

SIGHTS AND ATTRACTIONS ● Take in the panoramic views from TV Hill Lookout on Millstream Road ● Soar over the Pilbara coast and outback on a scenic flight, or take a safari tour of the region ● Explore Aboriginal heritage on the Jaburara Heritage Trail, a three-hour walk featuring Aboriginal rock carvings and artefact scatters ● Boat across to the Dampier Archipelago for bushwalking, swimming, fishing and wildlife-watching

VISITOR INFORMATION
4548 Karratha Road (08) 9144 4600

Carnarvon

On the mouth of the Gascoyne River, Carnarvon (population 6357) is the commercial centre of the region with strong sheep, beef, cattle and fishing industries.

SIGHTS AND ACTIVITIES ● Go game-fishing for marlin and sailfish, or cast out a line for snapper and groper ● Travel back in time on a steam train from One Mile Jetty to the town bridge ● See The Big Dish (involved in NASA's Gemini and Apollo space missions 1964–1974) at Brown Range ● Be blown away by the awesome 20-metre sprays at the Blowholes, 73 kilometres north of town, or head just south of there for a superb sheltered beach complete with rock oysters

VISITOR INFORMATION
11 Robinson Street (08) 9941 1146

Denham

Denham (population 1140) is Australia's most westerly town and is located on the peninsula of Shark Bay, a World Heritage area renowned for its wild dolphins. The area also protects dugongs, humpback whales, green and loggerhead turtles, important seagrass feeding grounds and a colony of stromatolites, an incredible and ancient life form.

SIGHTS AND ACTIVITIES ● Jump aboard one of the daily catamaran cruises, featuring dugong-watching ● Get up close and personal with the bottlenose dolphins that come to feed in the clear shallow waters of Monkey Mia ● Discover the unique crystal waters of Shell Beach, where there are no waves, no sand, just miles of tiny white shells

VISITOR INFORMATION
71 Knight Terrace (08) 9948 1253

TOURISM AUSTRALIA

Shell Beach, south of Denham

Kalbarri

Located between Geraldton and Carnarvon, Kalbarri (population 1788) is in a picturesque setting at the mouth of the Murchison River flanked by Kalbarri National Park.

SIGHTS AND ACTIVITIES ● Saddle up and go horse riding at the Kalbarri Big River Ranch, with trail rides or four-day tours through the rich and wild countryside ● Explore the breathtaking wild beauty of the Kalbarri National Park, encompassing the lower reaches of the Murchison River, as it winds its way through spectacular red gorges to the Indian Ocean.

VISITOR INFORMATION
Grey Street (08) 9937 1104

MEET THE LOCALS

Loggerhead turtle
The sandy beaches of Turtle Bay, on Dirk Hartog Island, are one of the few nesting sites in Western Australia for the endangered loggerhead turtle. During the summer months you can take an eco-tour to observe egg laying and hatching.

MEET THE LOCALS

Underwater artist Roger Swainston
Most artists would go anywhere to find subjects for painting, though would you dive to the bottom of the ocean? Acclaimed Western Australian natural-history artist Roger Swainston has done just that. He paints pictures of the underwater world with extraordinary precision, and his artwork has helped raise awareness of the beauty of Ningaloo Reef.

MEET THE LOCALS

Gentle giants
Ningaloo Marine Park, on the north-west coast, is one of the only known places to be regularly visited by the whale shark. Arriving each year from March to May, the sharks gather off the coast to feed on plankton, making Ningaloo one of the best places in the world for tourists to snorkel with these gentle giants.

TOURISM AUSTRALIA

ABC Midwest Wheatbelt

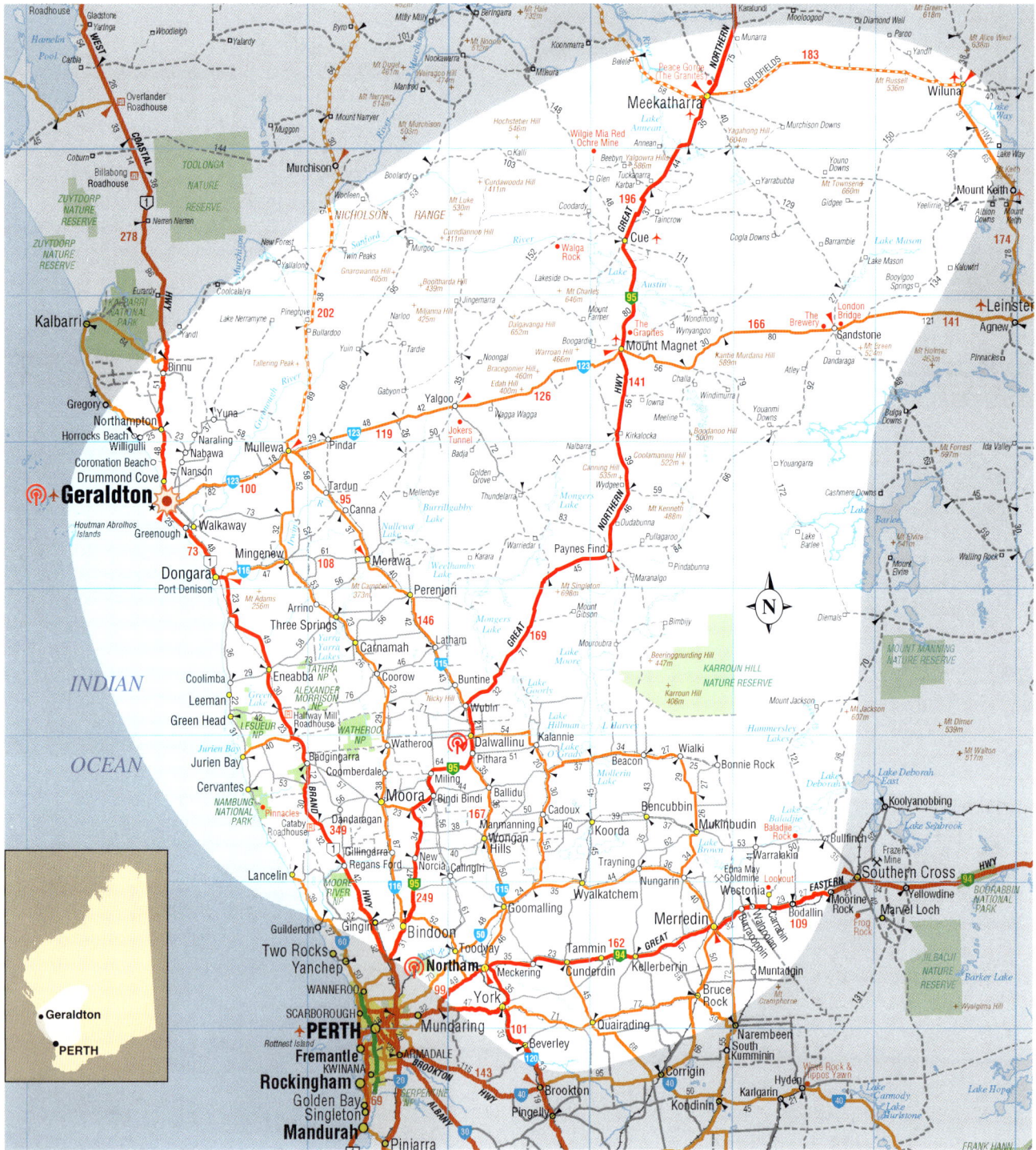

Location of ABC Local Radio studio

Towns in red have their own AM transmitter

Fields of gold in the State's wheatbelt

The Midwest Wheatbelt region of Western Australia covers an area of 396 519 square kilometres and 500 kilometres of the west coast, including the Abrolhos Islands. It is an area of wide-open spaces, white-sand beaches and beautiful offshore reefs where fish and coral abound. In some places, seals can also be seen. The area has a fascinating maritime history, with the wreck of the *Batavia* and the loss of HMAS *Sydney* just two of the interesting tales to tell. Add to this the wonderful wildflower displays and intriguing historic towns, and there's more than enough for every visitor. Over half of the grain produced in Western Australia comes from this region, and the western rock-lobster industry (centred on Geraldton) extends over the entire coastal area. Tourism is also worth a million dollars a week to the region, the peak period being during wildflower time in spring.

ABC Midwest Wheatbelt broadcasts to this diverse region from its headquarters in Geraldton, catering to an audience with a broad range of interests. As a major tourist destination, it also provides plenty of news and current affairs to keep locals and visitors abreast of world events.

NOT TO BE MISSED

- See the striking limestone pillars of the Pinnacles Desert in **Nambung National Park**
- Be awed by the big-sky country of the central wheatbelt
- Enjoy the spectacular display of **wildflowers** from August through to summer
- Feast on lobsters fresh from the many small ports along the coast, and see the live trade operation in **Geraldton**
- Take a boat or plane for a day trip to the famed **Houtman Abrolhos Islands** to see the Batavia wreck site or to go diving to see the superb coral reefs that surround them

Houtman Abrolhos Islands

LOCAL EVENTS

Jan **Geraldton:** Windsurfing Classic
Jurien Bay: Windsurfing Carnival
Lancelin: Ledge to Lancelin Ocean Classic

Feb **Beverley:** Yabby Races

Easter **Dongara:** Horse Races
Lancelin: Dune Buggy Championships

June **Geraldton:** *Batavia* Celebrations

Aug **Badgingarra:** Shears Competition
Beverley: Quick Shear; Agricultural Show
Mullewa: Wildflower Show
Northam: Avon Descent (white-water race)

Sept **Beverley:** Duck Race (with plastic ducks)
Lancelin: Lily Festival

Oct **Northampton:** Airing of the Quilts
Geraldton: Sunshine Festival
Merredin: Vintage Car Festival (odd-numbered years)
Northam: Multicultural Festival

Nov **Dongara:** Blessing of the Fleet
Jurien Bay: Marine Expo and Blessing of the Fleet

Dec **Cervantes:** Slalom Carnival (windsurfing)

LOCAL KNOWLEDGE

Wildflowers

It's not that hard to find superb blooms of wildflowers during spring and early summer in Western Australia. But to find out where they're blooming best, listen to ABC Local Radio for tips. You can also check out the Wildflower Directory on the Backyard website at www.abc.net.au/wheatbelt/wildflowers.htm

MICHELLE HAVENSTEIN

Geraldton

The commercial and administrative centre for the region, Geraldton (population 25 500) boasts agriculture and fishing, especially rock lobsters, as its main industries. Tourism is also growing, as visitors discover the pleasant year-round climate and the city becomes a hub for tours to the nearby Abrolhos Islands. In town, numerous museums, memorials, buildings and monuments are of particular interest (heritage-trail brochure available).

SIGHTS AND ACTIVITIES • Visit the excellent Maritime Museum for information on the famous wreck of the *Batavia* in 1629, and the sinking of HMAS *Sydney* in 1941 • Learn about the fascinating live lobster handling facility on a lobster-factory tour • Try sailboarding at Mahomets Beach in town, one of Australia's top windsurfing destinations • Visit the restored buildings of Greenough village (just south of town) that date from the 1880s

VISITOR INFORMATION
Bill Sewell Complex, cnr Bayly Street and Chapman Road (08) 9921 3999

MICHELLE HAVENSTEIN

Greenough historic village

Dongara

One of the larger fishing towns along this prosperous stretch of coast, Dongara (population 1874) boasts excellent beaches, sheltered bays and good fishing.

SIGHTS AND ACTIVITIES • Take the heritage trail (brochure available) to see the town's many historic buildings and its Moreton Bay fig-lined main street • Visit the cemetery where graves date as far back as 1874 • Dine on succulent, freshly caught rock lobster

VISITOR INFORMATION
Library, 9 Waldeck Street (08) 9927 1404

Pinnacles, Nambung National Park

LOCAL TIPS

- At **Meckering** see the large fault line produced by an earthquake in 1968
- Just outside **Jurien** there are attractive secluded beaches and stunning sand-dune systems, great for picnics and sand surfing
- See and learn about stromatolites, one of the world's oldest living fossils, near **Cervantes**
- Pick up a license and try your hand at catching western **rock lobsters**, or ask the locals where the best place is to wet a line

Jurien Bay

Another of the attractive small towns along the mid-west coast, Jurien Bay (population 636) is an angler's paradise due to its substantial marina and boating facilities.

SIGHTS AND ACTIVITIES • Tour the rock-lobster processing factory during the fishing season • Marvel at the famous Pinnacles in the Nambung National Park, south of town • Hire a sailboard to find out why this coast is renowned for this sport (the winds are great)

VISITOR INFORMATION
Council Offices, 110 Bashford Street (08) 9652 1020

Merredin

If it's wide-open spaces you're after, Merredin (population 2911) is the place – the heartland of Western Australia's wheat industry.

SIGHTS AND ACTIVITIES • Walk or drive the Merredin Peak Heritage Trail for wildflowers, and historical and geological sites • Take in the sights from Kellerberrin Hill • Save yourself a trip to Wave Rock with a visit to the remarkably similar Totadgin Rock, just outside town

VISITOR INFORMATION
Barrack Street (08) 9041 1666

Northam

The regional centre of the fertile Avon valley, Northam (population 6300) services the eastern wheatbelt and is a major rail hub.

SIGHTS AND ACTIVITIES • Take a heritage tour (brochure available) of the town's numerous historical buildings • Cross one of Australia's longest swing bridges, the footbridge over the Avon River • Go bird-watching and possibly see white swans along the river near Peel Terrace • Float away in a hot-air balloon (from the airport between April and November)

VISITOR INFORMATION
2 Grey Street (08) 9622 2100

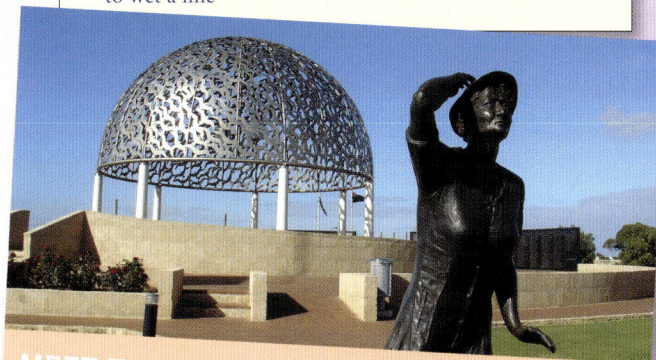

MEET THE LOCALS
A timely memorial

In 1941, after engaging with the heavily armed German raider *Kormoran*, HMAS *Sydney* was sunk with the loss of her entire crew of 645. Remarkably, it took until 2001 for an appropriate memorial to be erected, on Mount Scott overlooking Geraldton. A central dome is constructed from 645 seabirds (one for each of *Sydney*'s crew) and the memorial also features a woman looking out to sea for the loved ones who haven't returned.

MEET THE LOCALS
Graceful migrants

Whale migrations are very well known on the east coast of Australia, so it should come as no surprise that whales also have to navigate around the west coast. Tours operate from Kalbarri, north of Geraldton, during the whale migration season (July to November). The ideal time is September and October, when the area's wildflowers are also at their best.

ABC Goldfields-Esperance

Coverage extends to the north-east and includes Warburton

Location of ABC Local Radio studio

Local Radio Frequencies

Coolgardie	648 AM
Esperance	837 AM
Kalgoorlie-Boulder	648 AM
Hopetoun	105.3 FM
Laverton	106.1 FM
Leinster	106.1 FM
Leonora	105.7 FM
Norseman	105.7 FM
Ravensthorpe	105.9 FM
Southern Cross	106.3 FM
Warburton	106.1 FM

Towns in red have their own AM transmitter
Towns in green have their own FM transmitter

ABC Local Radio can also be heard in many of the remote localities to the north of the area shown on the map.

There are some parts of Australia where what you expect and what you actually find can be vastly different things. The perception of the region that extends north from the sea at Esperance into the harsh and unforgiving interior of Western Australia is that it's an area full of tough people engaged in difficult and dangerous mining operations. Yet it turns out that the region is diverse, fascinating and has a lifestyle that is quite beguiling. Many Kalgoorlie-Boulder locals are people who came for a few months and have stayed for a lifetime.

The main industries include the ubiquitous mining, as well as farming, pastoralism, fishing, shipping and tourism. Visitors will find historic mining towns and

Exchange Hotel, Kalgoorlie-Boulder

enormous mining operations, but they'll also find stunning desert landscapes, striking coastal scenery and lively festivals and events.

The ABC has had a presence in Kalgoorlie-Boulder since 1937 and has played a significant part in the cultural life of the area over that time. Late in 1998 the station moved into new studios on Hannan Street, enhancing the ABC's profile as well as providing some of the most technologically advanced broadcasting equipment available. In addition to its main regional office in Kalgoorlie-Boulder, the ABC has a small modern studio in Esperance, staffed by a rural reporter who covers the primary industries around this south coast town.

NOT TO BE MISSED

- Get down to earth at **Esperance** Municipal Museum with its genuine Skylab debris
- See how many orchid species you can find in spring in **Cape Arid National Park**
- Drive to **Kambalda**'s Red Hill Lookout for great views over Lake Lefroy
- Take a steam-train journey from **Kalgoorlie-Boulder** and see the famous Golden Mile

St Barbara's Festival, Kalgoorlie-Boulder

Kalgoorlie-Boulder

Once a wild frontier town where gold was discovered by Paddy Hannan in 1893, the twin towns in the heart of the Goldfields are now a thriving cosmopolitan centre of 28 087 people. Mining remains the main industry (with more than 1300 tonnes of gold extracted so far), but tourism is also thriving, as is the local wool industry. The town and surrounding district are full of surprises. It's incredibly remote, extremely prosperous and renowned for its superb historic buildings and spectacular open-cut operations.

SIGHTS AND ACTIVITIES ● Take a walk around Hannan Street's heritage buildings and sculptures (brochure available) ● Visit the city's historic two-up school (no longer operational), just outside town ● Be awed by the sheer scale of mining with the view from the Superpit lookout ● See gold pouring and tour both above and below ground at Hannans North Historic Mining Reserve ● Use Kalgoorlie-Boulder as your base for touring the region's many other mining towns

VISITOR INFORMATION
250 Hannan Street (08) 9021 1966

Historic two-up school

Esperance

Tucked between the Southern Ocean and the Nullarbor Plain, this beautiful town (population 8647) is renowned for its pristine beaches, scenic coastline and the extraordinary wildlife that inhabits the Archipelago of the Recherche, just offshore. The town operates as the port for local agriculture and fisheries.

SIGHTS AND ACTIVITIES ● Take a dive course and explore the spectacular marine environment of the archipelago ● Go fishing or watch out for the sea lion off Tanker Jetty ● Enjoy the region's spectacular wildflower displays in spring and summer ● Drive the Great Ocean Drive loop road ● Cruise to Woody Island, for camping, fishing and wildlife-watching

VISITOR INFORMATION
Museum Village, Dempster Street (08) 9071 2330

MEET THE LOCALS

A cast of fifty

Inside Australia is an extraordinary art installation. The work of British sculptor Antony Gormley, it comprises 50 locals from around the mining town of Menzies whose naked bodies were computer-scanned then cast in metals from the mineral-rich landscape. Each sculpture was then erected in the salt bed of Lake Ballard. Says Gormley, 'The art here is not the subject. [It's] an excuse for coming here and thinking about this place and the people who dwell in it.' See more at www.abc.net.au/goldfields/stories/s806941.htm

Leonora

Situated 250 kilometres north of Kalgoorlie-Boulder, Leonora (population 1143) is the railhead for the north-eastern gold, copper and nickel mines. Its wide main street with verandahed shopfronts is an outback classic.

SIGHTS AND ACTIVITIES • Tour the three gold-mining operations nearby including the famous Sons of Gwalia • Visit the 'living ghost town' of Gwalia, and see the home of the area's most famous mine manager, Herbert Hoover, who went on to become president of the United States • Picnic at Malcolm Dam, just east of town

VISITOR INFORMATION
34c Tower Street (08) 9037 6888

Norseman

The gateway to the Goldfields, Norseman is the first (or last) major town (population 1516) for those crossing the Nullarbor. The town once boasted one of the richest quartz reefs in Australia, and it's still popular with amateur prospectors and gem fossickers.

SIGHTS AND ACTIVITIES • See a statue of the horse the town is named after in Roberts Street; Norseman is said to have uncovered a nugget after pawing the ground • Enjoy spectacular sunrises and sunsets from Beacon Hill Lookout • Marvel at the granite outcrops at Cave Hill Nature Reserve north of town

VISITOR INFORMATION
68 Roberts Street (08) 9039 1071

LOCAL TIPS

- Go op-shopping in **Kalgoorlie-Boulder**
- Watch lightning storms (spectacular and free!)
- Visit the lake at the old **South Windarra** open-cut mine near Laverton
- Enjoy the wildflowers of **Leonora**
- Photograph the old bluestone windmill near **Kambalda**
- Visit the historic Art Deco-style Palace Theatre in **Boulder**
- Be captivated by the view from **Mount Jimbilana** near Norseman
- Take a dip in **Bromus Dam** on the highway between Norseman and Kambalda
- Refresh yourself at the **Ora Banda** Hotel
- Camp at **Burra Rock**

MEET THE LOCALS

Belly dancer

It's perhaps appropriate that a town on the edge of the desert should feature some exotic compensations for all that heat and sweat. But it's not the influences of the Afghan cameleers that inspire Kalgoorlie-Boulder's belly-dance troupes. Former local Kathy Kont, pictured, sees it as part of the increasingly cosmopolitan Kalgoorlie-Boulder she's come to know.

LOCAL KNOWLEDGE

Creating leather from fish

While in Esperance, one of the must-buys is one of the leather goods made from fish. It's a small-scale operation, but 'breaming' with possibilities. Now the fashion industry is hooked on the idea, it could put a whole new complexion on leather jackets.

MEET THE LOCALS

Stacks of gents

Ladies, if you're looking for a man, you'll find more than two for every woman in Australia's blokiest town, Leinster. Situated in the north-eastern goldfields, the mining-dominated town of 1400 is 70.4 per cent male, according to the latest Census statistics.

LOCAL KNOWLEDGE

Desert fishing

It's hot, it's dry and fishing is the last thing you'd think of doing. But for one day in September all that changes in the desert town of Kambalda. That's when several hundred fish are tipped into the de-chlorinated East Kambalda swimming pool and it's on for young and old from 6.30am to 7pm. It might be Ian Thorpe's worst nightmare, but it's every Kambalda angler's dream.

ABC South Coast and Great Southern

INDIAN OCEAN

SOUTHERN OCEAN

Cervantes
NAMBUNG NATIONAL PARK
Cataby Roadhouse
Dandaragan
Lancelin
Guilderton
Gingin
Two Rocks
Yanchep
NEERABUP NP
WANNEROO
SCARBOROUGH
PERTH
Fremantle
Rottnest Island
KWINANA
Rockingham
Golden Bay
Singleton
Mandurah
North Dandalup
Pinjarra
Dwellingup
Boddington
Waroona
YALGORUP NATIONAL PARK
Harvey
Australind
Bunbury
Collie
Capel
Cape Naturaliste
Dunsborough
Yallingup
Geographe Bay
Busselton
Gracetown
Margaret River
LEEUWIN-NATURALISTE NATIONAL PARK
SCOTT NP
Nannup
Bridgetown
Balingup
Boyup Brook
Manjimup
Deanmill
Augusta
Cape Leeuwin
Cape Beaufort
Pemberton
D'ENTRECASTEAUX NATIONAL PARK
Point D'Entrecasteaux
Sandy Is
Northcliffe
MOUNT FRANKLAND NP
Walpole
Nornalup
WALPOLE-NORNALUP NP
Peaceful Bay

Chomberdale
Miling
Bindi Bindi
Ballidu
Moora
Dandaragan
Manmanning
Cadoux
Koorda
Wongan Hills
Calingiri
New Norcia
Goomalling
Toodyay
Northam
Meckering
Mundaring
York
Beverley
Brookton
Pingelly
Cuballing
Williams
Wickepin
Dudinin
Narrogin
Boscabel
Duranillin
Collie
Darkan
Kojonup
Frankland
SHANNON NP
Denmark
William Bay
Little Grove
TORNDIRRUP NATIONAL PARK
Blowholes
Albany

Mollerin Lake
Bencubbin
Mukinbudin
Koorda
Trayning
Wyalkatchem
Nungarin
Tammin
Cunderdin
Kellerberrin
Bruce Rock
Quairading
Corrigin
Kondinin
Kulin
Yealering
Jitarning
Karlgarin
Hyden
Wave Rock & Hippos Yawn
Pingaring
Dumbleyung
Kukerin
Lake Grace
Newdegate
Nyabing
Pingrup
Katanning
Broomehill
Gnowangerup
Ongerup
Cranbrook
STIRLING RANGE NATIONAL PARK
Mt Hassell 1016m
Mount Barker
HASSELL NATIONAL PARK

Lake Deborah East
Koolyanobbing
Lake Seabrook
Bullfinch
Frazers Mine
Edna May Goldmine
Westonia
Bodallin
Moorine Rock
Southern Cross
Yellowdine
Marvel Loch
JILBADJI NATURE RESERVE
Barker Lake
Merredin
Narembeen
South Kumminin
Karlgarin
Lake Carmody
Lake Varley
Lake Hurlstone
Varley
FRANK HANN NATIONAL PARK
Lake King
Ravensthorpe
FITZGERALD RIVER NATIONAL PARK
Mt Drummond +309m
Whale-watching
Pt Ann
Mt Bland
Hopetoun
Jerramungup
Bremer Bay
Peppermint Grove
Chesne Bay
Cape Riche
Ledge Point
Bald Island
Two Peoples Bay

Wagin

Legend: Location of ABC Local Radio studio

Inset map: PERTH · Wagin · Albany

Local Radio Frequencies

Albany	630 AM	
Bremer Bay	630 AM	
Bridgetown	630 AM	1044 AM ABC South West
Cranbrook	630 AM	
Denmark	630 AM	
Hyden	558 AM	
Jerramungup	558 AM	
Katanning	558 AM	
Lake Grace	558 AM	
Mount Barker	630 AM	
Narrogin	558 AM	
Tambellup	558 AM	
Wagin	558 AM	
Walpole	630 AM	

Towns in red have their own AM transmitter

Coastal scene near Albany

ABC Radio in the south of this vast State covers an area almost the size of Victoria. Programming is provided through the South Coast studio in Albany and the Great Southern studio in Wagin.

Albany is the regional centre for the South Coast and serves a population of more than 50 000. The city nestles between two hills on the shores of King George Sound, one of the largest natural harbour systems in Australia. It is a traditional English seaside town, where the Victorian colonial architecture has survived and is protected.

The regional centre of the Great Southern, Wagin, is the sheep capital of the State. The importance of the wool industry is celebrated in its annual Wagin Woolorama.

NOT TO BE MISSED

- Walk in the treetops at the Valley of the Giants, **Walpole**
- Watch the sunrise from the War Memorial overlooking **Albany**'s King George Sound
- Sample the superb wines of the **Mount Barker** region
- Hike through the spectacular scenery of the **Stirling Ranges National Park**
- Discover the fascinating history of **Albany**, Western Australia's oldest European settlement

TOURISM AUSTRALIA

Valley of the Giants walk

TOURISM AUSTRALIA

Albany

The oldest town in Western Australia (population 20 493), Albany is set in one of Australia's most beautiful and spectacular locations, on the edge of King George Sound. Formerly a whaling station, it is now the State's major holiday destination, with boating, fishing, food and local wines vying for top position on most visitors' lists. There are some lovely inlets, sheltered beaches and great scenic viewpoints all around town.

SIGHTS AND ACTIVITIES • Take a stroll around the many historic buildings in the city centre (brochure available) • Find out nearly everything there is to know about whales at Albany Whaleworld • See spectacular coastal scenery and blowholes in Torndirrup National Park • Enjoy the views from Western Australia's southernmost point, West Cape Howe National Park, located between Albany and Denmark

VISITOR INFORMATION
Old Railway Station, Proudlove Parade (08) 9841 1088

Denmark

One of the gems of the south coast, Denmark (population 1978) is primarily a timber town but there is also a thriving artistic community. Art and craft shops abound, there are some excellent cafes, plus great fishing, pristine white beaches and great forest drives.

SIGHTS AND ACTIVITIES • Visit the shops in town, including Kurrabup Aboriginal Art Gallery, the Old Butter Factory and the Cottage Industries Shop • Head up Mount Shadforth for superb views over the Denmark River and Wilson Inlet • Take the Mount Shadforth and Scotsdale scenic drives, and explore wineries, galleries, lookouts and forest walks • Enjoy a heritage walk, a cruise on the river or head into the hills on a pony trek

VISITOR INFORMATION
60 Strickland Street (08) 9848 2055

MEET THE LOCALS

Roger the stud marron

Among the many attractions of the south-west corner of Western Australia is its many marron farms. This superb delicacy is just delicious, but consider the breeding program. Roger, the stud marron was part of one farm's brood stock, and after about eight years he weighed 600 grams and measured 275 centimetres from head to tail. And what happens to stud marron in retirement? Well, they're not put out to pasture (or should that be pondage?). Roger was auctioned, his vendors hoping he'd go to a good plate.

LOCAL KNOWLEDGE

Perth under water

That's the former Australian Navy frigate, not the city. The decommissioned ship was sunk in Albany's King George Sound in 2001, and now provides an artificial reef for fish, and a superb wreck dive in the local area. But you don't have to get wet to experience this major tourist drawcard, you can go for a virtual dive at www.abc.net.au/southcoast/stories/s426021.htm

Mount Barker

Wheat fields to the north, Stirling Ranges to the north-east, the Porongurup Range to the east and vineyards in every single direction – there's something for everyone in this pleasant Great Southern town (population 1648).

SIGHTS AND ACTIVITIES • Drive the 30-kilometre heritage trail through town and the surrounding area (map available) • Sample some of the region's excellent wines, available at cellar doors in town and around the district • Head for the Stirling or Porongurup ranges for a picnic with some wine and superb local produce – awesome scenery is part of the menu

VISITOR INFORMATION
Unit 6, Lot 22, Albany Highway (08) 9851 1163

Wagin

Located in the centre of the prosperous grain, crop, cattle and sheep industries of the famous Great Southern, Wagin (population 1337) is also one of the most important rail centres for the area. It has some fascinating history and historic buildings, and is an excellent base for exploring the many attractive sights and towns of the region.

SIGHTS AND ACTIVITIES • Explore Wagin Historical Village, with pioneer artefacts displayed in authentic old buildings • Take the heritage trail around Victorian buildings and shopfronts • Get your photo taken with the Giant Ram (all 7 metres of him), or if you're lucky, in March you could check out Woolorama which attracts 28 000 sheep farmers from around Australia • Find out about emu farming at Corralyn Emu Farm • Picnic, hike or enjoy the views at Mount Latham

VISITOR INFORMATION
Council Offices, Arthur Road (08) 9861 1177

LOCAL TIPS

- For hikers, the 963-kilometre **Bibbulmun Track** passes through the south of this region, providing a great way to experience as much of the coast and bush as you can handle
- The walking track around **Walpole's** waterways provides several good bird-watching and sunset vantage points
- Keep an eye out for **southern right whales** and their newborn calves between August and November
- For excellent surfing Denmark's **Ocean Beach** is highly recommended

MEET THE LOCALS

Mosaic garden
The town is called Lake Grace, and it also does things with style. In the midst of drought in 2002, a project for a garden at the local hospital became an opportunity for the community to take its mind off its troubles. The result is a wonderful mosaic garden, comprising 261 tiles arranged to portray the character of the region, and a central water feature. The tiles were made by local individuals, families and schoolchildren.

MEET THE LOCALS

Ute muster
If you think Wagin's annual Woolorama is just about sheep, well, you're wrong (not that anyone could blame you). In fact, it's about lots of things to do with the rural sector, and one of the most obvious things is the good old Aussie ute. Woolorama features one of Western Australia's biggest ute musters, where enthusiasts can gather to show off their pride and joy.

MEET THE LOCALS

A real dragon
These exquisite creatures are leafy sea dragons, and they're unique to the southern coasts of Australia. They're obviously related to seahorses, and their extraordinary appearance allows them to virtually disappear in the seaweeds and grasses they inhabit. The best way to find them is on a guided dive trip but, remember, take great care not to disturb any that you see.

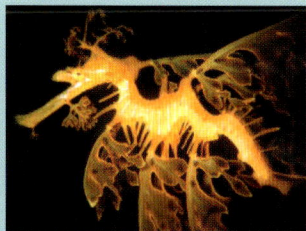

ABC South West

PERTH
● Bunbury

INDIAN

OCEAN

SOUTHERN

OCEAN

N

Mandurah — North Yunderup, North Dandalup, Halls Head, Miami, Furnissdale, Florida, Dawesville, Melros, Cape Bouvard, South Yunderup, North Pinjarra, Pinjarra, Meelon, Dwellingup, Coolup, Lane - Poole CP, Nanga, Amphion, Elmilyn, Marrinup

Pingelly, Boonering Hill 529m, Wandering, Popanyinning, 121, Cuballing, Narrogin

Lake Clifton, YALGORUP, Preston Beach, NATIONAL, PARK, Lake Preston, Hamel, Wagerup, Warawarrup, Waroona, Yarloop, Mt Keats +474m, Marradong, 128, Bannister, Crossman, Dwarda, Quindanning, Williams, Geeralying, Minniging, 120, Dumberning, Josbury, 32

108, Harvey, Wokalup, Benger, Beela, Myalup, Binningup, SOUTH, WESTERN, Stirling Dam, Harris R., Bingham River, Mt Saddleback 575m +, Wild Horse Hill 395m, Boraning, Culbin, Tarwonga, Dardanine, Arthur River, 107

Brunswick Junction, Roelands, Worsley, Allanson, 107, 55, Boolading, Hillman, Darkan, 30, Hillman River, **Australind**, Eaton, Burekup, Waterloo, **Bunbury**, Picton, Shotts, 61, 146, Buckingham, Bowelling, Duranillin, Boscabel, Gelorup, Dardanup, **Collie**, Collie Burn, Collie Cardiff, Mumballup, Corderipy, 30

Stratham, Boyanup, Lowden, McAlinden, Lake Ngartinilla, 98, 30, Capel, Preston R., Donnybrook, Wilga, Geographe Bay, TUART FOREST NP, Cape Naturaliste, Sugarloaf Rock, Eagle Bay, Newlands, 93, WESTERN, Grimwade, Gregory Tree, Kulikup, Muradup, Kojonup

Busselton, Dunsborough, Yallingup, Canal Rocks, Quindalup, Vasse, Carbunup River, Yunderup, VASSE, 36, Jarrahwood, Kirup, Mullalyup, Balingup, 31, Boyup Brook, Dinninup, Mayanup, 91, Jingalup

LEEUWIN-NATURALISTE, NATIONAL PARK, Willyabrup, Cowaramup Point, Gracetown, 145, RUSSELL, Cowaramup, 48, THE RAPIDS CP, Mt Yates, 104, Greenbushes, 26, 31, Tweed, Henry Hill, 91

Margaret River, Cape Mentelle, Prevelly, 10, Witchcliffe, 135, Nannup, HWY, **Bridgetown**, HWY,

Cape Freycinet, LEEUWIN-NATURALISTE NATIONAL PARK, 30, BROCKMAN, 75, 10, 10, HWY, 76, The Four Aces, Palgarup, Dingup, 102, Frankland, 80

Karridale, Kudardup, SCOTT NP, 14, Scott, GINGILUP SWAMPS NR, One Tree Bridge, Deanmill, Jardee, **Manjimup**, King Jarrah, Nyamup Tourist Village, Quabicup Hill, 95, Rocky Gully, 102

Augusta, Cape Hamelin, Flinders Bay, Cape Leeuwin, Cape Beaufort, Diamond Tree Fire Lookout, SIR JAMES MITCHELL NP, Pemberton, Quinninup, Tone, 96, MOUNT, FRANKLAND, NATIONAL, Mt Frankland 422m +

BEEDELUP NP, WARREN NP, Marianne North Tree & Bicentennial Tree, BROCKMAN NP, GLOUCESTER NP, SHANNON NP, Shannon, 1, WESTERN, SOUTH, Lymburner Falls, Lake Muir

D'ENTRECASTEAUX, Warren, 31, 10, Northcliffe, Bootara Tree, Lane Poole Falls, Granite Peak 402m, 272, Ferndale Falls, Tingle Tree Top, Bow Bridge Roadhouse

Warren Beach, NATIONAL, PARK, Windy Harbour, Point D'Entrecasteaux, Sandy Is, Ledge Is, Broke Inlet, **Walpole**, Nornalup

☀ Location of ABC Local Radio studio

Towns in red have their own AM transmitter
Towns in green have their own FM transmitter

Augusta and Nannup are serviced, via satellite, by the Karratha transmitter.

One of Margaret River's main attractions

O nly three hour's drive from Perth, Western Australia's south-west corner stretches from the resorts on Mandurah's sandy inlets and lakes, south through the Limestone Coast's rocky headlands and surf beaches, and ends at Cape Leeuwin where the Indian and Southern oceans meet. Just inland is the region's premier wine-growing district, the world-famous Margaret River.

Built on industries such as the mining of mineral sands and tin, dairying, horticulture, prime lamb, woodchips, beef and fishing, tourism and viticulture are now the boom industries.

The ABC has been an integral part of life in the south-west since 1961 when studios were set up using equipment salvaged from the old Perth studios. Today the station broadcasts to the 80 000 people who have made this region home, as well as to the numerous tourists who flock to the south-west attracted by its mild climate, beautiful landscapes and famous wineries.

NOT TO BE MISSED

- Take a winery tour and discover why the region's reputation for premium wines is built on its cabernet sauvignon and chardonnay
- Get a bird's eye view of the beautiful wildlife by climbing the spiral ladder to the top of the 61-metre Gloucester Tree in the **Gloucester National Park**
- Grab a board and go **surfing** at some of the world's most spectacular surf beaches.
- Visit the restored 1859 homestead, **Wannerup House**, 10 kilometres east of Busselton
- Explore the region's old-growth forests of karri and the spectacular deep-red hardwood jarrah at **Dwellingup**'s Forest Heritage Centre which also features canopy walks
- Pick an apple in **Donnybrook**, home of the Granny Smith and Lady William apples
- Energise your soul by taking the 140-kilometre **Cape to Cape Walk** (Cape Naturaliste to Cape Leeuwin)
- Go underground to see **Mammoth Cave**, which contains fossils dating back more than 35 000 years; it's a high-tech, self-discovery tourist attraction

Scenery on the Cape to Cape Walk

MEET THE LOCALS

Cherry spittin' champion

The cherry trees in Manjimup blossom in readiness for the Christmas harvest, and each November Manjimup hosts the Cherry Harmony Festival. The weekend's events include street theatre, a parade, a cherry-spitting contest, a long lunch, a rock concert, a Cherry Fairy and, of course, lots of cherry eating.

Bunbury

Known as the 'harbour city' and the commercial centre of the south-west, Bunbury, with a population of 29 945, is situated on the junction of the Preston and Collie rivers. This town enjoys a warm temperate climate, flanked by beautiful beaches and fringed by the distant Darling Range.

SIGHTS AND ACTIVITIES • Travel back in time to see domestic life in the early twentieth century at Kings Cottage historical museum • Catch a wave, or a fish, at one of the great surf beaches, then enjoy the view from the surf club on Ocean Beach • Dive with the dolphins at the Dolphin Discovery Centre, or take a stroll along the mangrove cave and shipwreck trail, through the southernmost mangrove colony in Western Australia • Try a glass of the Semillon Sauvignon Blanc at the Capel Vale Winery, 27 kilometres south • Take the Bunbury–Australind Tourist Drive along the old coast road for beautiful coastal scenery and picnic spots

VISITOR INFORMATION
Old Railway Station, Carmody Place (08) 9721 7922

Busselton

One of the oldest towns in Western Australia, Busselton (population 10 642) is a seaside holiday destination on the shores of Geographe Bay and the picturesque Vasse River. Inland are jarrah forests, dairy and beef-cattle farms, and vineyards.

SIGHTS AND ACTIVITIES • Stay at the historic Prospect Villa (1855), now a restored B&B • Take a stroll, or even a train ride, along the longest jetty in the Southern Hemisphere (2 kilometres) on the beachfront near Queen Street • Visit the Nautical Lady Entertainment World on the beachfront for a day of adventure with giant water slides, flying foxes, bumper boats, lookout tower and nautical museum • Pack a picnic and head to the sheltered waters of Geographe Bay for swimming, diving, boating, fishing and dolphin-watching

VISITOR INFORMATION
38 Peel Terrace (08) 9752 1288

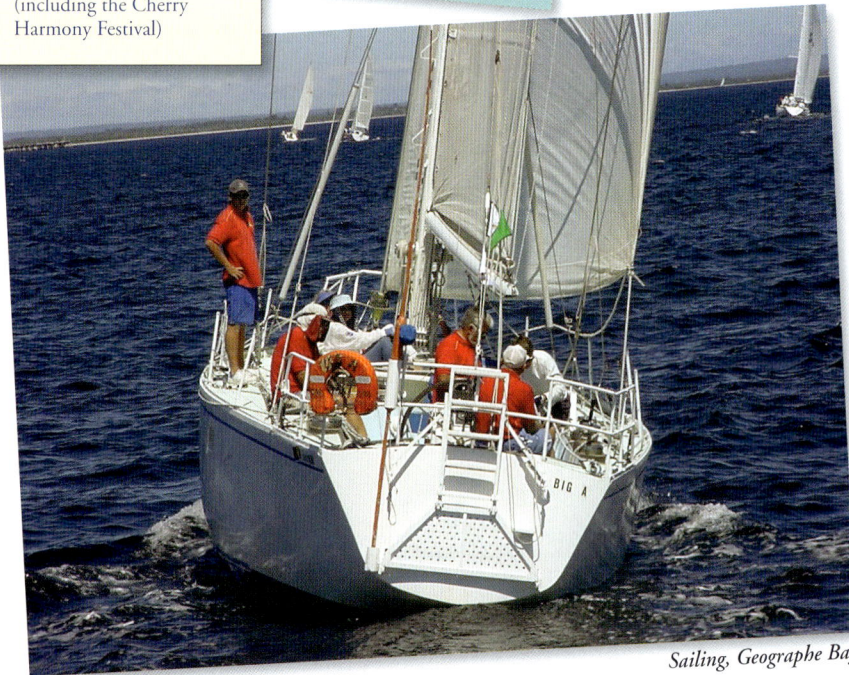

Sailing, Geographe Bay

Margaret River

The area around this beautiful township on the Margaret River is renowned for its world-class wines, magnificent coastal scenery, excellent surfing beaches and spectacular cave formations.

SIGHTS AND ACTIVITIES • Wander around the Margaret River Gallery, Margaret River Pottery and the Melting Pot Glass Studio for the finest in local art and crafts • Pick up a wine directory and plan the ultimate wine-tasting tour – in the heart of the wine-making district you are spoilt for choice • Call in to the Fonti Farm and Margaret River Cheese Factory to sample their flagship brie

VISITOR INFORMATION
Cnr Turnbridge Road and Bussell Highway (08) 9757 2911

Pemberton

Pemberton (population 994) is a small town in a quiet valley surrounded by karri forest with some of the tallest hardwood trees in the world and, in spring, brilliant flowering plants. It is a centre for the highest quality woodcraft.

SIGHTS AND ACTIVITIES • Take a breathtaking ride on the 1907 replica tram through the heart of the great karri forests • Find a quiet spot by a stream and try your hand at catching the local trout, perch and marron (licence required), or visit the Trout and Marron Hatchery • Purchase some fine wine direct from the cellar door – there are around 28 wineries in the area, some of which have restaurants serving the freshest local produce • Take a drive to the Beedelup National Park where you'll find rocky waterfalls, bushwalking tracks (with suspension bridge), the 'Walk-through-Tree' and magnificent wildflowers in the spring

VISITOR INFORMATION
Brockman Street (08) 9776 1133

LOCAL TIPS

- Surfers head for the great breaks off **Yallingup** and **Prevelly Beach**, while non-surfers often watch from the headlands
- While sampling wine around **Margaret River,** keep an eye out for other local items such as venison and marron
- Take a dive course and visit the wreck of the HMAS *Swan* in **Geographe Bay**
- You can spend a day exploring the small towns, fishing and swimming opportunities on the short drive from **Dunsborough** around the coast to **Cape Naturaliste**

MEET THE LOCALS

Ghost stories

The classic lighthouse tower on Cape Naturaliste near Dunsborough was officially opened in 1904 and has since enjoyed a fascinating history. The first light on the Cape was a simple lantern on a pole, then replaced with a limestone tower which is today valued at around five million dollars. Tour guide Dawn Brians is as well acquainted with its history as she is its ghosts, Happy Harry and Bloody Mary. These ghost stories are just part of the richness of both the Cape and its people.

MEET THE LOCALS

The wooden clockmaker

In a region renowned for its timber products, it's little wonder that wood-working is a time-honoured local tradition. Now, though, Nannup local Kevin Bird has taken things one step further and revived the centuries-old skills of wooden clock making. He operates a business making the clocks full-time, while creating timeless pieces that he considers 'kinetic sculpture'.

Grandstand

On-the-spot reporting

If James Hird kicks the winning goal for Essendon, Darren Lockyer crosses for the winning try for the Broncos, Shane Warne takes another Test wicket or Australia wins Gold at the Olympics, chances are you'll hear it live on ABC Local Radio. This is possible thanks to the far flung resources of an extraordinary operation that's known to fans across the country as 'Grandstand'.

It's just like being there, or as Peter Longman, Editor Radio Sport, says: 'The main strengths of the program are the range of sports covered throughout the year, the quality of the sports broadcasters and the breadth of the coverage around Australia.'

Normally, 'Grandstand' airs on Saturday and Sunday afternoons – a complex operation involving coverage from many different venues. The host studio then has to decide which event to cross to, a difficult call when a lot of things are happening at once, often with high drama involved. An Executive Producer co-ordinates these decisions, a job that takes experience and a cool head.

In winter 'Grandstand' splits into northern and southern versions, and these are further refined to regionalise coverage and cater for local football teams. For instance North Queensland, Newcastle, Wollongong and Canberra listeners get commentary of all their local National Rugby League games, as well as other match coverage. In the AFL, South Australian listeners get all Crows and Port matches, while West Australian listeners get all Fremantle and West Coast games, as well as other match coverage.

In summer, there's cricket. Each year 'Grandstand' broadcasts more than 150 hours of international cricket that's played in Australia. This results in day after day of pure enjoyment for listeners, as the raconteurs of radio give full rein to their wit, wisdom and wordplay, and every nuance and shifting fortune of the game.

Supporting the commentators is a complex technical operation that has to allow for such things as crowd noise, sound from the stumps, statistics and interviews from around the ground with cricketers or the crowd. In addition, you can now see the commentary team as well, with frequently updated photographs posted on the ABC's match website.

It's all come a long way from the 1930s, when the first ball-by-ball broadcasts of cricket started on ABC Radio. By the late 1940s it had become an ABC Radio staple, and had advanced to 'synthetic' broadcasts, with commentators calling Tests played in England 'live', creating appropriate sound effects

while reading cables sent from the match. Now, with satellite communications, ball-by-ball descriptions can come from anywhere in the world in the blink of an eye. Not that there aren't occasional glitches, as happened recently when commentators had to call a Test match in India using mobile phones to overcome technical difficulties.

The style of broadcasting has also changed greatly. Commentators still have to tell the listener what is happening on the field and give the score regularly. They also have to make the broadcasts as entertaining as possible, even if the cricket isn't that exciting. For this they need to have an encyclopaedic and topical knowledge of the game, so they can cite facts and figures, and discuss relevant issues at length during rain delays or if the play is really slow.

So successful are they that there is now a diverse group of listeners tuned to broadcasts. There are the cricket 'tragics,' who only want to know the facts of the game but, increasingly, listeners are tuning in purely for the entertainment value of the commentators. Kerry O'Keefe typifies the change in style with his combination of great insight into the game and entertaining stories. An example is this contribution to a discussion on batsman Sachin Tendulkar's 'slump': 'Slump. I'll tell you about a slump. I retired in 1981 and all I wanted to do was be a cricket commentator. I finally achieved it in 2000. Now that's what I call a slump.'

Of course, the pinnacle for 'Grandstand' is the coverage of the Olympic Games, when the greatest show on earth runs for 16 continuous days. To cover sports as diverse as water polo and dressage, Grandstand employs dozens of expert commentators on a contract basis. Says Peter Longman: 'The experts are well-respected figures in their various sports, having played or coached at the highest level.' Meanwhile, if an Australian looks like winning a medal, we all want to know as soon as it happens, and more often than not, 'Grandstand' is right on the spot. No-one has to wait until after the ad break on their ABC.

Opposite (top): *Jim Maxwell interviews cricketer Glenn McGrath;* (centre) *Peter Longman, Editor Radio Sport* (back to camera) *and Technician Bruce Jackson;* (bottom) *View from the commentary box*

Top: *An early photo of commentators simulating live cricket coverage*

Above: *Kerry O'Keefe mixing with the crowd at the cricket*

Northern Territory

From the world-famous wetlands of Kakadu to the iconic Uluru, the Northern Territory exerts a fascination unlike any other State or Territory. There's a frontier quality that manifests itself in dangerous reptiles like the saltwater crocodile, and unforgiving landscapes such as the MacDonnell Ranges. It is a place of great natural beauty and quite unlike anywhere else on the planet. The locals are often referred to as 'rugged Territorians' – and sometimes they need to be. Fortunately, they also know how to pamper visitors keen to experience the lifestyle and natural wonders of this remarkable land.

See inside back cover for a list of ABC Local Radio stations and their frequencies.

ABC Darwin

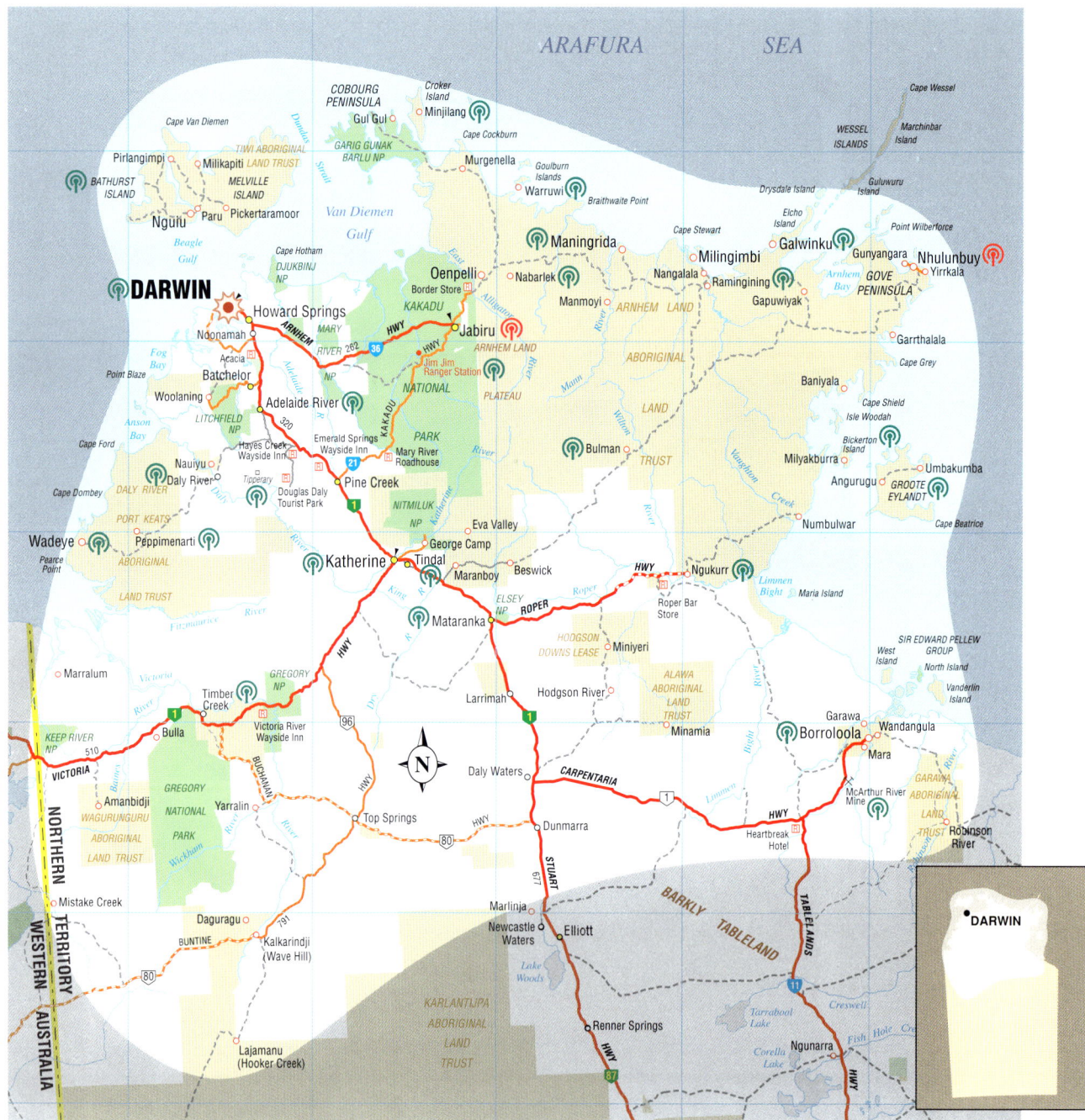

ARAFURA SEA

Cape Wessel

COBOURG PENINSULA
Croker Island
Minjilang
Gul Gul
WESSEL ISLANDS
Marchinbar Island

Pirlangimpi
Milikapiti
TIWI ABORIGINAL LAND TRUST
GARIG GUNAK BARLU NP
Cape Cockburn
Murgenella
Goulburn Islands
Warruwi
Braithwaite Point
Drysdale Island
Guluwuru Island
Point Wilberforce

BATHURST ISLAND
MELVILLE ISLAND
Van Diemen Gulf
Elcho Island
Galwinku
Gunyangara
Nhulunbuy
Yirrkala

Nguiu
Paru
Pickertaramoor
Maningrida
Milingimbi
Nangalala
Ramingining
GOVE PENINSULA
Arnhem Bay

Beagle Gulf
Cape Hotham
DJUKBINJ NP
Oenpelli
Border Store
Nabarlek
Manmoyi
Gapuwiyak
Garrthalala

DARWIN
Howard Springs
Noonamah
ARNHEM HWY
Jabiru
KAKADU
ARNHEM LAND
Cape Grey

Acacia
MARY RIVER
36
HWY
Jim Jim Ranger Station
ABORIGINAL
Baniyala
Cape Shield
Isle Woodah

Point Blaze
Batchelor
Woolaning
KAKADU NATIONAL PARK
LAND
Bickerton Island
Milyakburra

Cape Ford
LITCHFIELD NP
Adelaide River
Emerald Springs Wayside Inn
Mary River Roadhouse
Bulman
TRUST
Angurugu
GROOTE EYLANDT
Umbakumba

Anson Bay
Nauiyu
Hayes Creek Wayside Inn
21
Numbulwar
Cape Beatrice

Cape Dombey
DALY RIVER
Daly River
Tipperary
Pine Creek
NITMILUK NP
Eva Valley
George Camp

Wadeye
PORT KEATS
Peppimenarti
ABORIGINAL
Katherine
Tindal
Maranboy
Beswick
HWY
Ngukurr
Roper Bar Store
Maria Island

Pearce Point
LAND TRUST
Mataranka
ELSEY NP
ROPER
Limmen Bight
SIR EDWARD PELLEW GROUP
West Island
North Island

Marralum
GREGORY NP
HODGSON DOWNS LEASE
Miniyeri
ALAWA ABORIGINAL LAND TRUST
Vanderlin Island

Timber Creek
Victoria River Wayside Inn
96
Larrimah
Hodgson River
Minamia
Garawa
Wandangula

Bulla
510
VICTORIA
BUCHANAN
Daly Waters
1
CARPENTARIA
Borroloola
Mara

Amanbidji
GREGORY NATIONAL PARK
Yarralin
Top Springs
Dunmarra
HWY
McArthur River Mine
GARAWA ABORIGINAL LAND TRUST
Robinson River

NORTHERN TERRITORY
WESTERN AUSTRALIA
80
Mistake Creek
Dagaragu
BUNTINE
791
Kalkarindji (Wave Hill)
Marlinja
Newcastle Waters
Elliott
BARKLY TABLELAND
Heartbreak Hotel
11

80
Lajamanu (Hooker Creek)
KARLANTIJPA ABORIGINAL LAND TRUST
Lake Woods
Renner Springs
Tarrabool Lake
Creswell
87
Ngunarra
Corella Lake
Fish Hole

DARWIN

⊙ Location of ABC Local Radio studio

Local Radio Frequencies

Jabiru	747 AM
Nhulunbuy	990 AM
Adelaide River	98.9 FM
Bathurst Island	91.3 FM
Bickerton Island	105.7 FM
Borroloola	106.1 FM
Bulman	102.9 FM
Daly River	106.1 FM
Darwin	105.7 FM
Galiwinku	105.9 FM
Groote Eylandt	106.1 FM
Jim Jim	105.9 FM
Katherine	106.1 FM
Maningrida	104.5 FM
Mataranka	106.1 FM
McArthur River Mine	105.7 FM
Minjilang	102.9 FM
Nabarlek	107 FM
Ngukurr	104.5 FM
Peppimentari	102.1 FM
Pine Creek	106.1 FM
Ramingining	107.3 FM
Timber Creek	106.9 FM
Tindal	91.7 FM
Tipperary	88.1 FM
Wadeye	102.1 FM
Warruwi	103.7 FM

Towns in red have their own AM transmitter
Towns in green have their own FM transmitter

Short-Wave

Katherine	5025 KHz

Aboriginal rock art

The Top End of Australia exerts a fascination for the rest of the country, which still regards it as about as remote as it's possible to get. Its major city Darwin only seems to make it into the news after events like the bombing raids in World War II, devastating cyclones or the occasional attacks by crocodiles.

Yet it's this frontier perception that draws tourists from around the world, and they're rarely disappointed. The scenery of the Top End is superb, and the wetlands are vast and teeming with great bird-watching and fishing opportunities. Even better, in the dry season the climate is just wonderful.

Closer to Asia than to any other Australian city, Darwin is an incredible mix of European, Asian, Aboriginal and Islander cultures, resulting in some great restaurants and stunning arts and crafts.

ABC Darwin brings together this extraordinary mix of cultures, while providing a vital window on the world to many of the Top End's far-flung and remote communities. When travelling between these distant towns, it can also be picked up on short-wave (see Local Radio Frequencies list).

NOT TO BE MISSED

- Handfeed fish at **Aquascene**
- See crocs in safety at **Crocodylus Park**
- Swim in croc-free **Howard Springs**
- Find the Lost City in **Litchfield National Park**
- Be amazed at the abundant wildlife at **Fogg Dam**, particularly at sunrise and sunset
- View the Aboriginal rock art, then watch the sunset from Ubirr Rock in **Kakadu National Park**
- Hook a **barra** in almost any river, while keeping an eye out for crocodiles

Outdoor dining at Stokes Hill Wharf

Darwin

The 90 000 people who live in Darwin, the capital city of the Northern Territory, constitute nearly half the population of the entire Territory. The city is still regarded by many as a frontier town, but the reality is very different. In recent years it has boomed as a tourist destination, thanks to its dry-season climate, superb dining, top-quality accommodation and its role as a launching pad to a fascinating part of this extraordinary country. Devastated by bombing raids in World War II, and again by Cyclone Tracy in 1974, it's a testament to the Territory spirit that it has picked itself up and recovered each time.

SIGHTS AND ACTIVITIES • Discover the historical and natural world of the Top End, plus its rich artistic heritage, at the Museum and Art Gallery of the Northern Territory • Enjoy the food and views at Cullen Bay Marina's many restaurants • Watch the sun set at Fannie Bay then dine and shop at the Mindil Beach Sunset Markets (Thursday and Sunday evenings, May to October) • Get some great seafood at Stokes Hill Wharf in the Wharf Precinct • Find even more great dining, most of it al fresco, along Mitchell Street in the city • Visit the oil storage tanks and East Point Military Museum to learn about the World War II attacks on Darwin • Shop for pearls, one of the Top End's major industries, in the city, and learn about pearling at the Australian Pearling Exhibition

VISITOR INFORMATION

Cnr Mitchell and Knuckey streets (08) 8936 2499

Painted boomerangs

Borroloola

One of the great frontier towns of times gone by, Borroloola (population 551) is now a popular fishing and four-wheel drive destination. Although the town is on Aboriginal land, visitor permits are not required.

SIGHTS AND ACTIVITIES • Take an air charter to the Lost City, or four-wheel drive to Cape Crawford's Bukalara rock formations and Caranbirini Conservation Reserve • Get into some of the gulf's best fishing, especially at Rosie Creek and Barranyi (North Island) National Park • See the world's longest road trains as they carry ore from the McArthur River Mine

VISITOR INFORMATION
Lot 384, Robinson Road (08) 8975 8799

Jabiru

The main service town for the Ranger uranium mine and the world-famous Kakadu National Park, Jabiru (population 1696) is in the heart of an area of superb wetlands, stone escarpments and Aboriginal rock art.

SIGHTS AND ACTIVITIES • Explore the best of Kakadu: within 100 kilometres of Jabiru are Nourlangie Rock, Yellow Water, Jim Jim Falls, Twin Falls and Ubirr • Gain fascinating insights into local culture in and near town: the Gagudju Crocodile Holiday Inn is shaped like a crocodile (the Gagudju people's totem); the Aurora Kakadu Lodge and Caravan Park are shaped in a traditional Aboriginal circular motif; and the Warradjan Aboriginal Cultural Centre is shaped like a pig-nosed turtle

VISITOR INFORMATION
6 Tasman Plaza (08) 8979 2548

Yellow Water

WHAT MAKES A LOCAL?

With so many Territorians originally from elsewhere, the ABC quizzed its audience on what made them a 'local'. These are some of the responses:

- You don't think Humpty Doo is a funny place name
- You're happy to drive 400 kilometres to go to a party
- You own several pairs of thongs for different occasions
- You mow your lawn and find a car
- You lived through Cyclone Tracy
- You've been fired from a construction job because of your appearance
- You think a stubby cooler is the greatest invention of all time
- You've got 15 recipes for mango chutney
- And your favourite dinner is pictured on the right

MEET THE LOCALS

The geckos

It's not uncommon for resorts across Northern Australia to be called to remove 'crocodiles' from guests' rooms. Inevitably they turn out to be geckos, which people mistake for the gecko's larger reptilian relative. And that's just what staff thought at a Top End resort when the alarm was raised by guests, err, screaming. The highly trained staff quickly identified the species at hand. Geckos are small, cute, with large eyes. This was 2.5 metres long, terrifying, with large pointy teeth! Wildlife officers evicted the female saltwater crocodile, aka the biggest gecko they'd ever seen! For lots of croc stories visit www.abc.net.au/farnorth/features/crocbites

MEET THE LOCALS

Introducing a pest

Yes, it's the cane toad (*Bufo marinus*) and sightings indicate it's moving rapidly west from Queensland, where it was first introduced to Australia in the 1930s. If you spot one, you can contribute to the register of sightings at www.frogwatch.org.au, which also happens to be a great website for all things amphibian in Northern Australia. The site includes pictures and sound grabs for nearly every frog (and toad) known in the Territory.

Nitmiluk Gorge

TOURISM AUSTRALIA

MEET THE LOCALS

Norforce

One thing visitors to the Top End can't help noticing is the strong military presence – army, navy and air force. If you're really lucky, you may notice members of Norforce, the Top End's military unit, famed for their ability to survive in the wild for weeks on end. They draw on Aboriginal experience to find bush tucker (and to avoid becoming bush tucker to one of the many crocs about).

Katherine

The second-biggest town in the Top End, Katherine (population 7979) is just over 300 kilometres south-east of Darwin and a major centre for the Top End's agricultural and grazing industries. It also services the nearby Mount Todd goldmine and Tindal RAAF base. The Katherine River flows through the town and is popular for fishing and canoeing, and there are great scenic spots in the surrounding area.

SIGHTS AND ACTIVITIES ● Watch the Jarraluk Dancers perform a corroboree (Wednesday evenings, in town) ● Take one of the self-guide walks (brochures available) ● See the spectacular Nitmiluk Gorge, with its sheer cliffs, extensive rock pools and ancient, Aboriginal rock paintings, from a flat-bottomed boat ● Tour the Cutta Cutta Caves, just south of town ● Enjoy the therapeutic powers of the Mataranka thermal pools, an hour south of town ● Visit Alfred Giles' homestead, Springvale, the oldest in the Northern Territory

VISITOR INFORMATION
Cnr Lindsay Street and Stuart Highway (08) 8972 2650

Nhulunbuy

Originally a service town for the mining industry, Nhulunbuy (population 3695) is now the administrative centre for the Gove Peninsula, held freehold by the Yolngu people. It's truly remote, accessible only by air or four-wheel drive (permit required).

SIGHTS AND ACTIVITIES • Take the Gayngaru Wetlands Interpretive Walk which skirts a lagoon renowned for its bird life • Visit Buku-Larrnggay Mulka, the Yirrkala community's renowned Aboriginal art museum • Be stunned by the tropical-blue waters of the local beaches particularly those at Dharmitjinya (East Woody Island) • Join a boat charter for game-, reef- and barra-fishing • Tour the bauxite mine (Fridays) • See traditional and contemporary art and craft at Nambara Arts and Crafts

VISITOR INFORMATION
Chamber of Commerce, Endeavour Square (08) 8987 1985

MEET THE LOCALS

Hook a local

What you're looking at is the best reason for anglers to visit the Top End. Meet *Lates calcarifer* (barramundi to most of us). This beauty was caught in the McArthur River near Borroloola by ABC fishing expert, Neil Croft (better known as Boof). Find out where they're chomping by tuning in to 105.7 ABC Darwin on Friday mornings around 8.40am.

LOCAL KNOWLEDGE

A new lease of life for Chinatown

Darwin is one of the most multicultural cities in Australia, with one of the largest proportions of people with Chinese origins. Yet they're so integrated that the city has always lacked a Chinatown complex – until now. Currently under construction, a new city development will be completed by 2006, and will include a Chinese food hall, retail and office space. It's already been blessed by Chinese lions from the Chung Wah society and Darwin's Buddhist monks.

ABC Alice Springs

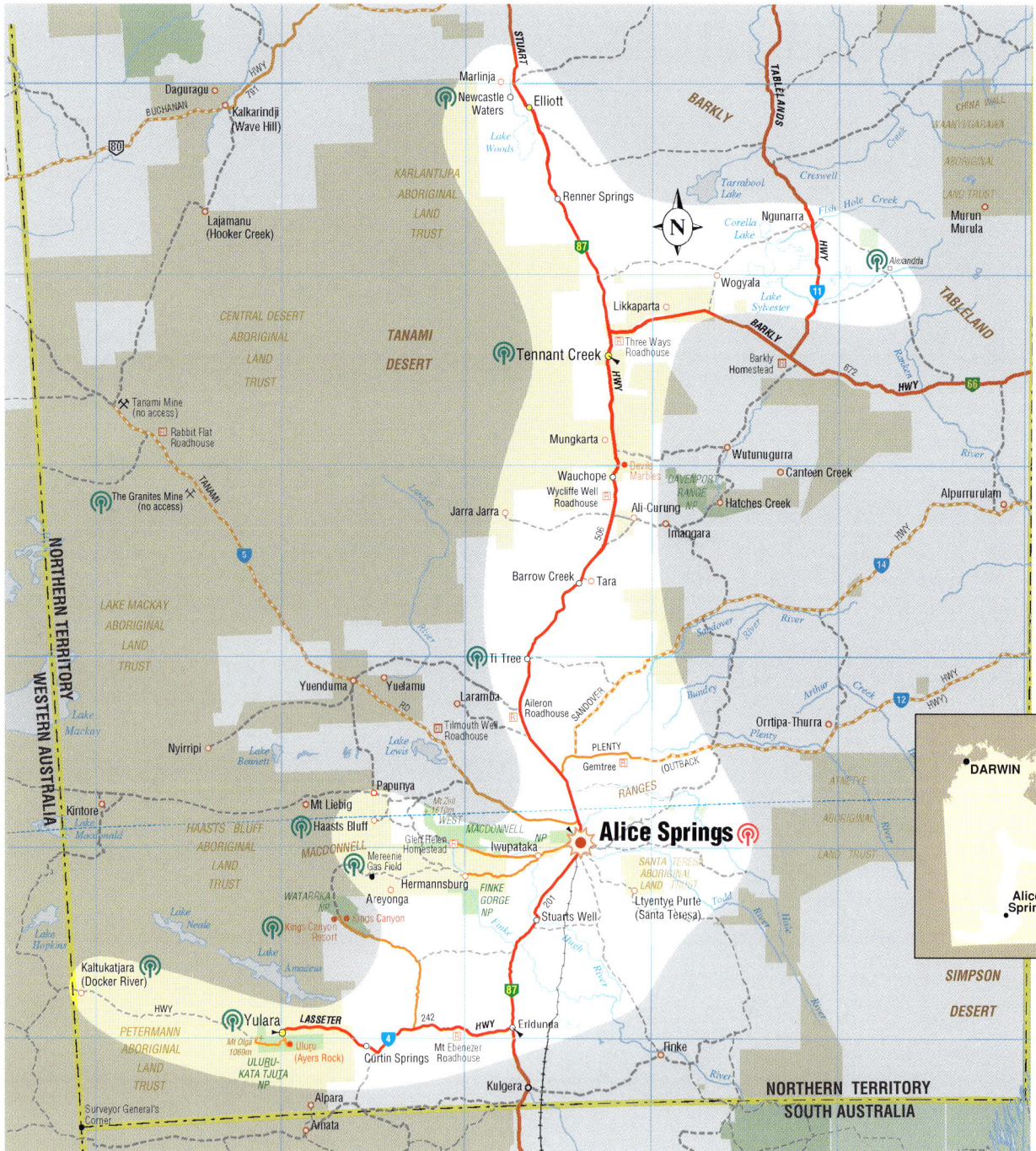

Location of ABC Local Radio studio

Local Radio Frequencies

Town	Frequency
Alice Springs	783 AM
Alexandria	105.5 FM
Docker River	107.7 FM
Haasts Bluff	105.9 FM
Kings Canyon Resort	89.1 FM
Mereenie Gas/ Oil Field	96.3 FM
Newcastle Waters	106.1 FM
Tennant Creek	106.1 FM
The Granites	96.1 FM
Ti Tree	107.7 FM
Yulara	99.7 FM

Towns in red have their own AM transmitter
Towns in green have their own FM transmitter.

Short-Wave

Town	Station	Frequency
Alice Springs	VL8A	4835 KHz
Tennant Creek	VL8T	4910 KHz

Uluru

You may never go to Mars but, for a sense of what it's like, there's always Central Australia. It really is another world, with spectacular landscapes and a climate that is found almost nowhere else on earth. It's also a vast area, extending from the Simpson Desert in the east to the Gibson Desert in the west, and north beyond the Tanami.

Of course, the region also has some of the country's greatest icons, such as Uluru and Kings Canyon, plus the spectacular MacDonnell Ranges, and one of its most famous towns, Alice Springs. In one of the world's toughest environments, there are plenty of characters – and there's a vibrant artistic community.

And part of that community is the local ABC. Note that radio coverage is generally restricted to the townships and will fade when you're covering the incredible distances between them. However, if you want to keep listening in when you're on the road, short-wave radio options are given below the list of Local Radio Frequencies.

NOT TO BE MISSED

- Walk in **Kata Tjuta**'s Valley of the Winds, then catch the sunset at **Uluru**
- Appreciate the landscape through works by **Hermannsburg**'s Aboriginal artists
- Learn about Central Australia's fauna at the **Alice Springs Desert Park**
- Marvel at the colours of the east and west **MacDonnell Range**
- Take a refreshing dip in **Ellery Big Hole**
- See Australia's Grand Canyon, **Kings Canyon**
- Play among the **Devils Marbles**, south of Tennant Creek

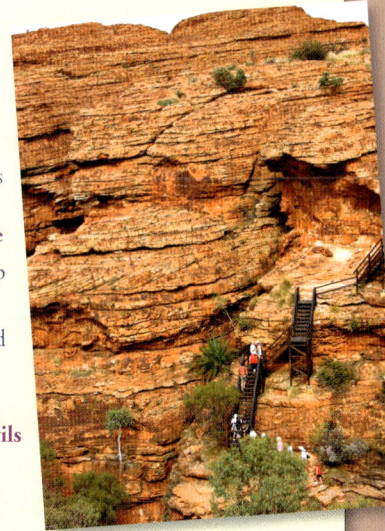

Kings Canyon

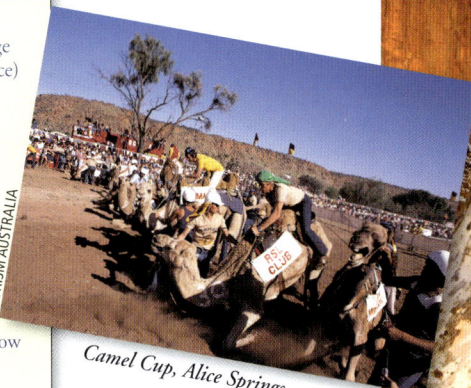
TOURISM AUSTRALIA

Camel Cup, Alice Springs

Standley Chasm, one of the highlights of the west MacDonnell Ranges

Alice Springs

The main centre of Central Australia, Alice Springs (population 22 488), has been made famous in literature and history as a frontier outpost. Yet the image of kangaroos hopping down the main street is a long way from reality. Todd Street is now a pedestrian mall with cafes, upmarket shopping and art galleries. Around town, there are many attractions and museums. And there are the numerous scenic and historic sites in the surrounding MacDonnell Ranges.

SIGHTS AND ACTIVITIES ● Visit the Royal Flying Doctor Base (tours daily) ● Listen to children on remote stations doing schoolwork at the School of the Air ● Discover the region's natural history at the Museum of Central Australia ● Purchase excellent Aboriginal art works and artefacts at numerous galleries around town ● Take a tour to the spectacular chasms of the west MacDonnells ● Fossick for gold at Arltunga, in the east MacDonnells, and visit the Bush Hotel and the Historical Reserve

VISITOR INFORMATION
60 Gregory Terrace (08) 8952 5800

LOCAL KNOWLEDGE

Sandover gallery

In Alice Springs you won't have any trouble finding galleries selling Central Australian Aboriginal art. There are so many that it can be hard to work out which one to visit, particularly if you cannot distinguish the good from the merely average. One new gallery well worth checking out is the sandover gallery, which presents the work of communities north-east of Alice Springs along the Sandover Highway – the Ampilatwatja, Urapuntja and renowned Utopia artists. Others include the Ngurrutjuta Corporation's gallery and workspace, which presents the many different styles of Western Desert art, and Papunya Tula, the first art centre to popularise and develop the modern Western Art movement.

LOCAL KNOWLEDGE

School of the saddle

How do you get Central Australian kids to go to school? At Warrego Primary School, 55 kilometres north-west of Tennant Creek, the secret was to throw in riding lessons as well. Not only that, the school curriculum is built around the riding program – dressage, for example, is the perfect way to teach geometry. And attendance rates: 100 per cent, thanks to a little horse sense.

Yulara

Located on the edge of the Uluru-Kata Tjuta National Park, this township with a population of 1200 is the site for the Ayers Rock Resort, which has facilities ranging from camping to five-star accommodation. It is the departure point for a wide range of day and night tours to the surrounding natural wonders.

SIGHTS AND ACTIVITIES ● Respect the Anangu people's wishes and take one of the walking tours around Uluru, rather than climb the rock ● Learn about bush foods on an Anangu tour. Mmm… grevillea honey ● Visit the Uluru-Kata Tjuta Cultural Centre to learn more about the local Aboriginal culture

VISITOR INFORMATION
Ayers Rock Resort (08) 8957 7377

Tennant Creek

Reputedly founded when a beer wagon broke down, this centre for gold and copper mining is a lively town (population 3856) with a surprising amount to see and do – not surprisingly, a lot of it is mining related.

SIGHTS AND ACTIVITIES ● Take a night tour of an early goldmine ● Visit the gold stamp battery, which is still working ● Enjoy water sports at Mary Ann Dam

VISITOR INFORMATION
Peko Road (08) 8962 3388

LOCAL TIPS

- On hot Wednesdays in **Alice Springs** you may see locals walking around the main shopping centre at high speed – they're exercising in air-conditioned comfort
- On cold days, check out the beanies in **Alice Springs** – locals are so proud of them they have a Beanie Festival in July
- UFOs are frequently seen around the **Wycliffe Well** Roadhouse. The locals will tell you they're spying on a secret US jet-testing facility in the Tanami Desert to the west – really

MEET THE LOCALS

Gum Tree 69

Jimmy Hooker is a true bushie. So much so that if you write to him at Gum Tree 69, Tennant Creek, your letter will be delivered. Not that he'll be able to read it. The 60-year-old never learned, but that hasn't stopped him becoming a poet and storyteller. He's even put out a CD. An expert on bush tucker, look him up and he'll share a bit of his knowledge, and have a bit of a yarn.

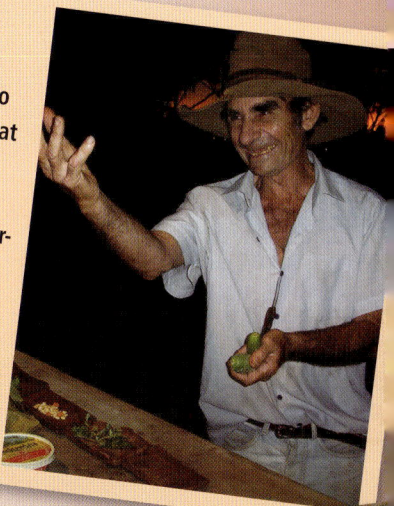

LOCAL KNOWLEDGE

Never mind the smell, look at that plumage

Where do you find waterbirds in a dry town like Alice Springs? The local sewage ponds, of course. The bird life is remarkable – pelicans, herons, spoonbills – some species even migrating from the Arctic Circle to visit the ponds. The locals have responded with bird identification signage, even a hide. Undeterred bird-watchers can easily find the sewage works: it's right next to the town dump.

MEET THE LOCALS

Dinky, the singing dingo

Originally an orphaned dingo pup, Dinky the dingo belongs to Jim Cotterill, proprietor of Jim's Place, as the Stuarts Well Roadhouse is known to locals. Dinky's love of music was discovered early, when someone was playing the piano and Dinky hopped up on the keyboard and joined in. He now amuses visitors, some of whom phone ahead to be sure of a recital. Armchair travellers can hear Dinky's singing at www.abc.net.au/central/stories/s820858.htm

Rural Broadcasting

Specialists in their field

The nation's longest running radio program, 'Country Hour', is heard across regional Australia on ABC Local Radio. It is produced by a unique team of specialist reporters who travel the country connecting rural communities. It also has quite a history, and the *Guinness Book of Records* recognises the ABC 'Country Hour' as Australia's longest running radio program – first broadcast on 3 December 1945. The enduring success of the program highlights the ABC's unique connection with all Australians.

The program is an institution in rural Australia, providing the latest news and views from the primary-industry sector and the rural communities it supports. Integral to its success is the team of rural reporters located across Australia who, in addition to contributing to 'Country Hour', also present an early morning 'Rural Report' as a part of local breakfast programs.

Rural reporters are specialists in their field, often armed with formal qualifications in agriculture, or having grown up on farms or in rural communities. In many respects they are the face of local stations, criss-crossing the broadcast area in the radio station's car, racking up thousands of kilometres a year, to meet and interview people, as well as attending field days and conferences. Whether it's joining a farmer on the tractor in the sowing season, standing in the cattle yards at sale time or wading into the creek to assess salinity levels (pictured above right), rural reporters are a very visible example of the ABC's connection with rural communities.

This unique connection goes further than the local level. The rural team also plays a vital role in connecting the city to the country, producing radio programs for Radio National and Radio Australia, and one of Australia's leading rural websites. It's no surprise to learn that more than half of the visitors to www.abc.net.au/rural are

'Heywire's purpose is to get the under-represented voices of regional and rural youth on the radio,' says Heywire co-ordinator Justine McSweeney. 'It's something that allows them to present their concerns in their own words and, by being heard, feel that they can make a difference.'

The broader community also benefits through a greater understanding of the issues that affect young people. 'Young people's interests are usually represented by government reports, media and community leaders. Heywire is the rural and regional experience told directly. Where there needs to be change for young people, knowing about the issues is a first step.'

During summer Heywire stories can be heard getting national airplay on Local Radio stations, Triple J, Radio National and Radio Australia. Stories are also posted on a Heywire website, www.abc.net.au/heywire, both as an audio file and a transcript, so the whole world can hear and read what Australian youth has to say. The winning entrants also travel to Canberra in February for the Heywire Youth Issues Forum, held at the Australian Institute of Sport. They receive leadership training before returning to their communities, better able to make a difference.

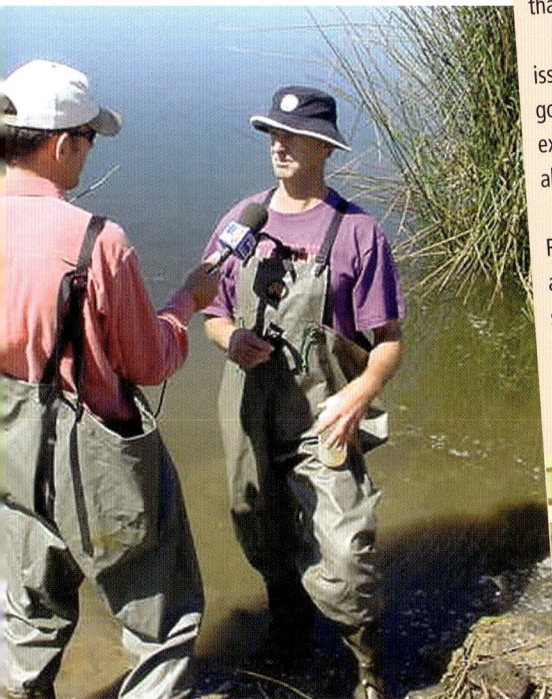

Opposite: *Rural reporters go wherever the story takes them*

Above: *ABC Gippaland's Rural Reporter Gerard Callinan up to his knees in a story at Lake Wellington in eastern Victoria, talking to a Waterwatch monitor about the health of the Gippsland Lakes*

'clicking on' from city locations to stay in touch with what's happening in the bush.

This close involvement of rural reporters in regional communities and awareness of their needs has led to a couple of important ABC Rural Radio initiatives. In 1993–94 the ABC launched 'Rural Woman of the Year', a national award that showcased the important role women play in the rural life of Australia. In 1998 the ABC recognised that the Rural Woman project had achieved its aim, and the decision was made to create a new project that gave a voice to rural youth – Heywire was born (see panel on right).

It may or may not be coincidence that a profile of ABC Radio staff shows that Rural Radio probably has the youngest staff demographic. It is certainly an area that calls for boundless energy and initiative.

Queensland

There's a diversity about Queensland that makes it hard to define in an easy way. The bustling capital, Brisbane is closer to Hobart than the State's northern extremity at Cape York. The coastal regions are incredibly fertile, with the spectacular Great Barrier Reef drawing tourists from around the world. The vast outback supports a multitude of livestock and mining operations. Spanning such large distances, radio is the glue that helps hold many communities together. And it's through radio that you can meet stockmen, miners, fishermen, crocodile farmers and some truly eccentric characters.

ABC Far North

ABC Western Queensland

Cairns

ABC North Queensland

Townsville

Mount Isa

ABC North West Queensland

ABC Tropical North

Mackay

Longreach

ABC Central Queensland

Rockhampton

ABC Western Queensland

Bundaberg

ABC Wide Bay

ABC Sunshine & Cooloola Coasts

Sunshine Coast

ABC Southern Queensland

Toowoomba

ABC Brisbane

BRISBANE

Gold Coast

ABC Gold & Tweed Coasts

See inside back cover for a list of ABC Local Radio stations and their frequencies.

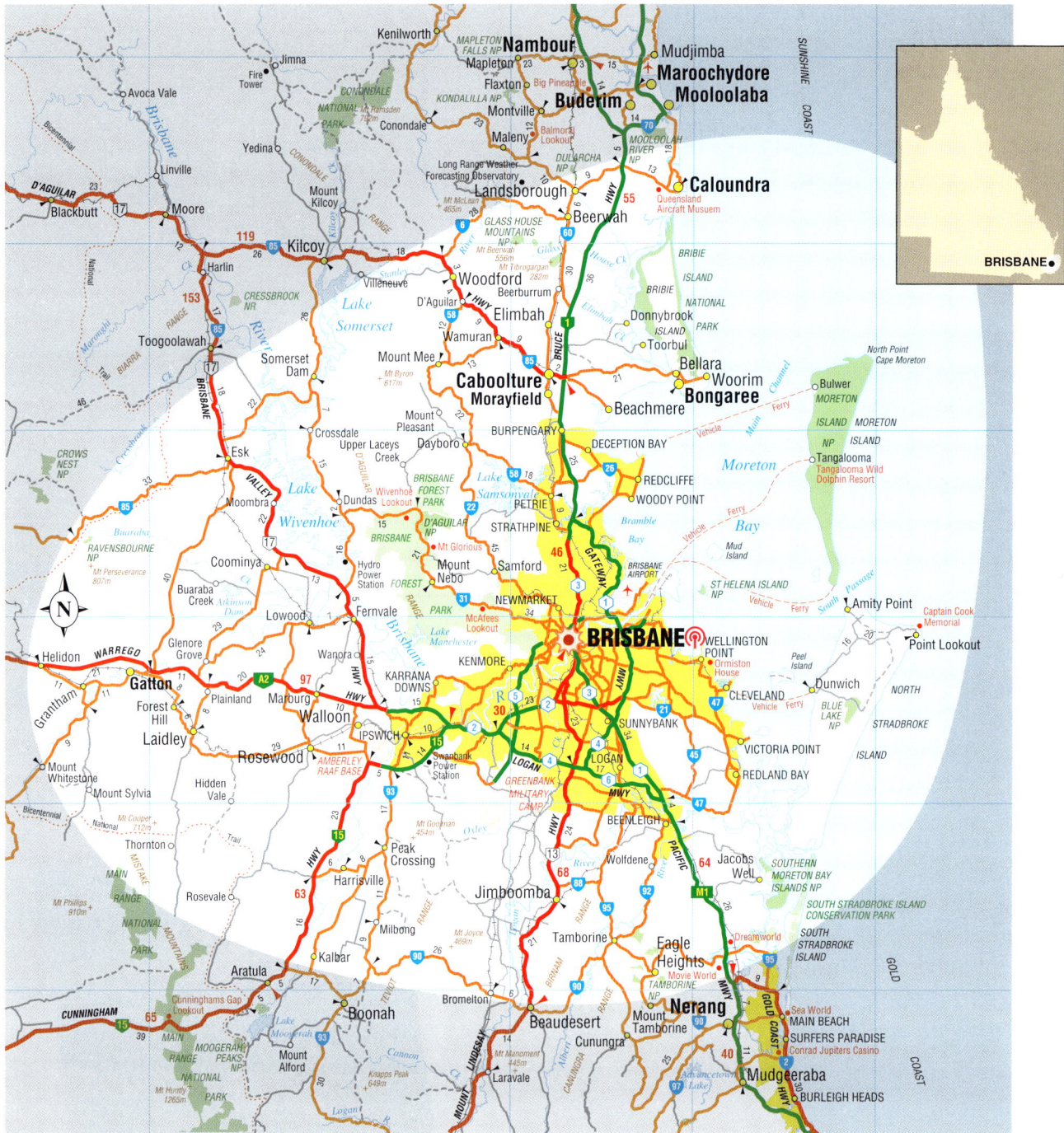

ABC Brisbane

☀ Location of ABC Local Radio studio

Local Radio Frequencies

Brisbane	612 AM
Beenleigh	612 AM
Caboolture	612 AM

Brisbane has the only transmitter (AM) in this region

TOURISM QUEENSLAND

The city of Brisbane straddles the meandering curves of the Brisbane River just inland from the river's mouth, where Moreton and Stradbroke islands create a barrier to the Pacific Ocean. Inland, the hilly subtropical landscape provides a beautiful backdrop to the city.

The city's architecture mixes the old with the new: golden-hued sandstone buildings and classic 'Queenslanders' sit beneath the gleaming metal and glass giants of the late twentieth century.

For more than 75 years Brisbane's local ABC radio station has played a distinctive role in the Queensland way of life. As part of Australia's only national, non-commercial broadcaster, 612 ABC Brisbane has shared its proud history and development with the growth of Queensland. Pictured are the original staff from 4QG in 1926.

NOT TO BE MISSED

- Stroll through the city to **Brisbane City Hall** – take a lift to the top for superb city views
- Cruise along the **Brisbane River**
- Cuddle up to a koala at the **Lone Pine Koala Sanctuary**
- People-watch over a coffee in the lively, inner-city suburb of **Fortitude Valley**, the heart of fringe art and culture
- Catch the latest in live productions at one of the **Queensland Cultural Centre**'s many theatres
- Cool off at **South Bank Beach**
- Hit the **city foreshore** for fine wine and dining in the former wharf and warehouse precinct – make sure you indulge in local specialities, like Moreton Bay bugs
- Explore the **City Botanic Gardens**' ornamental plantings, lawns and glittering ponds

TOURISM QUEENSLAND

'The Ekka'

City Centre

This busy city (population 1 653 000) is fairly easy to get around, thanks to a good public transport system and wide, pedestrian-friendly streets. There's an eclectic selection of restaurants and bars, cultural institutions and modern galleries, and a strong historical heritage to be explored.

SIGHTS AND ACTIVITIES ● Get your bearings and bargains at the Queen Street Mall where there's more than 1200 shops ● Take a stroll to King George Square, the location of the impressive Brisbane City Hall, a superb example of the grand, Greek Revival style that dominated Australian architecture during the early twentieth century ● Go to Roma Street Parkland (a former rail yard) which features restaurants, cafes and shops, as well as a tropical rainforest, lake and boardwalks ● Visit Gothic-styled St John's Cathedral, one of the finest churches in the Southern Hemisphere

VISITOR INFORMATION
Queen Street Mall (07) 3006 6290

MEET THE LOCALS

Anthony Lister

In 2000 the Brisbane City Council called for artists to beautify the electrical switchboxes that dot the city. Local artists responded to

the call and were soon painting switchboxes across the greater Brisbane area. They created flowers, street scenes, huge red pencils on a yellow background, yachts sailing on a bright blue harbour and evil-looking clowns. 'Every day it came out differently,' says one of the artists, Anthony Lister, 'and I walked away from every box feeling it was my best one.'

RAE ALLEN

Switchbox painted by Maria Field

City Foreshore

This one-time wharf and warehouse district has been recently redeveloped and is now one of the city's most attractive and vibrant areas, while still retaining the old-world charm of buildings like the Customs House and Old Government House.

SIGHTS AND ACTIVITIES • Head to the Eagle Street Pier for great restaurants and nightlife (especially on Friday nights) – it's also home to the lively Riverside Markets each Sunday • Picnic in the beautiful City Botanic Gardens on the Brisbane River

South Bank

Developed for World Expo '88, the landscape created at South Bank represents the Australian environment, from its beaches to rainforests, and features a flower-covered walkway that winds through the park.

SIGHTS AND ACTIVITIES • Make a splash at South Bank Beach, a palm-fringed sandy beach, slap-bang in the middle of this big city! • Trace the history of the area at the Queensland Maritime Museum, with its impressive collection of shipwreck relics and nautical models, and the World War II frigate, HMAS *Diamantina* • Take a tour of the Queensland Museum or the Queensland Art Gallery (with its emphasis on Aboriginal and contemporary Asian works) • Wander around South Bank's famous markets on Friday, Saturday and Sunday, with its lively art and craft scene, and fresh growers' markets on the first and third Saturday of every month

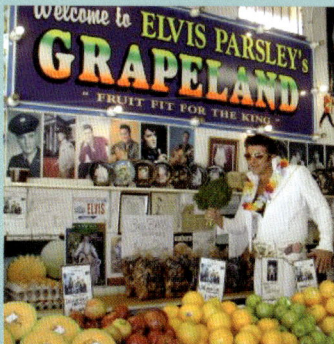

TOURISM QUEENSLAND

LOCAL TIPS

- There's a self-guide **heritage tour** to suit almost every interest; brochures are available from Tourism Information centres

- For **nightlife**, nightclubs and music venues abound in Caxton Street, Kangaroo Point and Fortitude Valley (details of gigs in Friday's *Courier-Mail*)

- For a different **dining** experience, try the refurbished wharf precinct at the city end of the Story Bridge

- Pick up some great Queensland-made art, craft, jewellery and more at the **Riverside Markets** (Eagle Street Pier, Sundays), **South Bank Art and Craft Markets** (all weekend) and the **Valley Markets** (Fortitude Valley, Saturdays and Sundays)

- For an excellent round of **golf**, try Indooroopilly (Saturday, members only), Brisbane or Victoria Park

- For a relaxing day trip or longer, take a **cruise** to one of the Moreton Bay islands such as Bribie, Moreton or North Stradbroke

MEET THE LOCALS

Elvis the Citrus

Elvis Parsley is alive and well, and living in Grapeland – Grapeland, Woodford, near Caboolture, that is. The King (aka Nick Comino) runs a fruit shop and serenades his customers with Elvis songs. This eccentric fruiterer's best-known tunes include 'Viva Las Vegies', 'Artichoke Hotel' and the all-time favourite 'Suspicious Limes'. You can read more about Elvis Parsley at www.abc.net.au/brisbane/stories/s932766.htm

MEET THE LOCALS

Ready, steady ...

Love the smell of burning rubber in the evening? Head for Willowbank Raceway on the outskirts of Brisbane, one of the world's best motor-racing facilities, with a drag track, touring-car track and go-karts. Best of all, you can have a go. Anyone can enter their own street cars, which are scrutinised to ensure they comply with the required safety standards. Willowbank is also an alcohol-free, family venue, so your partner and kids can watch as you unleash your inner hoon.

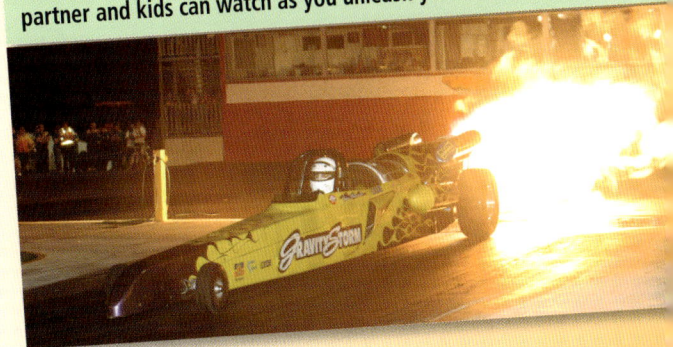

TOURISM QUEENSLAND

TOURISM QUEENSLAND

Inner North-East

Fortitude Valley, settled in 1849 by 'free settlers' arriving aboard the *Fortitude*, has retained the style of its nineteenth-century heritage. Encompassing Chinatown and the Brunswick Street Mall, this is now a very hip suburb, studded with good-value restaurants, cafes and the best in eclectic shopping.

West of the City

Lying just behind South Bank, this area is renowned for its restaurants and bars. Further west is the world's largest koala sanctuary and Mount Coot-tha Botanic Gardens.

SIGHTS AND ACTIVITIES • Hold a koala or feed kangaroos, wallabies and emus at Lone Pine Koala Sanctuary, Fig Tree Pocket • Take in the view of Brisbane and Moreton Bay from the summit of Mount Coot-tha • Wander through Redhill and Paddington for fine cafes, restaurants and bars

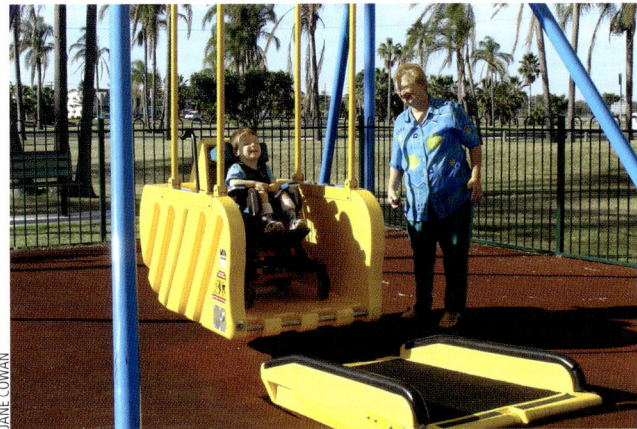

JANE COWAN

Matthew Alback enjoying a swing

LOCAL KNOWLEDGE

A swing with wheelchair access

It wasn't that long ago that disabled access was something rarely seen; where it existed, it was usually the result of intense lobbying by individuals and groups who believed everyone should be able to go everywhere. But what about disabled access to playgrounds? In Brisbane there is the Liberty Swing, designed by Wayne Devine and located at Pelican Park, Clontarf. To book the swing, phone the Redcliffe Visitor Information Centre on (07) 3283 0240. You can find out more at www.abc.net.au/brisbane/stories/s1046064.htm

MEET THE LOCALS

Meet one with plenty of knowledge

He may look bird-brained, but listeners tune in for their 'Letter From Lez' on 612 ABC Brisbane early every Wednesday morning during the 'Breakfast Show'. Lez from Logan brings a unique point of view to local and international events, and you can hear many of his witty and wise monologues at the website: www.users.on.net/lezman. (His views don't necessarily represent those of the ABC.) Lez can also be heard at other times adding his opinion to radio talkback.

LESLIE SANDERS

On the Coast

The calm waters of Moreton Bay are protected from the Pacific Ocean's crashing surf by Moreton and Stradbroke islands.

SIGHTS AND ACTIVITIES • Visit the Alma Park Zoo with its subtropical surrounds, landscaped gardens, exotic animals and Australian wildlife • Swim, fish or picnic at the lovely beaches in the Wynnum-Manly area, 15 kilometres east of the city

The Brisbane Hinterland

This subtropical haven lies just 20 minutes west of the city, with the main access point through the hamlet of Mount Glorious. Travel further west to reach the heritage city of Ipswich.

SIGHTS AND ACTIVITIES • Admire the diverse and pristine rainforest, towering trees, cascading waterfalls, deep pools and mountain streams at the Brisbane Forest Park – the Walk-About Creek Wildlife Centre features a freshwater creek environment populated with water-dragons, frogs, platypuses, pythons and fish • Tour the Workshops Rail Museum in Ipswich, where Queensland's first train line was begun in 1864 • Drive the Mount Glorious–Samford Road, one of the State's most scenic routes

The Brisbane Islands

There are more than 350 islands in and around the fringe of Moreton Bay, including North Stradbroke, St Helena, Bribie and Moreton islands. Despite development these islands have retained an aura of wilderness, with endless white beaches, creeks, lakes and amazing wildflowers and wildlife.

SIGHTS AND ACTIVITIES • Use the Island Hopper to visit the islands (details from www.ourbrisbane.com) • Visit St Helena Island which was used as a prison from 1867–1932; historic ruins remain and tours of the island depart from Manly and Breakfast Creek • Explore the coastal and bush paradise on North Stradbroke Island • Spot whales (June–November), dolphins, dugongs and turtles off the beautiful coastal beaches on Moreton Island, most of which is a national park

TOURISM QUEENSLAND

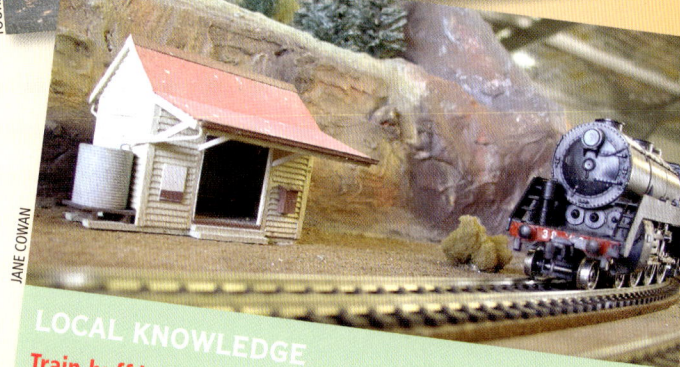

JANE COWAN

LOCAL KNOWLEDGE

Train-buff heaven

We might all be model-train enthusiasts if we had enough room to have our layout permanently set up. So enthusiasts visiting Brisbane should check out the new facilities for the Railway Modellers' Club of Queensland in Brendale. There are monthly meetings every second Saturday, and informal get togethers throughout the month. Visits can be organised by contacting the club though its website: www.rmcq.mixedpk.com

MEET THE LOCALS

Tracking Clayton

When Queensland Parks and Wildlife rangers first met the orphaned Clayton, he weighed a mere 360 grams and had problems with his paws and eyes. As he was nursed back to health, his spirit and determination touched everyone. When Clayton had recovered from his injuries, he still needed a safe environment in which to live. He was released into an enclosed plantation at the Capalaba Water Treatment Works, complete with a transmitter and antenna to help rangers track him and monitor his progress.

TOURISM QUEENSLAND

ABC Gold and Tweed Coasts

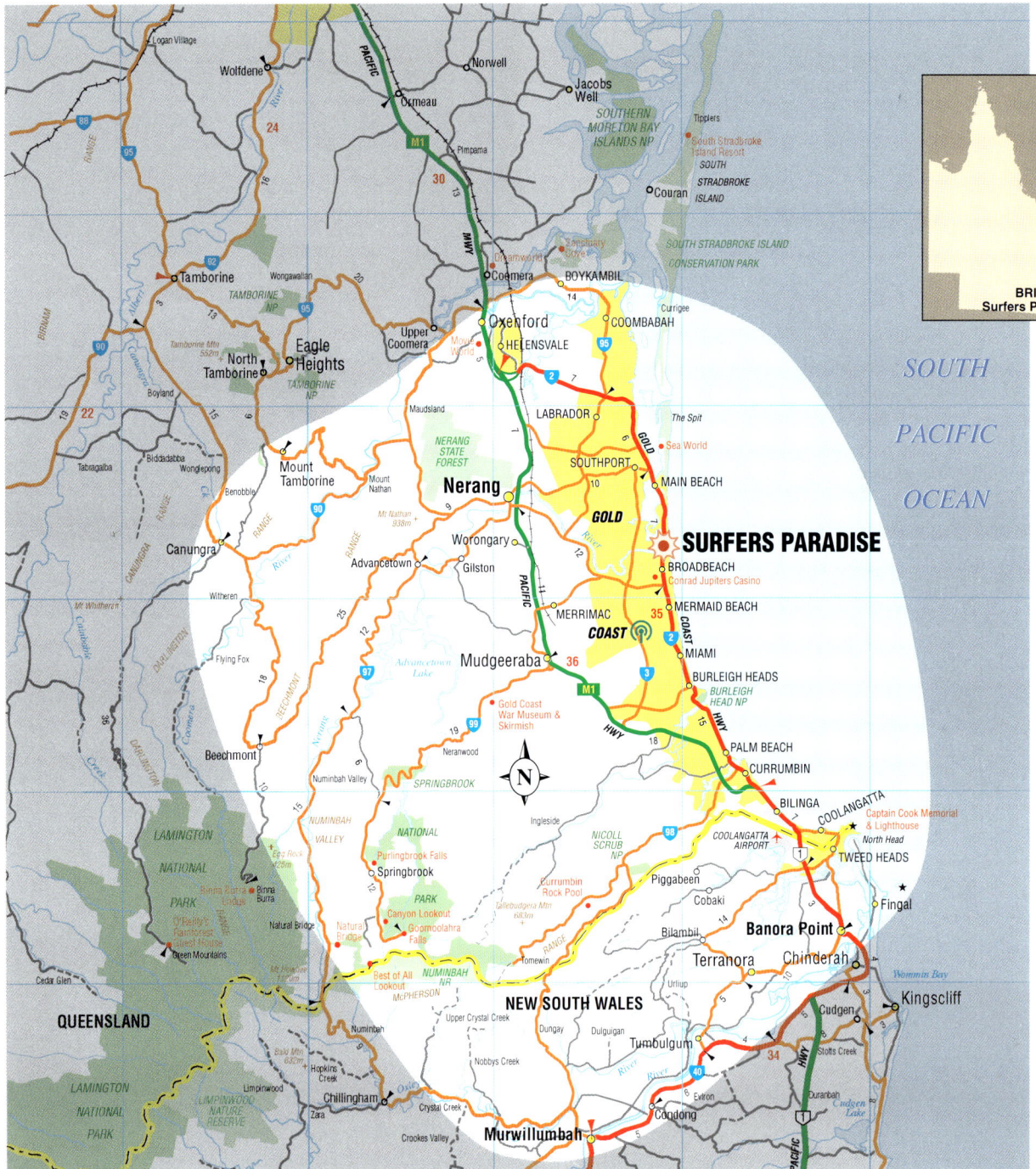

☀ Location of ABC Local Radio studio

Local Radio Frequencies

Banora Point	91.7 FM
Coolangatta	91.7 FM
Gold Coast	91.7 FM
Mermaid Beach	91.7 FM
Mudgeeraba	91.7 FM
Mount Tamborine	91.7 FM
Nerang	91.7 FM
Oxenford	91.7 FM
Surfers Paradise	91.7 FM
Tweed Heads	91.7 FM

Gold Coast has the only transmitter (FM) in the region

ABC Coast FM is also broadcast live through ABC Online. Most areas can also receive 612 AM ABC Brisbane and 720 AM ABC North Coast (New South Wales).

ABC Gold and Tweed Coasts encompasses two of the most popular tourist destinations in Australia: the Gold Coast, including Surfers Paradise, Southport, Coolangatta, Palm Beach and Currumbin; and the Tweed Coast, including Murwillumbah, Tweed Heads, Kingscliff and Cabarita.

The 35 gold-sand beaches and the unbelievably good weather – an average of 300 days of sunshine each year – are trademarks of Australia's biggest and busiest tourist destination. Around four million tourists spend an estimated 2.5 billion dollars each year, attracted by 70 kilometres of magnificent surf beaches and beautiful national parks including Mount Warning, Tamborine and the World Heritage-listed Lamington National Park.

The area's industry base is diverse and ever-widening, with education, film-making, manufacture, ship building and integrated technology among the many enterprises based in the area. ABC Coast FM brings the world to a loyal local audience on the Gold and Tweed Coasts.

TOURISM QUEENSLAND

Lamington National Park

NOT TO BE MISSED

- Surf locations like **Kirra Point** and **Currumbin** are said to be among the 10 best breaks in the world
- Play a round of golf at one of **Sanctuary Cove**'s championship courses, the Pines or the Palms, or hit one of the Gold Coast's 38 other courses
- Drop straight down at 70 kilometres per hour on the Wild West Falls Adventure Ride, or see the business of movie-making up close at **Warner Bros Movie World**
- Camp on **South Stradbroke Island** surrounded by beautiful beaches – no cars are permitted so you can really get away from it all
- Walk through the World Heritage-listed **Lamington National Park**, a wonderland of rainforest and volcanic ridges
- Take a scenic flight from **Carrara** aboard a Tiger Moth
- Drive to the galleries, cafes and antique stores in the villages of the **Tamborine Mountain** area

TOURISM QUEENSLAND

Surfers Paradise

World-class hotels and restaurants, golden-sand beaches, a subtropical climate and a year-round holiday atmosphere make this part of the coast ideal for a wide range of holiday-makers.

SIGHTS AND ACTIVITIES • Relax at a cafe on Cavill Avenue then stroll round to Orchid Avenue for designer-clothes shops, funky bars and clubs, or head to the beach for the art and craft markets on Friday evening • Take in a bird's eye view from the Flycoaster or Bungee Rocket thrill rides on Cypress Avenue • Try your luck at Conrad Jupiters Casino at Broadbeach • End the day with a swim on one of the most beautiful beaches on the east coast • Experience the thrills and spills of one of the Gold Coast's theme parks – from the operational film set at Warner Bros Movie World or Wet 'n' Wild's giant slides and aquatic park to Dreamworld's Tower of Terror and Tiger Island or the legendary Sea World

VISITOR INFORMATION
Cavill Walk (07) 5538 4419

Mount Tamborine

Sitting on the edge of the escarpment behind the Gold Coast, Mount Tamborine, with its nearby tropical rainforests, national parks and mountain retreats, sits in perfect contrast to the coast.

SIGHTS AND ACTIVITIES • Explore the national parks • Discover local treasures in the village, which is home to many art and craft galleries, cafes and teahouses • Look out from one of the many fine viewing points – at 560 metres, there are many

MEET THE LOCALS

Venetta Fields

She's sung with Aretha Franklin, The Rolling Stones, The Supremes, Barbra Streisand and Bob Dylan. As a backing vocalist once based in Los Angeles, Venetta Fields is now a Gold Coast local, having fallen in love with Australia back in the 1980s. A regular on ABC radio, you can also catch her in performance around the Gold Coast; she gives singing lessons as well (www.venettafields.com).

TOURISM QUEENSLAND

LOCAL KNOWLEDGE

Tedder Avenue

If you're looking for a special dining experience while you're on the Gold Coast, ask a local for directions to Tedder Avenue. Located a few blocks behind Main Beach it's worth seeking out for refined and cosmopolitan outdoor dining – perfect for the Gold Coast climate. Candles and starlight replace the neon and spotlights, and you'll find Thai, Chinese, Japanese and Italian cuisine, as well as wine bars, tapas bars and cafes.

TOURISM QUEENSLAND

Tweed Heads/Coolangatta

Coolangatta (population 6618) is the gateway to the Gold Coast; its much larger twin town in New South Wales, Tweed Heads, has a population of 37755.

SIGHTS AND ACTIVITIES • Try skydiving or take a joy flight from the airport • Visit the Captain Cook Memorial Lighthouse and enjoy the excellent panoramic views over the ocean and coast; dolphins may be seen off the coast from the pleasant cliff-edge walk • Laze around on the one of the nearby sheltered white-sand beaches

VISITOR INFORMATION
Shop 14b, Coolangatta Place (07) 5536 7765

LOCAL TIPS

- A visit to **Tamborine Mountain** is not only a good idea for galleries, cafes and more, but you can watch hangliders riding the updrafts as well

- Play a round or two on some of the best and best-known golf courses in Australia, such as **Sanctuary Cove**

- For good fishing, try the breakwall inside the entrance to the **Broadwater**

- A pleasant day trip is a drive to **Springbrook National Park** and such sights as the Natural Bridge and the Best Of All View. On the New South Wales border, you'll also get superb views over Murwillumbah and the Mount Warning Caldera

- See platypus in the creek and taste wines at the cellar door at **Canungra Valley Vineyards** on the road to O'Reilly's Rainforest Guesthouse

MEET THE LOCALS

JANE COWAN

Warren Young
You probably don't want to meet this bloke, let alone get his kiss of life, but it's nice to know he's there. Warren Young is the Gold Coast's chief lifeguard, and a regular personality on ABC Coast FM. He's there with the latest on surf conditions, tides and water temperatures, and he's quite a character. He takes beach safety very seriously – so always swim between the flags.

MEET THE LOCALS

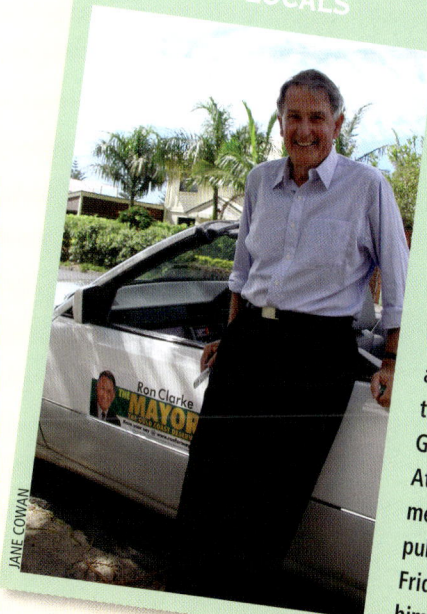
JANE COWAN

Mayor Clarke
He once ran for his country, but the man who lit the Olympic flame in 1956 has now run for office. And, as often happened in his career, record-breaking Ron Clarke has won again – this time it's the job of Mayor of Gold Coast City Council. Attend a council meeting (open to the public and usually held Friday) and you can see him in action.

ABC Sunshine and Cooloola Coasts

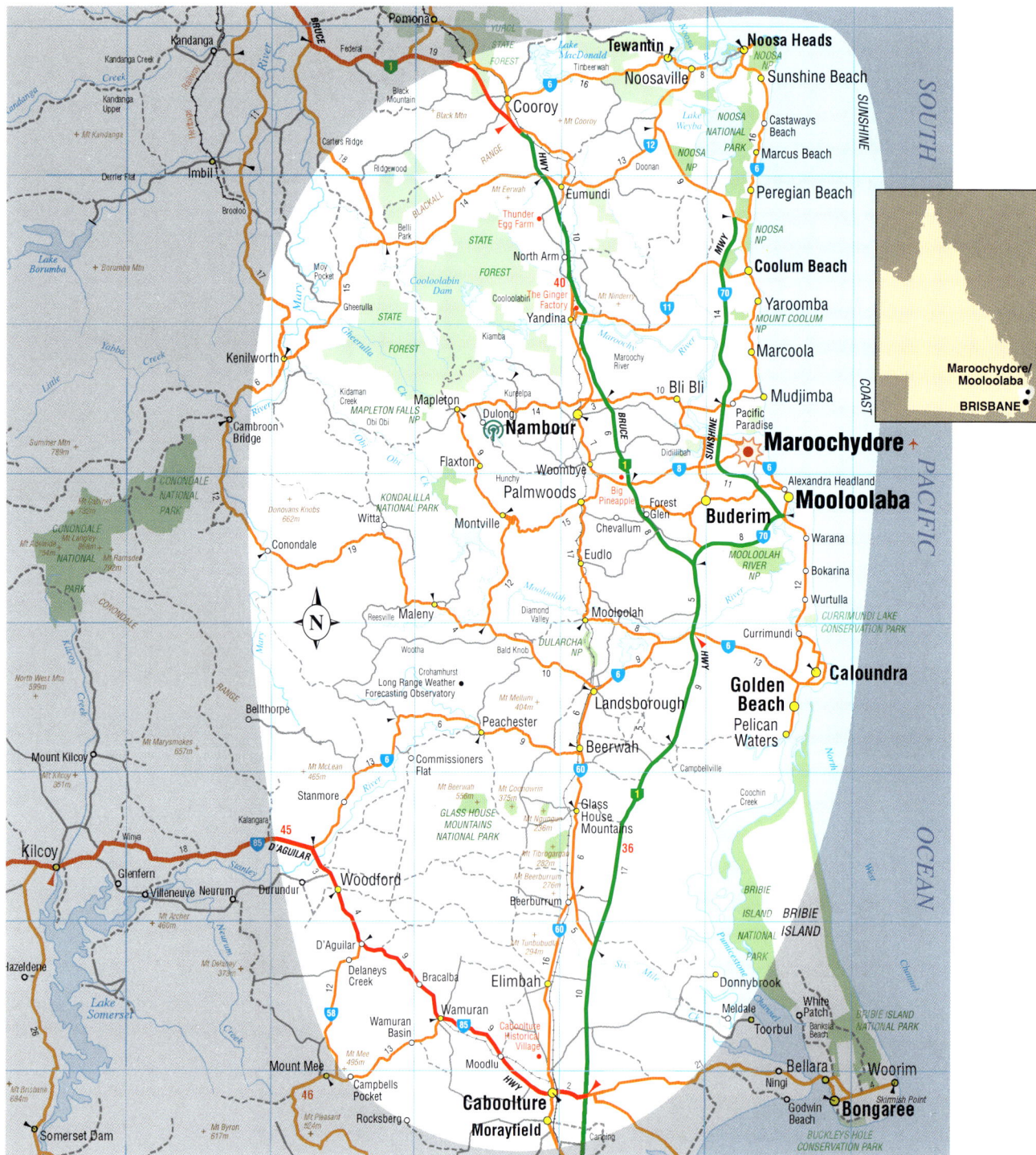

Location of ABC Local Radio studio

Local Radio Frequencies		
Buderim	90.3 FM	
Caboolture	90.3 FM	
Caloundra	90.3 FM	
Cooroy	95.3 FM	
Eumundi	95.3 FM	90.3 FM
Maleny	90.3 FM	
Maroochydore	90.3 FM	
Montville	90.3 FM	
Mooloolaba	90.3 FM	
Nambour	90.3 FM	
Noosa	95.3 FM	90.3 FM 855 AM ABC Wide Bay
Tewantin	95.3 FM	90.3 FM

Nambour has its own FM transmitter

ABC Coast FM is also broadcast live through ABC Online.
Most areas can also receive 612 AM ABC Brisbane.

Glass House Mountains

Beautiful beaches bathed by the blue South Pacific and fringed by native bush stretch from north of Noosa Heads south to the tip of Bribie Island to form the Sunshine Coast. Inland lie forested folds and ridges, and the striking volcanic formations of the Glass House Mountains. The Sunshine Coast hinterland is marked by charming hilltop villages and waterfalls, an area perfect for walks and scenic drives.

And to add to the attractions, the area's local produce is the envy of much of the rest of Australia. With such quality produce on their doorstep, it is not surprising that world-class chefs are attracted to the region's restaurants, particularly at Noosa Heads. It's also little wonder that the area is considered a perfect weekend escape from nearby Brisbane, and a winter playground for the southern States.

Calling itself ABC Coast FM, ABC Sunshine and Cooloola Coasts covers the geographical area from Bribie Island north past Cooroy and back through the surrounding hinterland. The station is an integral part of the region, and the quality of its programming draws an extremely loyal following from a potential audience in excess of 260 000.

NOT TO BE MISSED

- Glide along the **Noosa River** in a gondola at sunset
- Experience the transparent tunnel at the UnderWater World complex in **Mooloolaba**
- Splash in the blue waters at **Noosa Beach**, then take a stroll down Hastings Street which has some of the finest restaurants on the coast
- Go **surf fishing** for bream, flathead, whiting and dart
- Wonder at the beauty of the multicoloured sands in the 40 000-year-old cliffs at **Teewah**
- Wander through antique shops and art galleries, or stop at a cafe in one of the mountain villages along the 70-kilometre scenic drive that starts at Landsborough and passes through **Maleny**, **Montville**, **Flaxton** and **Mapleton**
- Chill out at the famous **Eumundi** markets on Saturday mornings, with everything from organic goat's cheese and fruit to local crafts, art, live music and more

Jan	**Yandina:** Ginger Flower Festival
Apr	**Regional:** Sunshine Coast Festival of the Sea **Mooloolaba:** Sydney– Mooloolaba Yacht Race
June	**Caboolture:** Medieval Tournament
July	**Pomona:** King of the Mountain (attracts mountain runners from around the world)
Aug	**Gympie:** National Country Music Muster
Aug– Sept	**Pomona:** Silent Movie Festival, Majestic Theatre
Sept– Oct	**Noosa Heads:** Jazz Festival **Bribie Island** Festival (includes a mullet-throwing competition)
Oct	**Gympie:** Gold Rush Festival **Mapleton:** Nambour Yarn Festival **Maleny:** Scarecrow Festival **Noosa Heads:** Beach Car Classic
Oct– Nov	**Noosa Heads:** Triathlon Multi-Sport Festival
Nov	**Maleny:** Festival of Colour (open gardens)
Dec	**Caboolture:** Rodeo **Woodford:** Folk Festival

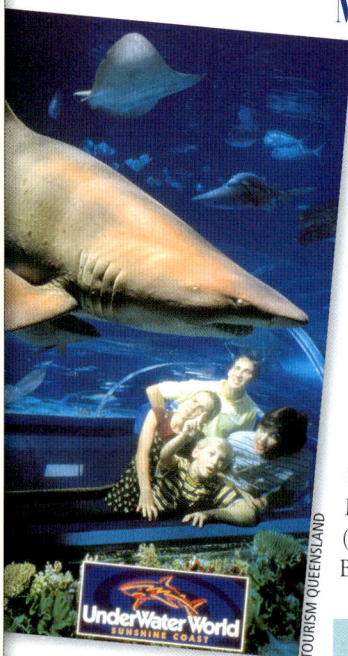

TOURISM QUEENSLAND

Maroochydore/Mooloolaba

These adjacent towns (population 28 509) combine to form a popular beach resort boasting both great surfing beaches and safe swimming. Mooloolaba also has excellent facilities for boating.

SIGHTS AND ACTIVITIES ● See a replica of Captain Cook's *Endeavour* on David Low Way ● Visit Nostalgia Town 7 kilometres north-west for a humorous look at history ● Drop by Bli Bli Castle, 10 kilometres north-west, a medieval castle with dungeon, torture chamber and doll museum ● Meet a shark eye-to-eye in the 80-metre underwater viewing tunnel at the wharf's UnderWater World complex ● Go game fishing or take a yachting charter to nearby reefs, which can be organised from the wharf

VISITOR INFORMATION
Maroochydore: Cnr Sixth Avenue and Aerodrome Road (07) 5479 1566. Mooloolaba: Cnr First Avenue and Brisbane Road (07) 5478 2233

MEET THE LOCALS

Pelican patrol

While holidaying on the Sunshine Coast, don't be alarmed if you see a couple of blokes grappling with a pelican while it throws up rotten fish all over them. It could be Michael McNamara and Darcy Eve (pictured), Maroochy and Noosa Councils' Riverwatch Rangers. Many pelicans become tangled with hooks and fishing lines discarded by careless recreational anglers. Catching the pelicans isn't too hard. Pelicans love fish. Meeting the Pelican Patrol isn't too hard either, especially if you're downwind.

JANE COWAN

MEET THE LOCALS

Noosa Farmers' Market

When it comes to fruit and vegies and all things home-grown or homemade, Shane Stanley's your man. As co-ordinator of the Noosa Farmers' Market he's passionate about fresh produce. He brings together local producers and the public, who find the experience of browsing in the open-air market preferable to the sterile, fluorescent-lit aisles of the supermarket. There's nothing like seeing and talking to the person who's grown or made the food you're going to eat.

Maleny

This small mountain village (population 880) in the Blackall Range is popular with alternative-lifestylers and has a number of co-operative stores and cafes as well as local art and craft galleries. Nearby Montville is arguably even more picturesque, with more galleries and cafes to enjoy.

SIGHTS AND ACTIVITIES • Admire the breathtaking views of the Glass House Mountains from McCarthy's lookout, south-east of town • Take one of the best scenic drives in this part of Queensland, north-east from Maleny through to Mapleton, passing through gorgeous mountain villages and with views of the Sunshine Coast, Moreton Island, Bribie Island and nearby pineapple and sugarcane fields • Don't miss Montville's main street, 7 kilometres north, lined with cafes, gift shops, potteries, art and craft galleries

VISITOR INFORMATION
25 Maple Street (07) 5499 9033

Nambour

With a subtropical climate and volcanic soils, the region is renowned for its produce, and Nambour's Big Pineapple is testament to this.

SIGHTS AND ACTIVITIES • Take a train, trolley or boat through the Big Pineapple complex • Sample some delicious produce at the Macadamia Nut Factory 7 kilometres east, and The Superbee Honey Factory 10 kilometres further south • Take a tour through Yandina's Ginger Factory, 10 kilometres north, to find out how ginger is processed or to buy a sample from a range of ginger products, including ginger ice cream

VISITOR INFORMATION
5 Coronation Avenue (07) 5476 1933

Noosa Heads

Offering luxury hotels, top restaurants and stylish bars, boutiques and galleries, the town is flanked by crystal clear ocean on one side, an estuary on the other and overlooked by the headland of the Noosa National Park.

SIGHTS AND ACTIVITIES • Discover the National Park's protected coves, surfing beaches and seascapes • Cruise along the Noosa River and explore the 40 kilometres of river systems through the Everglades • Jump in the car and head to the Noosa Regional Gallery, Big Shell and House of Bottles at Tewantin, 8 kilometres west • Further north, see the coloured sands of Teewah

VISITOR INFORMATION
Hastings Street roundabout (07) 5447 4988

LOCAL TIPS

- Visit **Pomona**'s Majestic Theatre (30 kilometres east), an authentic silent movie theatre with a cinema museum and home to the Silent Movie Festival in August–September

- The Appollonian Hotel at **Boreen Point** is a beautiful timber Queensland colonial pub wreathed in bougainvillea and renowned for its folk nights and Sunday spit roast

- **Point Glorious**, located at the northern end of the Blackall Range near Kenilworth, is as good as it gets, and has sensational views of the Sunshine Coast

- A walk up the massive stone flanks of **Mount Coolum** or **Mount Ninderry** takes a strenuous 20 to 30 minutes, but is worth it for the superb views up and down the coast

- For a romantic sunset, locals reckon **Dunethin Rock**, on the Maroochy River, is the place to enjoy a spectacular view over the river, cane fields and hinterland beyond

- Get away from it all – take a trip to the Cooloola section of the **Great Sandy National Park**

The Big Pineapple complex

TOURISM QUEENSLAND

LOCAL KNOWLEDGE

Mayor Bob Abbot

Try to imagine what the mayor of an upmarket resort destination like Noosa might look like, and Bob Abbot might be the last person to spring to mind. Bob was re-elected in 2004 with 74 per cent of the vote. Weighing in at around 145 kilograms (23 stone), with a full beard, jeans and riding boots, he's a salt-of-the-earth type and the locals love his straightforward approach to local issues. Where can you meet him? Council meetings are open to the public, and you may also catch him playing blues harmonica at Joe's Waterhole in Eumundi.

NOOSA SHIRE COUNCIL

ABC Wide Bay

Location of ABC Local Radio studio

Whale-watching at Hervey Bay

TOURISM QUEENSLAND

Local Radio Frequencies

Agnes Water	855 AM	100.1 FM
Biggenden	855 AM	100.1 FM
Eidsvold	855 AM	100.1 FM
Fraser Island	855 AM	100.1 FM
Gympie	1566 AM	95.3 FM ABC Sunshine Coast 612 AM ABC Brisbane
Monto	855 AM	100.1 FM
Mundubbera	855 AM	100.1 FM
Pialba (Hervey Bay)	855 AM	100.1 FM
Seventeen Seventy	855 AM	
Bundaberg	100.1 FM	855 AM
Childers	100.1 FM	855 AM
Gayndah	100.1 FM	855 AM 747 AM ABC Southern Queensland
Gin Gin	100.1 FM	855 AM
Hervey Bay	100.1 FM	855 AM
Maryborough	100.1 FM	855 AM
Miriam Vale	88.3 FM	
Murgon	100.1 FM	855 AM 612 AM ABC Brisbane 747 AM ABC Southern Queensland
Tiaro	100.1 FM	855 AM 612 AM ABC Brisbane
Tin Can Bay	100.1 FM	855 AM 612 AM ABC Brisbane
Wide Bay (near Biggenden)	100.1 FM	
Wondai	100.1 FM	855 AM 612 AM ABC Brisbane 747 AM ABC Southern Queensland

Towns in red have their own AM transmitter
Towns in green have their own FM transmitter

W ide Bay gets its name from the expanse of water south of Fraser Island but it encompasses a much broader area than that. The coverage of ABC Radio Wide Bay extends across the Burnett region as well, servicing a population of 185,000.

The people live in the major centres of Bundaberg, Hervey Bay, Maryborough, Childers and Gympie, and smaller centres such as Monto, Mundubbera, Murgon, Gayndah, Eidsvold and Biggenden. It is an extremely fertile and prosperous area where agriculture thrives. Local produce includes tomatoes, avocados, subtropical fruit and even wine. The region produces about a fifth of Australia's sugar.

Tourists are drawn to the region by the annual humpback whale migration to Hervey Bay, the world-heritage listed Fraser Island and the idyllic climate. Yet there's more to the area than that. Turtle rookeries and dugong feeding grounds can be found on the coast, rare fish are in the rivers, many of the small towns boast National Trust-listed Queensland colonial architecture, and the parks and gardens feature spectacular subtropical plants and trees.

NOT TO BE MISSED

- Rum goings-on at the **Bundaberg Rum Distillery**
- Watch loggerhead turtles laying eggs (November to January) or babies hatching (January to March) at **Mon Repos Turtle Rookery**
- Marvel at the annual whale migration in **Hervey Bay** (August to October)
- Visit the wrecks and other treasures of **Fraser Island**
- Devour the superb food and wine of the **Wide Bay** and surrounding region

Lungfish sculpture

Bundaberg

The centre of the Wide Bay region (population 41 025), Bundaberg is an important provincial city. It's the hub of a diverse agricultural industry that includes sugar, beef, fruit and more. There are many fine parks and gardens, and the town was home to aviator Bert Hinkler, singer Gladys Moncrieff, cricketer Don Tallon and footballer Mal Meninga.

SIGHTS AND ACTIVITIES • Take a tour of the Bundaberg Rum Distillery • Talk to the animals at Alexandra Park and Zoo • Explore the city's local history (brochure available) • Visit the Whale Wall, a six-storey high mural in Bourbong Street • Drop into Bert Hinkler House or one of the other museums in the Botanical Gardens, or just smell the gorgeous flowers • Learn about lungfish (*Neoceratodus*) that inhabit the Burnett River, or check out the sculpture on the riverbank in town

VISITOR INFORMATION
271 Bourbong Street (07) 4153 8888

MEET THE LOCALS

Burnett River snapping turtle

One local you'd be very lucky to meet is the Burnett River snapping turtle. That's not because it's all that rare, but because it has the ability to remain underwater for several days. No, it doesn't have incredible lung capacity. A gill system in its backside gives the creature its remarkable skill. They're not small either. The female can weight up to seven kilograms.

Gympie

Originally a gold town after its discovery there in 1867, it's now the major centre for the fertile Cooloola region (population 10 813). In town, the streets are lined with attractive poinciana, jacaranda and flame trees.

SIGHTS AND ACTIVITIES • Tour the Woodworks, Forestry and Timber Museum • Pan for gold in Deep Creek or visit the Gold Mining Museum • Visit the cottage of Andrew Fisher, the first Queenslander to become Prime Minister • Ride the rails of the Mary Valley Heritage Railway (or see people Race the Rattler in June)

VISITOR INFORMATION
Matilda's Roadhouse Complex, Bruce Highway, Kybong (07) 5483 5554

Hervey Bay/Fraser Island

Tourism is the primary industry of this idyllic town (population 32 054) that takes its name from the adjoining bay. A mecca for southerners escaping the chill of winter, the bay offers year-round safe swimming, sheltered from the Pacific swells by Fraser Island. The island is the world's largest sand island and is also famous for its beaches, lakes, wrecks, wildlife and World Heritage listing.

SIGHTS AND ACTIVITIES • Watch whales from August to October • See the one-kilometre pier at Urangan as well as memorials to Matthew Flinders (who landed in 1799) and the Z-Force commandos (who trained there on the *Krait*) • Immerse yourself in the numerous theme parks and wildlife exhibitions • Head for Fraser Island for four-wheel drive adventures, camping, fishing, swimming and more

VISITOR INFORMATION
Cnr Urraween and Maryborough-Hervey Bay roads (07) 4124 2912

Maryborough

Historic buildings dating back to when the region was first explored by Europeans in 1842 make Maryborough (population 21 286) a must-visit for history buffs. There are numerous museums, a replica of Queensland's first steam train and the historic Wharf Street precinct.

SIGHTS AND ACTIVITIES • Hand feed waterbirds at Ululah Lagoon, a scenic waterbird sanctuary • Stroll back in time with a self-guide historic tour (brochure available) • Hear one of Queensland's last sets of pealing bells at St Paul's bell tower (1887)

VISITOR INFORMATION
BP South Complex, Bruce Highway (07) 4121 4111

Maryborough Heritage Centre

LOCAL TIPS

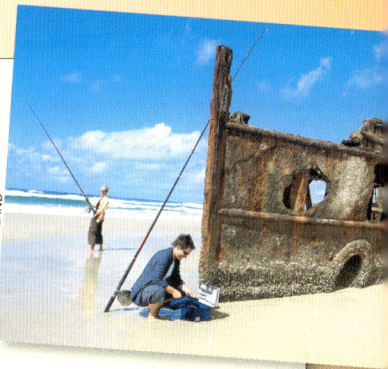
TOURISM QUEENSLAND

- On **Fraser Island**, the wreck of the *Maheno* is still visible
- **Hervey Bay** is renowned for its whales, but dugong are also found and closely monitored
- **Gin Gin**'s Wild Scotchman Festival in March commemorates bushranger James McPherson. It's also Queensland's friendliest town (they're thinking of changing the name to Grin Grin) with an excellent bakery and a winery with an anti-oxidant enriched red wine
- In **Bundaberg**, keep an eye out for the water towers, which ensure good pressure in the water supply. They're not just functional, they also express a range of architectural styles and are local landmarks
- **Childers** features the memorial to the Palace Hotel backpackers fire. Visitors can also see excellent displays at Snakes Down Under and the Bird Sanctuary
- **Miriam Vale**'s speciality is mud-crab sandwiches

MEET THE LOCALS

The Bundy Undy

'Gentlemen, drop your trousers!' That could well be the way they start one of Australia's strangest races, the Bundy Undy 500. Yet every year Bundaberg locals drop their daks and run in their undies for 500 metres – all in the name of charity. The June event also features a 'Rub A Runner' auction and a Lingerie Fashion Show, which raise money for the Queensland Cancer Fund. It puts a whole new complexion on 'jockeying' for position.

ABC Central Queensland

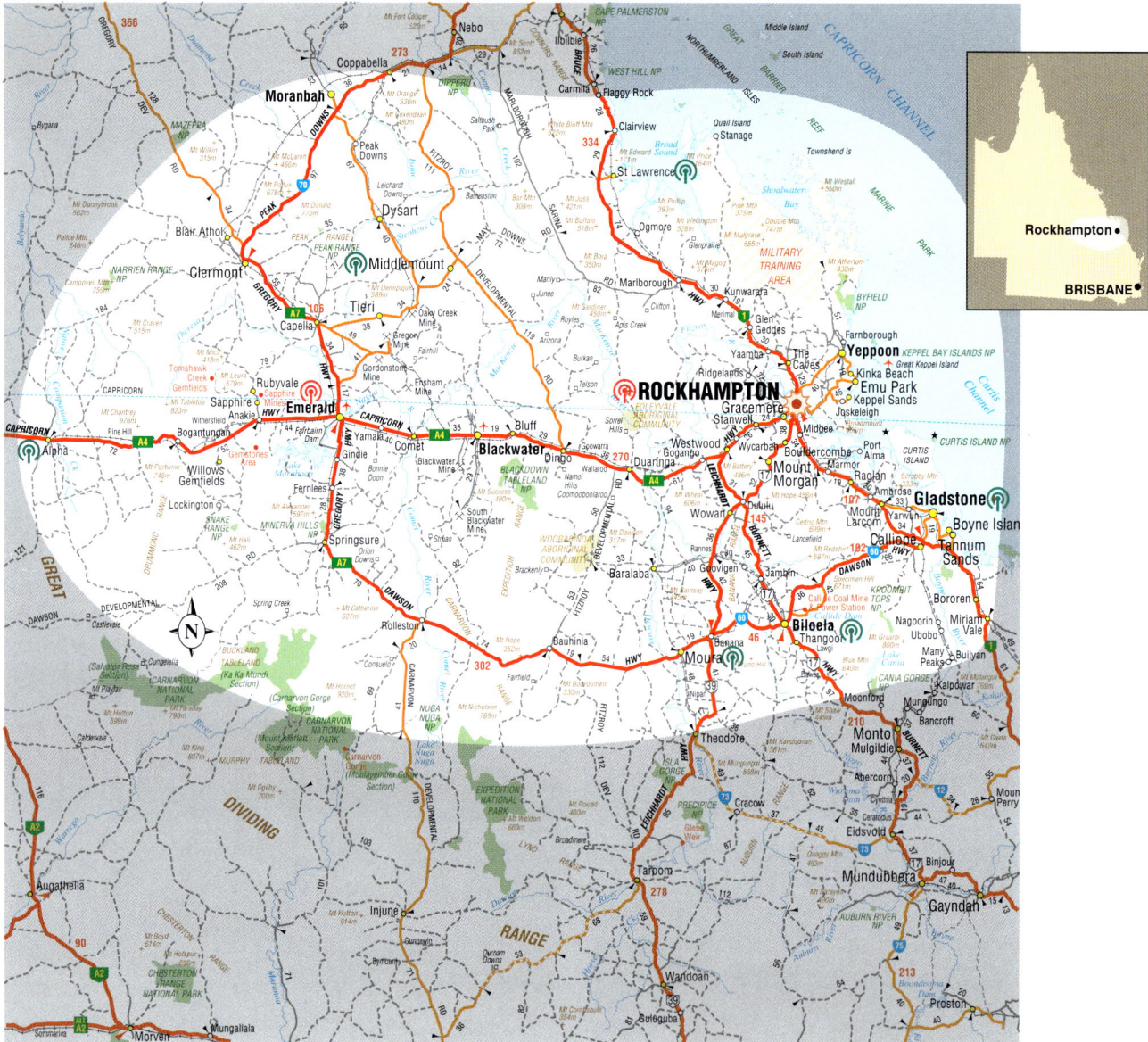

Location of ABC Local Radio studio

Beef is a mainstay of the local economy

TOURISM QUEENSLAND

Local Radio Frequencies		
Anakie	1548 AM	504 AM ABC Western Queensland
Blackwater	1548 AM	837 AM
Blair Athol	1548 AM	
Bororen	837 AM	88.3 FM ABC Wide Bay 855 AM ABC Wide Bay
Capella	1548 AM	
Clermont	1548 AM	
Dingo	1548 AM	837 AM
Emerald	1548 AM	
Marlborough	837 AM	
Miriam Vale	837 AM	88.3 FM ABC Wide Bay 100.1 FM ABC Wide Bay 855 AM ABC Wide Bay
Mount Morgan	837 AM	
Ogmore	837 AM	
Rockhampton	837 AM	
Rubyvale	1548 AM	
Sapphire	1548 AM	
Springsure	1548 AM	540 AM ABC Western Queensland
Yeppoon	837 AM	
Alpha	105.7 FM	1548 AM 504 AM ABC Western Queensland
Biloela	94.9 FM	837 AM 855 AM ABC Wide Bay
Gladstone	99.1 FM	837 AM 855 AM ABC Wide Bay 100.1 FM ABC Wide Bay
Middlemount	106.1 FM	1548 AM 837 AM
Moura	96.1 FM	837 AM
St Lawrence	94.9 FM	837 AM 1548 AM
Tannum Sands	99.1 FM	837 AM 855 AM ABC Wide Bay 100.1 FM ABC Wide Bay

🎙 Towns in red have their own AM transmitter
🎙 Towns in green have their own FM transmitter

ABC Central Queensland (Capricornia) is one of the ABC's few original regional stations dating back to the inception of the ABC on 1 July 1932. In fact the Rockhampton station has been broadcasting since 1931.

ABC Capricornia has a strong history of community service which continues today and is demonstrated by the station's exceptionally high community profile. ABC Capricornia stages a number of the area's major annual events and also actively supports the local beef industry as host broadcaster of the regular triennial beef expos.

It is also closely linked with the region's history. Its offices are housed in the heritage-listed former headquarters of the Mount Morgan Gold Mining Company, situated in the Fitzroy riverbank precinct of Rockhampton. Nearby Mount Morgan was at one time the single richest gold mine in the world, and one of the studio's editing rooms is in the old vault where the gold was stored!

As well as a local breakfast and morning program, the station also broadcasts a daily networked regional late afternoon program to a large part of Queensland, and provides a daily syndicated program service to other Queensland ABC stations.

NOT TO BE MISSED

- Step back in time to the **Mount Morgan** gold-mining days
- Tour **Gladstone**'s massive industrial projects
- Enjoy the **Rockhampton** Botanic Gardens
- Fossick for gemstones around **Anakie**, **Sapphire**, **Rubyvale** and **Willows** gemfields
- Hike scenic trails in **Blackdown Tableland National Park**
- Relax in the sun and sea of the **Capricorn Coast**

Rockhampton

Capricornia's regional centre (population 59 120), Rockhampton also prides itself as the Beef Capital of Australia. That explains the bulls that adorn major routes into town, but there's more to this city than that.

SIGHTS AND ACTIVITIES • Journey back in time in Quay Street, Australia's longest National Trust-classified street, with more than 20 listed buildings • Wet a line and try to catch a mighty barramundi • Straddle the Tropic of Capricorn alongside the 14-metre Capricorn Spire at Curtis Park • Nearby, there's Rockhampton Heritage Village, Capricorn Caverns and air access to Great Keppel Island • Experience Aboriginal and Torres Strait Islander culture at the Dreamtime Cultural Centre • Take a ride on the Purrey steam tram at the historic Archer Park railway station

VISITOR INFORMATION
Customs House, 208 Quay Street (07) 4922 5339

Biloela

Located 142 kilometres south of Rockhampton, this thriving town has a population of 5161 and is the agricultural centre for a region of lucerne, cotton, sorghum, wheat and sunflowers. The town's name is the local Aboriginal for 'white cockatoo'.

SIGHTS AND ACTIVITIES • Tour historic Greycliffe Homestead (open by appointment) • Take a guided tour of nearby Callide power station • Go boating, fishing and swimming at Callide Dam • Catch a bus tour of the town during the week

VISITOR INFORMATION
Callide Street (07) 4992 2405

Emerald

The gateway to the largest sapphire fields in the Southern Hemisphere, Emerald is a very attractive town (population 9345) that also enjoys prosperous cattle, grain, oilseed and soybean industries.

SIGHTS AND ACTIVITIES • Enjoy tree-lined Clermont and Egerton streets, and the National Trust-classified railway station (1901) • Tour the Pioneer Cottage and Museum in Harris Street • Visit local cattle stations • Fossick for gems around the district (licences are available) • Descend underground at Rubyvale's walk-in mines (60 kilometres north-west)

VISITOR INFORMATION
Clermont Street (07) 4982 4142

TOURISM QUEENSLAND

Fossicking for gems

Gladstone

With a population of 26 415, Gladstone has one of Australia's busiest harbours – a major hub for the export of Central Queensland's mineral and agricultural industries. The world's biggest alumina refinery processes bauxite from Weipa, and tourism is also thriving.

SIGHTS AND ACTIVITIES • View the harbour and nearby islands from Auckland Hill Lookout • Book Barrier Reef dive and fishing trips in Marina Drive • Tour major industries • Picnic and swim at the beautiful parks and beaches of nearby Boyne Island

VISITOR INFORMATION
Marina Ferry Terminal, Bryan Jordan Drive (07) 4972 4000

Yeppoon

The resort centre of Capricornia (population 8810), Yeppoon is located on the shores of Keppel Bay, which has a string of beaches stretching to the south and Great Keppel Island just offshore.

SIGHTS AND ACTIVITIES • Relax on the sand or take a drive or adventure tour • See the rare Byfield fern in Byfield National Park • Hear the 'singing ship' memorial to Captain Cook at Emu Park, where hidden pipes are played by the wind • Visit Cooberie Park to cuddle a koala, and Koorana Crocodile Park to see baby crocs hatch

VISITOR INFORMATION
Scenic Highway (07) 4939 4888

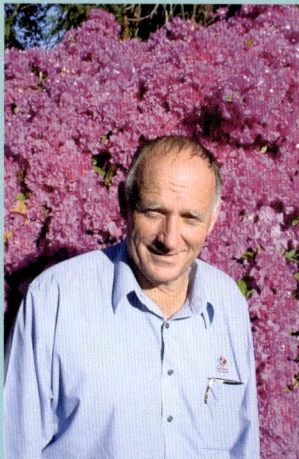

LOCAL TIPS

- In **Blackdown Tableland National Park** there's great swimming at Rainbow Falls, and Sunset Lookout is a perfect place to end the day
- The town of **Theodore** and the national capital, Canberra, have a lot in common: both were designed by Walter Burley Griffin
- The bell in front of **Mount Morgan**'s scout hall is made from coins and watches donated by locals in 1900

MEET THE LOCALS

Disco bull

You've heard of a mirror ball. How about a mirror bull? Every three years Rockhampton hosts Australia's Beef Expo, and as part of the excitement locals are encouraged to erect bulls of all shapes and sizes in their front yards. For Beef 2003 that included Recyla-bull, Invisi-bull, Incredi-bull, Enjoya-bull, and of course, Disco Bull. Judging from his platform, he's into roller-disco.

MEET THE LOCALS

The bent-wing bat

View the annual visit of these tiny creatures to rear their young at Mt Etna Caves National Park, just outside Rockhampton. Guided tours are conducted through rainforest and limestone formations to Bat Cleft, with rangers explaining the significance of the region and the emergence flight as the bats leave their cool, dark homes each evening between November and January to forage.

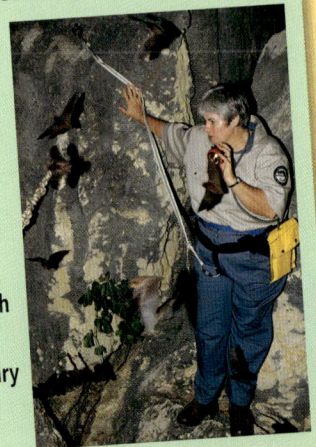

MEET THE LOCALS

Tom Wyatt

In Rockhampton meet Tom Wyatt, Director of Parks and Gardens with the Rockhampton City Council. He's been ABC Capricornia's talkback, gardening host for more than 25 years, and has also done much to expand the Rockhampton Botanic Gardens. The gardens are regarded as Rockhampton's 'hidden jewel' with their fine tropical displays, orchids, a fern house and a Japanese-style garden, plus monkeys, koalas and a walk-in aviary.

ABC Tropical North

Location of ABC Local Radio studio

Towns in green have their own FM transmitter

Pool area, Brampton Island

C ane, coal, coral. These three things might summarise this Queensland region, but they're only shorthand for an area that is blessed with superb natural wonders and resources. The main city of the region, Mackay, is certainly the biggest sugar town in Australia, producing a third of the nation's crop. Go a little north and you'll come to Bowen, renowned for its fabulous mangoes and tomatoes. Inland, you'll find the gigantic coal-mining projects around Dysart and Moranbah. And go to the stunningly beautiful Hibiscus Coast and you'll find the fabulous islands of the Whitsundays. Then there are the towns with a proud history that's reflected in some stunning buildings and beautiful parks and gardens.

There's all this and more in a region well served by its local ABC, which supports several major cultural events and does live broadcasts from many more. As they say, 'The coverage we provide reflects the warm and friendly atmosphere that is typical of our envied tropical lifestyle.' Why would you stay in the studio?

For the visitor, it's usually the tropical resorts that are the attraction. But there's plenty more to this area and its locals than cane, coal or coral.

NOT TO BE MISSED

- Take a trip to the islands and reefs from **Shute Harbour** or **Airlie Beach**
- Wet a line with a youngster and learn how to use a cast net to catch sunfish during Take A Kid Fishing Day at **Shoal Point** (May)
- Walk on the rainforest trails in **Eungella National Park** and visit pristine beaches at **Cape Hillsborough National Park** (check marine-stinger status before entering the water)

Cape Hillsborough National Park

- Savour **Bowen** tomatoes and mangoes
- Follow the big yacht action during **Hamilton Island** race week in August

Art-deco styled Maguire's Hotel

JUDY KELLY

Mackay

It's certainly one of the biggest sugar-producing towns in the world, with the largest bulk-sugar loader in the world and no less than five mills in town. It's also the centre of a thriving mining and tourism sector, with a great climate for good measure. Little wonder the population is growing rapidly (almost 100 000 including the surrounding towns).

SIGHTS AND ACTIVITIES • Set sail or fly to nearby Brampton and Lindeman islands • Tour Fairleigh sugar mill (July to October) • Be captivated by the town's superb Art Deco and 1930s architecture (self-guide walk brochure available)

VISITOR INFORMATION
The Mill, 320 Nebo Road (07) 4952 2677

Airlie Beach

This and nearby Shute Harbour are the gateways to paradise. Tropical paradise that is, with Shute Harbour the largest water-transport terminal in Australia after Sydney's Circular Quay. Airlie overlooks the Whitsunday Passage and is a resort centre in its own right.

SIGHTS AND ACTIVITIES • Snap a snappy local at Vic Hislop's Shark World • Embark from here or Shute Harbour for the Whitsunday islands • Go butterfly- and Prosperpine wallaby-spotting at Conway National Park

VISITOR INFORMATION
277 Shute Harbour Road (07) 4946 6665

MEET THE LOCALS

Just a bit of digging

If you happen to be near the Norwich Park coal mine, you may be mightily impressed by the gigantic shovels that operate on the open cut, scooping coal into the trucks. You may be further impressed by Gerry Gillespie (that's ABC presenter Anne O'Keeffe in the jaws of Gerry's machine), the first female shovel operator at the mine who is able to scoop up 220 tonnes of coal at a time.

Whitsunday Passage

TOURISM QUEENSLAND

Bowen

The first settlement in north Queensland now has a population of 8985. It was named after the State's first governor and is the centre of an incredibly fertile agricultural region.

SIGHTS AND ACTIVITIES • Take the signposted Golden Arrow Tourist Drive • View the 22 historical murals that adorn the central city area • Linger at the many beautiful bays just east of town

VISITOR INFORMATION
Bruce Highway, Mount Gordon (07) 4786 4222

Moranbah

Before 1971 this town didn't exist. Now it's the bustling centre of the Bowen Coal Basin, population 6508.

SIGHTS AND ACTIVITIES • Tour BHP's Peak Downs Mine (tours leave the town square Thursday mornings)

VISITOR INFORMATION
Library, town square (07) 4941 7221

LOCAL TIPS

- In **Eungella**, ask if local youngster Mattie McEvoy is doing a poetry recital. She's terrific. Or you can hear her recital of Jack Drake's 'Cattle Dogs Revenge' at www.abc.net.au/tropic/stories/s962337.htm

- At **Slade Point**, take the 600-metre cultural Kommo Touera or water boardwalk, through the melaleuca forest and learn about the Yuibera people's bush foods and medicines

- In September or October, learn about 6000 years of local indigenous culture at **Airlie Beach**'s Paddling Through History Festival

- Try each of **Bowen**'s 10 beaches, each quite small and secluded with exellent swimming, then enjoy the sunset at Grave's Bay

JUDY KELLY

MEET THE LOCALS

In the spotlight

Eungella National Park boasts one of the best rainforests in Queensland, plus regular guided night tours by park

JUDY KELLY

rangers. Among the nocturnal discoveries are this spectacular Azure kingfisher, taking off in a blur of colour after being woken.

MEET THE LOCALS

The weather lady

Listen in to ABC Tropical Queensland just after the 10am news and weather, and from time to time you'll hear Suzannah from Eungella updating conditions in the Eungella Range, and life in the idyllic region where she lives. Suzannah also runs a cafe there and, if you ask nicely, may show you her extraordinary sculpture garden where rose quartz (the crystal of love and relationships) is the dominant theme.

AVOID A LOCAL

Making life safer

Keep an eye out on the roads around Queensland's Tropical North and you may see a brilliant local initiative that's making life safer for the council's road workers. The signs really work: motorists slow down much more, and the chances of injury are greatly reduced.

mY DAddY WoRKs hERe!
PLEASE SLOW DOWN
JUDY KELLY

ABC North Queensland

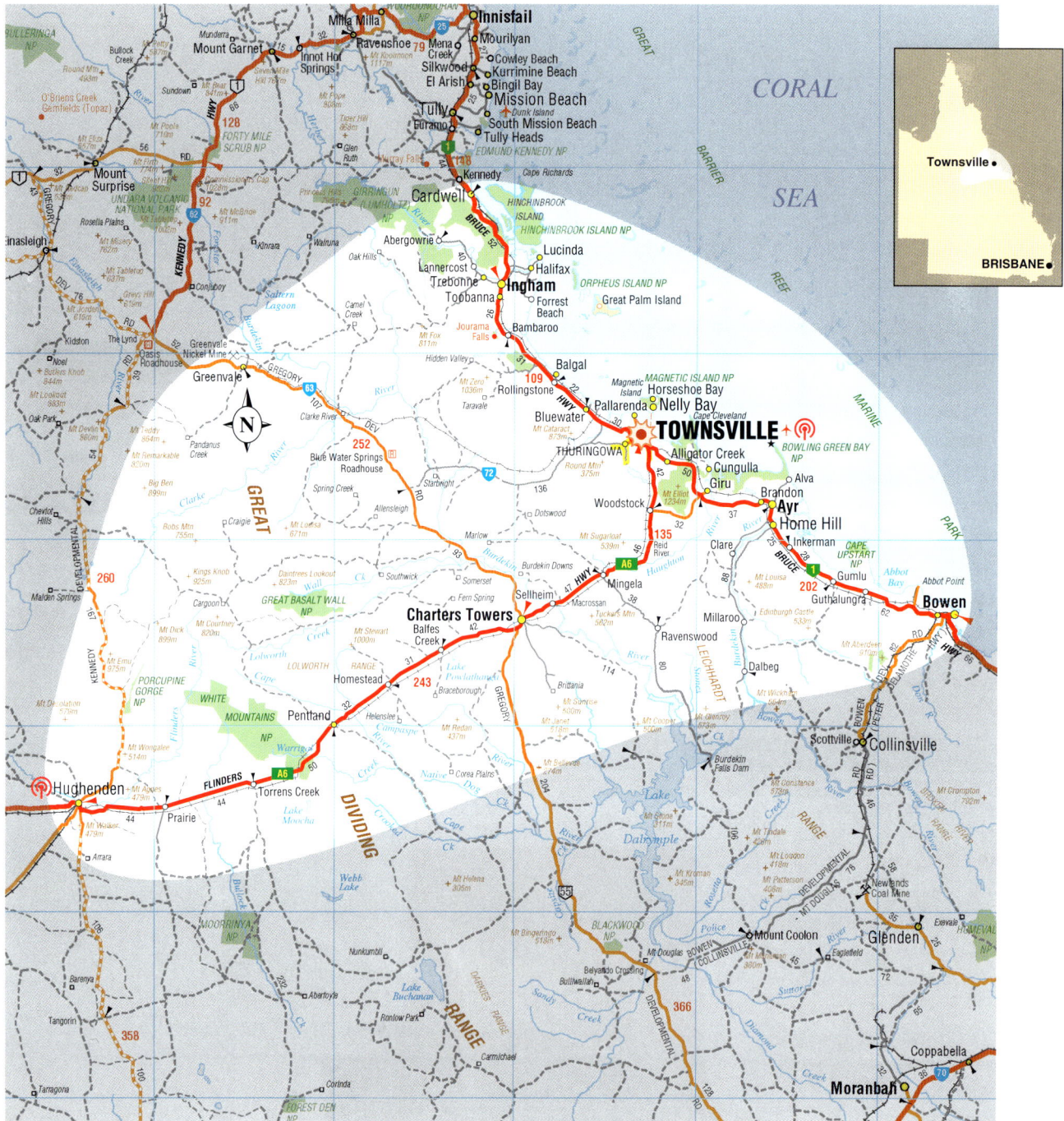

Location of ABC Local Radio studio

Towns in red have their own AM transmitter

TOURISM QUEENSLAND

Snorkelling on the Great Barrier Reef

N orth Queensland's stretches of sandy shoreline, warm tropical waters, bush-covered headlands and pockets of rainforest are an ideal holiday alternative to some of the Queensland coast's busier areas. The Great Barrier Reef and islands are accessible from several coastal points. Inland lie beautifully preserved historic towns.

It's a region of cattle and cane that also has a major military presence around its leading city, Townsville. James Cook University, a major tertiary institution, plays a crucial role in understanding and protecting northern Australia's remarkable environments, both aquatic and on land.

Bringing the world to this diverse community through its primary transmitter based at Brandon, south of Townsville, 630 ABC North Queensland broadcasts on the AM band. Built in the 1950s, it covers most of North and North-West Queensland and into parts of the Far North, and can be picked up as far away as Port Moresby in Papua New Guinea.

NOT TO BE MISSED

- Swim, saunter and savour the atmosphere at **The Strand**, a waterfront development in Townsville
- Explore the wonders of the Great Barrier Reef without getting wet, at **Reef HQ** in Townsville
- Dive the wreck of the **SS Yongala**, 16 kilometres off Cape Bowling Green

TOURISM QUEENSLAND

The Strand

- **Magnetic Island**'s Jazz Festival in October–November turns this idyllic island into one of the best venues in Australia to kick back and listen to live music.
- Hire a houseboat or yacht from **Cardwell** port and discover the beauty of the Great Barrier Reef and its islands
- Take a trip to the Wallaman Falls in the **Girringun (Lumholz) National Park** to see the fall's 305-metre sheer drop, the longest in Australia

TOURISM QUEENSLAND

Townsville

Townsville, with a population of just over 75 000, is one of Australia's largest tropical cities, and was settled in 1864 to service the cattle industry. The city's busy port handles minerals from Mount Isa and Cloncurry, beef and wool from the western plains, sugar and timber from the coastal regions and the products from its own manufacturing and processing industries. Northern Queensland's capital for administrative, commercial, educational and industrial activities, it has a reputation as a centre for research into marine life and is the headquarters for the Great Barrier Reef Marine Park Authority.

SIGHTS AND ACTIVITIES • Explore The Strand's tropical parks, waterfall, overhanging bougainvillea gardens and rock pool for year-round swimming • Try your luck at Jupiter's Townsville Hotel and Casino • Walk through the underwater viewing-tunnel at Reef HQ, which also features an aquarium with touch-tank • Cruise to Magnetic Island or take a day cruise on the reef • Catch the koala and crocodile feeding at The Billabong Sanctuary on the Bruce Highway • Visit Cotters Market in Flinders Mall (every Sunday) • Join a rainforest or white-water rafting tour

VISITOR INFORMATION
Bruce Highway (07) 4778 3555

LOCAL KNOWLEDGE

Strand ephemera

As part of the annual Townsville Arts Festival, every two years The Strand's popular walking track is turned into one long tropical art gallery. This exhibition, Strand Ephemera, includes pieces from local and international artists showcasing everything from frocked-up palm trees, to giant sun-worshippers to turf table settings.

MEET THE LOCALS

Do not disturb

One of the most majestic animals you're likely to come across in North Queensland – especially over summer – is the sea turtle. Turtles lay their eggs throughout the region at this time, and will nest anywhere from deserted beaches to Townsville's popular Strand. These animals must be treated with respect – keep your distance if you see a mother laying her eggs, and avoid using bright lights and camera flashes.

TOURISM QUEENSLAND

Cardwell

Great natural beauty is the main feature of Cardwell (population 1421). There are stunning views of Rockhampton Bay and the nearby islands of the Great Barrier Reef, and the channel between the mainland and Hinchinbrook Island is an excellent spot for fishing and snorkelling.

SIGHTS AND ACTIVITIES • Get acquainted with the regional landscape, flora and fauna at the Rainforest and Reef Information Centre in town before heading to the islands or taking one of the many walking tracks • Drive through Cardwell Forest for spectacular coastal vistas

VISITOR INFORMATION
142 Victoria Street (07) 4066 8601

Charters Towers

Queensland's second-biggest town during the 1870s gold rush, the population is now 8893 and the town showcases beautifully preserved buildings including the Bank of Commerce (restored as the World Theatre complex). Today, mining and cattle-raising are the main industries in the area, with several large gold mines still operating.

SIGHTS AND ACTIVITIES • Take a tour of the gold mines, the processing plants, the stock exchange or the museum • See the 'ghosts of gold' come alive at the Venus Battery • Discover the town's rich history by walking the preserved streetscapes of nineteenth- and twentieth-century architecture • Visit Towers Hill historic display

VISITOR INFORMATION
Mosman Street (07) 4752 0314

Ingham

A major sugar town (population 5012) near Hinchinbrook Island, Ingham has a strong Italian and Spanish Basque heritage. There are guided tours around the sugar mills available during the crushing season (July to November) and the Raintree Markets are held every third Sunday.

SIGHTS AND ACTIVITIES • Take a tour (July to November) of Victoria Sugar Mill • Visit Hinchinbrook Island, one of the world's largest national park islands

VISITOR INFORMATION
Cnr Bruce Highway and Lannercost Street (07) 4776 5211

LOCAL TIPS

- Try the fishing on the **Burdekin River** and **Groper Creek**. There are fishing charters available seeking barramundi, crabs and more

- Take a walking tour of **Innisfail**'s Art Deco buildings, such as the Shire Hall and Catholic Church, built after much of the town's buildings were lost in a severe cyclone in 1918

- Enjoy the healthy climate of **Magnetic Island**, with its relatively low humidity and remarkably constant warm temperatures that are particularly kind to arthritis sufferers

- On a clear day take a drive down the **Paluma Range** road with superb views from Windy Corner over Crystal Creek and out to sea.

LOCAL KNOWLEDGE

Anemones

Millions of people around the world fell in love with clown fish and sea anemones in the film *Finding Nemo*, but North Queensland scientist Dr Jackie Wolstenholme is far more passionate than most. She's been travelling Australia studying nearly 1000 different sea anemones, along the way becoming one of the world's only experts on the creatures. Sea anemones differ from other coral as they are a single invertebrate creature. Their beautiful colour and movement is not only attractive to scuba divers – plenty of reef fish call anemones home. See them at Townsville's superb Reef HQ.

MEET THE LOCALS

The thong man
Some people collect stamps, others collect teddy bears, but Alva local, Russell Doig has been collecting thongs for more than 10 years. He now has more than 4700 that he has picked up from his local beach, south of Townsville, and has created a 'fence of thongs' at his home. Russell says he finds small ones, big ones, coloured ones and even barnacled thongs. 'They just look good – especially now I've got 4700!' he says.

RUSSELL DOIG

ABC Far North

TOURISM QUEENSLAND

Local Radio Frequencies		
Atherton	720 AM	
Cairns	801 AM	
Daintree	639 AM	
Mossman	639 AM	
Thursday Island	1062 AM	
Weipa	1044 AM	
Babinda	94.1 FM	
Cairns	106.7 FM	
Cairns North	95.5 FM	
Cardwell	106.7 FM	630 AM North Queensland
Coen	105.9 FM	
Cooktown	105.7 FM	
Dimbulah	91.7 FM	
Edward River (Pormpuraaw)	106.1 FM	
Greenvale	105.9 FM	630 AM North Queensland
Innisfail	94.1 FM	106.7 FM
Kowanyama	106.1 FM	
Lakeland	106.1 FM	
Laura	106.1 FM	
Lockhart River	106.1 FM	
Mission Beach	89.3 FM	
Mount Garnet	95.7 FM	
Mount Molloy	95.7 FM	
Tully	95.5 FM	

Towns in red have their own AM transmitter
Towns in green have their own FM transmitter

Most of the remote northern regions of Australia are tremendously evocative places, and that's certainly the case with the Cape York Peninsula. The perception is that it's a wild, untamed place filled with crocodiles, frontier characters, mosquitoes and swamps. The reality is that it is a region of remarkable contrasts.

Fast-growing Cairns is the major city and one of the busiest tourism centres in the country. Contrast this with the distant Torres Strait islands, a thousand kilometres north, or Weipa on the Gulf of Carpentaria – incredibly remote communities often only accessible by air or sea when the wet season closes all overland access. Contrast this again with inland regions such as Chillagoe, in the semi-arid outback.

This is the extraordinary country where ABC Far North broadcasts. Transmissions go back to 1941 when the ABC took over station 4AT Atherton on 27 January 1941. ABC Far North's second transmitter, 4QY Cairns, came into service on 20 January 1950. The Far North region is home to a population of around 230 000 and the ABC coverage reflects the warm, friendly, tropical lifestyle of the people who choose to live in this much-envied corner of the world.

NOT TO BE MISSED

- White-water raft down the mighty **Tully River**
- Blow your budget at the **Kuranda** country markets
- Swim with giant groper among the coral of the **Great Barrier Reef**
- Explore the heritage-listed **Daintree National Park**
- Enjoy superb seafood from **Cardwell** to **Cape Tribulation**

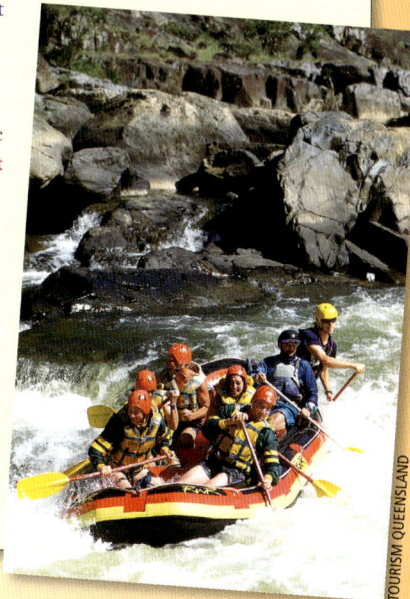

TOURISM QUEENSLAND

LOCAL EVENTS

May **Chillagoe:** Races, Concert and Festival
Kuranda: Folk Festival
Port Douglas: Village Carnivale

June **Cardwell:** Coral Sea Memorial
Cooktown: Endeavour Festival; Rodeo at nearby Helenvale
Mission Beach: Mudfest (music and culture festival)

July **Atherton:** Agricultural Show
Cairns: Agricultural Show
Innisfail: Agricultural Show; Harvest Festival
Mareeba: Rodeo
Chillagoe: Tablelands Country Music Festival
Tully: Agricultural Show

Aug **Mission Beach:** Banana Festival

Sept **Cairns:** Festival
Mareeba: Air Show
Torres Strait: Cultural Festival (Thursday Island, even-numbered years)

Oct **Kuranda:** Festival
Mareeba: Country Music Festival (even-numbered years)
Mission Beach: Aquatic Festival

Nov **Mossman:** Music Festival
Tully: Rodeo

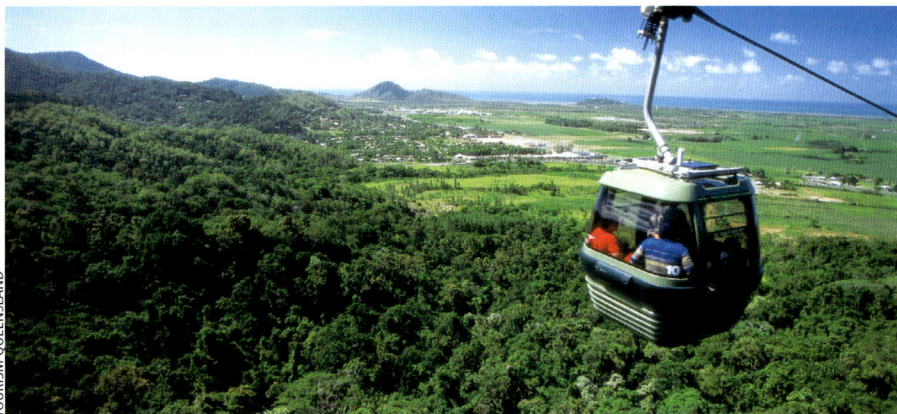

TOURISM QUEENSLAND

Cairns

Considered the capital of the region, Cairns is a fast-growing city with a population of 92 273. Cairns has it all – the Great Barrier Reef just offshore, incredible beaches to the north and south, and the rainforest-clad Great Dividing Range to the west. Oh, and fantastic seafood everywhere, and a cosmopolitan mix of local artists and tourists from all over the world.

SIGHTS AND ACTIVITIES • Absorb the effect this region has on artists at the superb Cairns Regional Gallery • Soar above the rainforest on the Skyrail Cableway to Kuranda, then return on the Scenic Railway • Immerse yourself in an ancient culture at the multi-award winning Tjapukai Aboriginal Cultural Park • Game-fish for the prized black marlin • Marvel at the beauty and diversity of tropical plants and bird life at the superb Flecker Botanic Gardens • Embark on the many tours to the islands, the inland and much, much more

VISITOR INFORMATION
51 The Esplanade (07) 4051 3588

Atherton

A mild tropical climate awaits in Tableland towns such as Atherton (population 5693). The rich agricultural land here is studded with pockets of rainforest, crater lakes and fascinating old mining towns.

SIGHTS AND ACTIVITIES • Discover local history and heritage at the Old Post Office Gallery and Chinese Heritage Museum • See beautiful timber works at nearby Tolga • Hike around or cruise on the crater lakes • Try to work out how people live in the tiny miner's cottages at Irvinebank

VISITOR INFORMATION
Cnr Silo Road and Main Street (07) 4091 4222

MEET THE LOCALS

Seaman Dan

He's been singing all his life but it wasn't until his seventies that Torres Strait elder, Seaman Dan was 'discovered'. A producer heard one of his songs, with blues, jazz and island music influences, and three albums – such as *Perfect Pearl* – have so far been the result. You may even be lucky enough to see Dan in performance around Torres Strait venues.

Cooktown

Famous as the site where Captain Cook beached the *Endeavour* in 1770, it was a gold-rush town of 18 000 in the 1870s, but now has a population of 1411.

SIGHTS AND ACTIVITIES • Replenish your supplies before heading north into the wilds of Cape York • Find out how good the fishing is off the wharf, which dates from 1880 • See an anchor from the *Endeavour* at the James Cook historical museum

VISITOR INFORMATION
101 Charlotte Street (07) 4069 5446

Mission Beach

Just one of the many beautiful beaches found to the north and south of Cairns, Mission Beach (population 1013) is now a haven for artists and craftspeople. It also has one of the best youth hostels in the country. The Barrier Reef is at its closest to the mainland here.

SIGHTS AND ACTIVITIES
• Take a water taxi to Dunk Island, or hire a catamaran and sail there • Keep a lookout for cassowaries on the Lacey Creek walking trail • Take a day cruise to fish or snorkel the reef

VISITOR INFORMATION
Porters Promenade
(07) 4068 7099

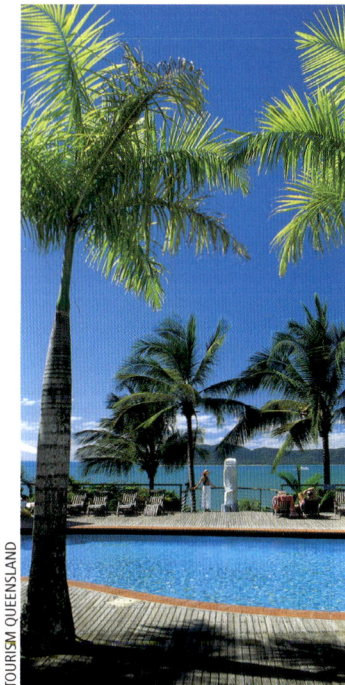

TOURISM QUEENSLAND

Resort, Mission Beach

LOCAL KNOWLEDGE
Controversial footwear
As part of its claim to have the highest ever annual rainfall in Australia, Tully's main street boasts the recently erected giant gumboot. The claim comes from a very wet year back in the 1950s but it's disputed by Babinda, which has the highest average annual rainfall. Now that Tully has thrown down the gumboot, how will Babinda answer the challenge? Maybe they'll line the main street with umbrella trees.

MEET THE LOCALS
Starshine
While doing the rounds of the galleries and cafes in Kuranda, take a moment to call in to the Kuranda Bat Rescue Centre. There you may meet Starshine, an extremely rare albino freetail bat, brought in after being attacked by a cat, and one of many bats being nursed back to health.

MEET THE LOCALS
Tractors
There are some things you just can't do without a tractor, and at Kurrimine, one of them is to go fishing. To launch and retrieve their boats, most of the locals have old tractors. And they're not rusty hulks. If you're in town, keep an eye out for the best-presented pride and joy. Make the right noises and you might get a free fish.

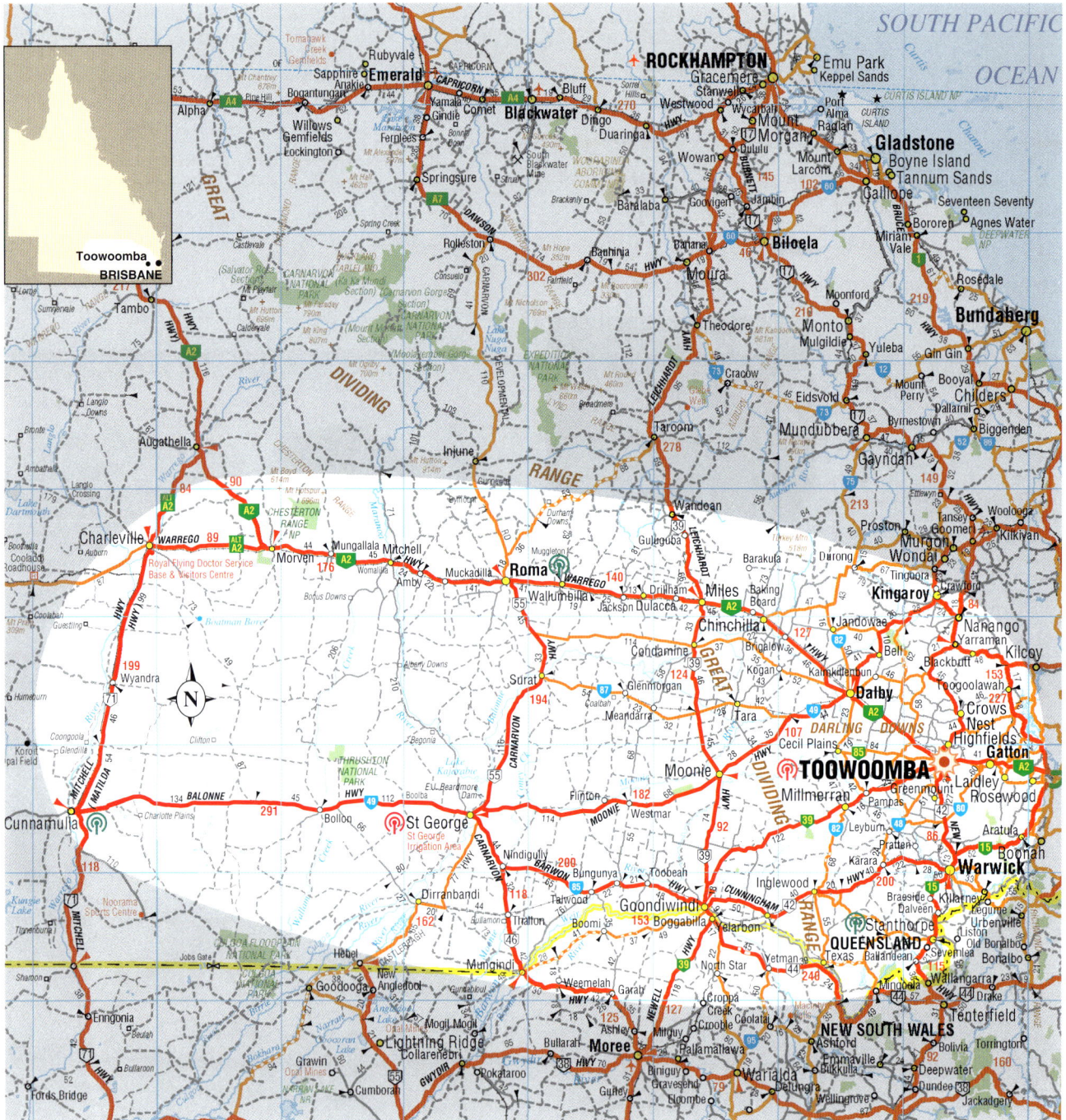

Location of ABC Local Radio studio

Local Radio Frequencies		
Boonah	747 AM	
Charleville	711 AM	603 AM
		540 AM ABC Western Queensland
Chinchilla	747 AM	
Crows Nest	747 AM	
Dalby	747 AM	
Gatton	747 AM	
Kilcoy	747 AM	
Kingaroy	747 AM	
Laidley	747 AM	
Miles	747 AM	
Mitchell	711 AM	106.1 FM ABC Western Queensland
Nanango	747 AM	
Rosewood	747 AM	
St George	711 AM	
Toowoomba	747 AM	
Wandoan	747 AM	98.1 FM ABC Western Queensland
Cunnamulla	106.1 FM	
Goondiwindi	92.7 FM	711 AM, 747 AM
Roma	105.7 FM	711 AM
Southern Downs (Stanthorpe)	104.9 FM	
Texas	104.9 FM	
Warwick	104.9 FM	

(radio icon) Towns in red have their own AM transmitter
(radio icon) Towns in green have their own FM transmitter

Towns in the east of this region may also receive 612 AM ABC Brisbane.

Blooms abound in the garden city of Toowoomba

TOURISM QUEENSLAND

S tretching from the eastern side of the Great Dividing Range on the edge of Brisbane, west over the rolling hills of the Darling Downs and on to the beginnings of Queensland's vast inland plain, ABC Southern Queensland is in the heartland of the State's prosperous agricultural industry. Everything from sheep, cattle and wheat to wine and famous horse studs can be found in this bountiful place.

Toowoomba in particular is the jewel of the region, renowned for its stunning gardens and parklands, which thrive due to the city's position atop the range and the rich soils that abound in the area. The other main towns – Roma, Warwick, Dalby, St George, Kingaroy, Stanthorpe and Goondiwindi – are also prosperous today while preserving a fascinating heritage.

ABC Local Radio's Toowoomba 4QS was established in 1948, and since then has been an integral part of this rich and varied community. Half a dozen transmitters now service the area from the rugged mountain ranges to the vast sweeping plains. ABC Southern Queensland is still headquartered in Toowoomba, but draws reports and a listening audience of hundreds of thousands from an area of many hundreds of square kilometres.

NOT TO BE MISSED

- Picnic with spectacular views at Toowoomba's **Picnic Point**
- Enjoy the beautiful public and private gardens around **Toowoomba**
- Step back in time at **Jondaryan Woolshed**, which has several other historic farm buildings
- Enjoy **Warwick**'s historic architecture
- Marvel at mountain scenery and waterfalls in the **Main Range National Park**, such as Queen Mary Falls
- Discover the Granite Country wineries around **Stanthorpe**

Jondaryan woolshed

TOURISM QUEENSLAND

Cobb & Co. Museum

Toowoomba

The major centre of the Darling Downs (population 83 350) is no drab service town. Toowoomba has a classic charm in its colonial architecture, a passion for beautiful parks and gardens, and a cosmopolitan style in its compact city centre.

SIGHTS AND ACTIVITIES • Relive the days of Cobb & Co. at the Cobb & Co Museum • Take a tour of the finest parks and gardens (brochure available) • Join the tens of thousands who celebrate the annual Carnival of Flowers in September • Visit historic towns and wineries around Dalby, Crows Nest, Warwick, Killarney and Stanthorpe

VISITOR INFORMATION
Cnr James and Kitchener streets (07) 4639 3797

Cunnamulla

On the far western edge of the ABC Southern Queensland listening area, Cunnamulla (population 1461), a major wool-handling centre, is celebrated in song and folklore.

SIGHTS AND ACTIVITIES • See The Robber's Tree, where bank robber Joseph Wells was bailed up in 1880 after he couldn't find his getaway horse • Enjoy the Outback Botanic Gardens and Herbarium • Keep an eye out for brolgas, swans, pelicans and eagles around nearby wetlands

VISITOR INFORMATION
Centenary Park, Jane Street (07) 4655 2481

Goondiwindi

A major crossroads on the beautiful Macintyre River and the New South Wales-Queensland border, Goondiwindi (population 4374) is also the centre of thriving cotton, wheat, beef and wool industries.

SIGHTS AND ACTIVITIES • Meet the famous 'Goondiwindi Grey' racehorse, Gunsynd, whose statue adorns Apex Park • Take a pleasant walk along the riverside walking track (brochure available)

VISITOR INFORMATION
Cnr McLean and Bowen streets (07) 4671 2653

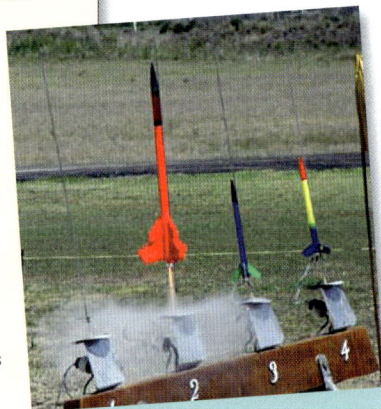

LOCAL KNOWLEDGE

Space program

Space, as they say, is the final frontier, and the last place you'd expect to find its explorers is Toowoomba. Yet the local Space Pilots Club is thought to be the oldest rocketry club outside the United States. For an uplifting experience all you need is a wide open space, and the sky's the limit.

Kingaroy

Famous for its peanut growing and for being the former home of Sir Johannes Bjelke-Petersen, Kingaroy (population 7013) is at the centre of an incredibly fertile agricultural region. It also has wineries and great scenic drives. Kingaroy's peanut silos are the town's most famous landmark.

SIGHTS AND ACTIVITIES • Take in the superb scenery of the Bunya Mountains • Watch videos about the peanut and navy-bean industries at the information centre • Stroll through rainforest in Bunya Mountains National Park to Pine Gorge Lookout, go bird-watching and see stands of Bunya pines

VISITOR INFORMATION
128 Haly Street (07) 4162 3199

Roma

The gateway to Western Queensland, Roma (population 5744) is rich in historic buildings and events, dating from the establishment of the first cattle property in 1847. Cattle and sheep continue to dominate the economy, but oil and gas exploration have joined them.

SIGHTS AND ACTIVITIES • See how they struck oil at the Big Rig complex, which includes a slab hut from 1893 • Marvel at the town's bottle trees, planted in memory of World War I casualties • Tipple at one of Queensland's oldest wineries • Admire the classic Queensland colonial buildings that abound

TOURISM QUEENSLAND

Bottle trees near Roma

VISITOR INFORMATION
2 Riggers Road (07) 4622 4355

St George

Situated at a major road junction, St George (population 2463) is on the edge of the wide open spaces of the outback. The town is regarded as the inland fishing capital of the State. Local waterways also supply local irrigation projects.

SIGHTS AND ACTIVITIES • Wet a line in the Balonne River or nearby dams and waterways • Thread your way to Cubbie Station, the largest private cotton property in the State (tours available)

VISITOR INFORMATION
Cnr The Terrace and Roe Street (07) 4620 8877

LOCAL TIPS

- **St George** is considered the inland fishing capital of Queensland – the rivers in the surrounding area are a great place to wet a line
- For coffee aficionados, **Toowoomba** has its own coffee roaster and uses it to roast beans imported from around the world
- For a classic outback pub experience, visit **Hebel**, on the New South Wales-Queensland border (Lightning Ridge is just to the south as well)
- Head north from Roma and enjoy a great drive through the Carnarvon Range and a visit to **Carnarvon Gorge**

LOCAL KNOWLEDGE

Driving dog sleds without snow
Winter in the Downs may be cold, but usually not cold enough for snow. Nevertheless, you can still see the local variation of dog-sled racing. Visit the Northern Exposure Gig Racing Club events in south-east Queensland and you'll see huskies and malamutes pulling scooters. The dogs love the competition and can pull a 'sled' 4 kilometres in just 15 minutes.

MEET THE LOCALS

The Light Horse
They were the best of the best, and their feats in the battles of World War I have become the stuff of legend. Keeping that legend alive are 30 Light Horse Troops comprising 850 members around Australia, such as this one in Toowoomba. They stage re-enactments, participate in ANZAC Day and engage in the same tests of skill as the original troops. The 11th Light Horse of Toowoomba has several former Light Horsemen ranging in age from 80 into their 90s, who still attend activities.

JESSICA DALY

GULF OF CARPENTARIA

CORAL

BARRIER

REEF

Longreach

BRISBANE

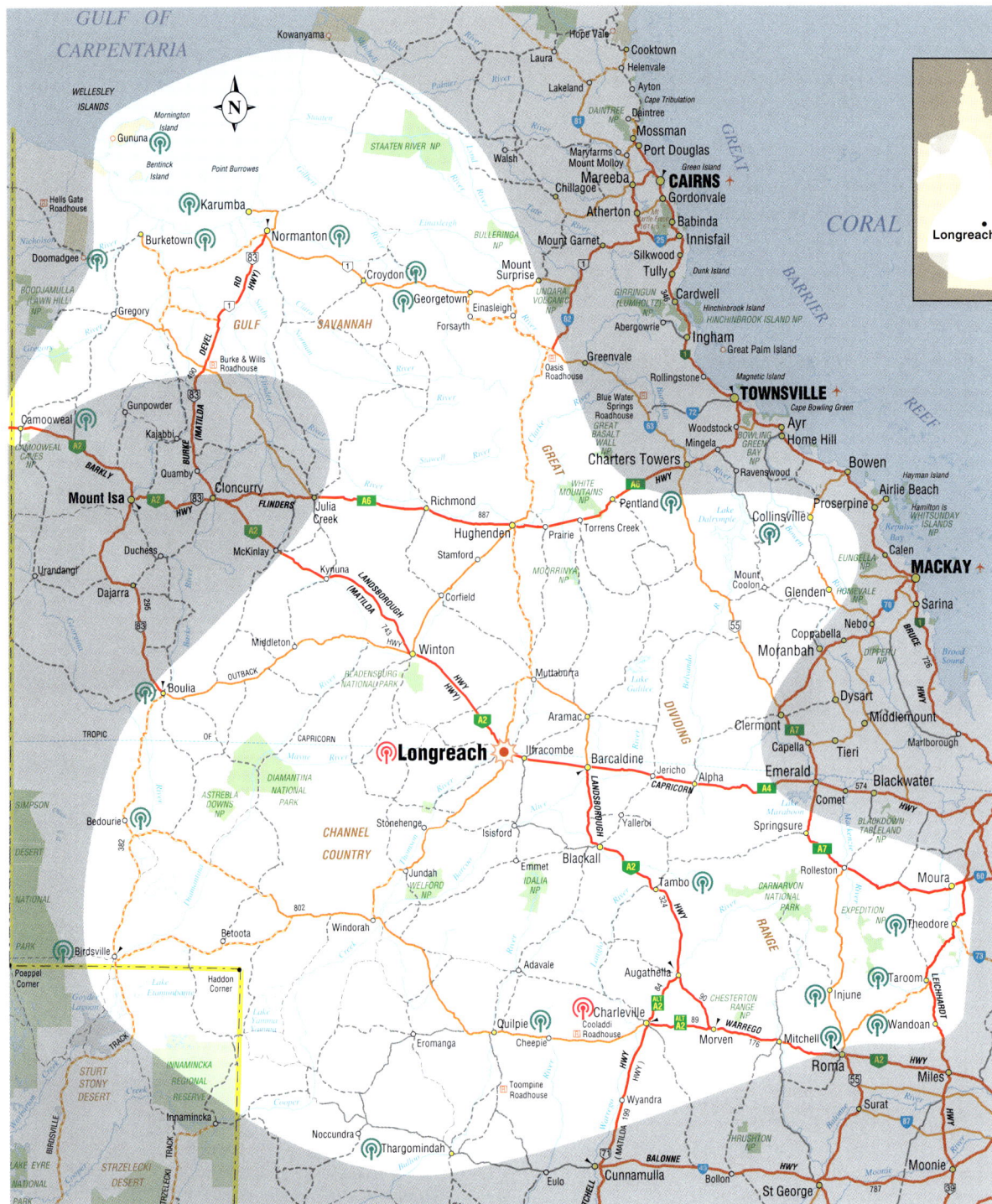

Location of ABC Local Radio studio

The broadcast area for ABC Western Queensland covers around two-thirds of the State – it's one of the largest broadcast zones in the southern hemisphere. The region is remote, sparsely populated and – in parts – stunningly beautiful. Many of the stories and legends of Australia's pioneering days were born here, and the themes of mateship, egalitarianism and a fair go are celebrated in the region's museums and monuments. The major industries are sheep and cattle grazing, and tourism. There are a few remote mining communities in the region extracting coal, opal and zinc.

ABC Local Radio is a vital part of life in this rural and remote part of the State. Whether it's a fire or a flood, or breaking news that affects the nation, for many people the ABC is the only daily medium of news and information. Consequently, ABC Western Queensland has very close connections with its audience.

Major towns in the region are Longreach (the base for ABC Western Queensland), Barcaldine, Birdsville, Charleville, Normanton and Winton.

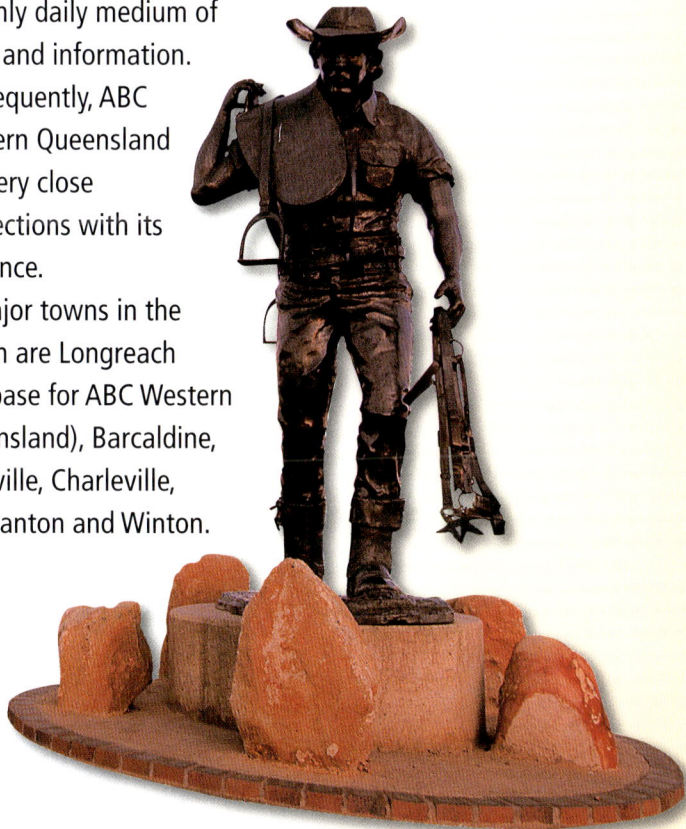

Stockman's Hall of Fame statue

Local Radio Frequencies

Alpha	540 AM	105.7 FM ABC Central Queensland 1548 AM ABC Central Queensland
Augathella	603 AM	
Barcaldine	540 AM	
Blackall	540 AM	
Charleville	603 AM	
Corfield	540 AM	
Isisford	540 AM	
Jericho	540 AM	
Longreach	540 AM	
Morven	603 AM	
Muttaburra	540 AM	
Winton	540 AM	
Bedourie	105.9 FM	540 AM
Birdsville	106.1 FM	540 AM
Boulia	106.1 FM	540 AM
Burketown	96.3 FM	567 AM ABC North West Queensland
Camooweal	106.1 FM	567 AM ABC North West Queensland
Collinsville	106.1 FM	540 AM 630 AM ABC North Queensland
Croydon	105.7 FM	567 AM ABC North West Queensland
Doomadgee	97.5 FM	567 AM ABC North West Queensland
Georgetown	106.1 FM	567 AM ABC North West Queensland
Gununa	92.7 FM	
Injune	105.9 FM	711 AM ABC Southern Queensland
Karumba	106.1 FM	567 AM ABC North West Queensland
Mitchell	106.1 FM	603 AM 711 AM ABC Southern Queensland
Normanton	105.7 FM	567 AM ABC North West Queensland
Pentland	106.1 FM	540 AM 630 AM ABC North Queensland
Quilpie	106.1 FM	540 AM 603 AM
Tambo	105.9 FM	540 AM 603 AM
Taroom	106.1 FM	855 AM ABC Wide Bay
Thargomindah	106.1 FM	540 AM 603 AM
Theodore	105.9 FM	855 AM ABC Wide Bay
Wandoan	98.1 FM	711 AM ABC Southern Queensland

Towns in red have their own AM transmitter
Towns in green have their own FM transmitter

NOT TO BE MISSED

- Explore the Stockman's Hall of Fame, **Longreach**
- Visit the Australian Workers Heritage Centre, **Barcaldine**
- Fish for barramundi in the **Gulf of Carpentaria**
- Waltz Matilda at **Winton**'s Waltzing Matilda Centre
- Climb Big Red, one of the giant sand dunes near **Birdsville**

TOURISM QUEENSLAND

Stockman's Hall of Fame

Longreach

Situated on the Thompson River, Longreach (population 3766) is the major centre of the Western Queensland region, and the headquarters of the region's ABC. It is also the centre for major sheep, cattle and transport industries.

SIGHTS AND ACTIVITIES ● See the Stockman's Hall of Fame and Outback Heritage Centre on the Matilda Highway and be impressed by this tribute to the men and women who opened up outback Australia for settlement, industry and agriculture ● Visit Banjo's Outback Theatre and Shearing Shed ● Discover the history of the second oldest airline in the world at the Qantas Founders Outback Heritage Museum at the airport ● Cycle through the Botanical Gardens ● Camp beside the billabong in true outback style at Broadwater Hole in Lochern National Park ● Enjoy the scenic view from Starlight's Lookout

VISITOR INFORMATION
Qantas Park, Eagle Street
(07) 4658 3555

MEET THE LOCALS

Hilton Jackson

It's hard to miss Hilton Jackson's house when passing through the tiny town of Ilfracombe between Longreach and Barcaldine. Outside is a collection of more than 15 000 items, including hubcaps, machinery and bottles like this Italian bottle with a clock in it. Hilton knows where every item is and will not part with a single one.

Mad Mick's Funny Farm

Barcaldine

Known as the Garden City of the West, thanks to its artesian water supply, Barcaldine (population 1592) is also considered by many to be the birthplace of the Australian Labor Party, in part thanks to the labour movement that grew around the shearers' strikes of the 1890s.

SIGHTS AND ACTIVITIES • Visit the 'Tree of Knowledge', a huge ghost gum where the shearers met in 1891 • See Mad Mick's Funny Farm

VISITOR INFORMATION
Oak Street (07) 4651 1724

Birdsville

One of Western Queensland's most remote towns, Birdsville is also one of its best known. It's a vital stop at the northern end of the Birdsville Track and for those intent on exploring the Simpson Desert to the west. Its population of 100 swells in the first weekend in September, when the Birdsville Races are held and around 6000 visitors come to town.

VISITOR INFORMATION
Wirrarri Centre, Billabong Boulevard (07) 4656 3300

LOCAL TIPS

- In **Longreach** meet the locals at the Seat of Knowledge (also known as the Senate) in the main street, where opinions of the day are discussed
- For sunsets, the big sky country on the open roads to **Jundah** are unsurpassed
- Near **Aramac**, visit the old coach stop at Grey Rock, where travellers have been carving their initials for nearly a century
- Lily Lagoon, near **Longreach**, has beautiful flora and birdlife

- A good spot for a picnic in **Jericho** is in the riverside park behind the school; there's also a walking trail to a small 'beach' and an island where the rare rufous heron is sometimes spotted
- At the open-top cinema in **Winton** you can see stars on screen and sparkling above

MEET THE TEDDIES
In Tambo

It may look like just another place for a break in your long journey across Western Queensland, but don't just slow down in the town of Tambo. Keep an eye out for teddy bears. This is the home of the Tambo Teddies, and the 'outback Teddy capital of Australia'. Prized locally and internationally, they're made from local wool and named after properties in the district or early settlers. They can also be dressed in moleskins, check shirts and 'Bear-as-a-bones'.

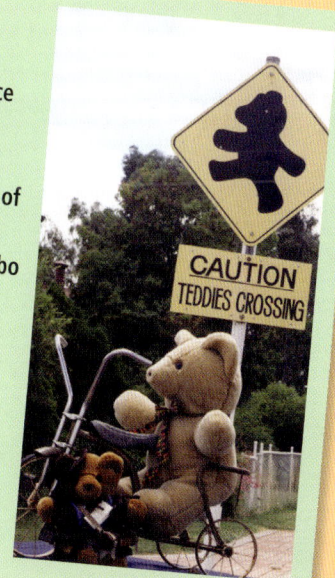

The singing fence

As part of the Queensland Festival of Music, held in 2003, percussionist Graeme Leak created a 'musical fence' in Winton that 'sings' to visitors. The fence uses wires strung just like a piano, or a guitar, but they do need amplification. It was built in two 30-metre sections, each with five strings and a resonator.

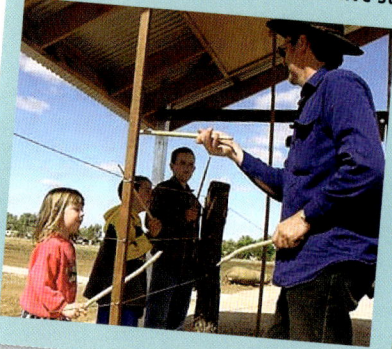

The fence is played using a variety of instruments such as sticks and bows. The creator has gone, but the fence still stands and can be played by any visitor to the area, or the wind can play it alone.

Reptiles race on the Paroo Track

Bidding is furious and alcohol flows freely in the south-west of the State when Eulo holds its annual World Lizard Racing Championships. For 36 years the locals have been catching, naming and tagging the lizards. Entrants bid for the lizards with the most interesting names, such as 'Matilda Highway' and 'Billabong'. Once the lizards are released into a roped-off circle, many just freeze initially. Eventually most usually make it over the line and some even make it into the spectator area. When the race ends, the lizards are released back into the wild – perhaps to race again another year.

TOURISM QUEENSLAND

One of Charleville's historic hotels, Corones

Charleville

The major town in the southern section of the Western Queensland region, Charleville (population 3327) has a history that reaches back to the days of Cobb & Co., and the first flight from London to Australia in 1919. Its main industries are sheep and cattle.

SIGHTS AND ACTIVITIES ● Visit the Royal Flying Doctor Service base ● See the Cobb & Co. craft shop ● Tour the night sky at Skywatch ● Visit the Historic House Museum ● Attend the Great Matilda Camel Races in July

VISITOR INFORMATION
Sturt Street (07) 4654 3057

The pub without a town ... but with parking meters

One-pub-towns are common in Western Queensland but what about 'no-town-pubs'? During the opal mining boom, the pub called Toompine (pictured) near Quilpie was the main Cobb & Co. stop before Charleville. Now it sits on 4000 hectares, has a cricket pitch, a golf course, a tennis court, lots of cows and a community hall.

The two parking meters here – the only two in the west – are not there to control parking, but to aid the Flying Doctor. And while the opal miners don't come anymore, the tourists and the local community do.

Normanton

The major town of the Gulf Savannah, Normanton (population 1328) is just south of the Gulf of Carpentaria. Nearby wetlands attract bird-watchers and its famous train attracts train buffs, but it's the fishing in the area that really draws the crowds.

SIGHTS AND ACTIVITIES • See the replica of Krys the Savannah King, an 8.6-metre crocodile • Admire the water birds on the nearby lakes • Take the Gulflander train from Normanton to Croydon

VISITOR INFORMATION
Shire Offices, Haig Street (07) 4754 1166

Winton

For a little town, Winton (population 1142) has played a big part in Australian history: it's the birthplace of Qantas and of Banjo Paterson's 'Waltzing Matilda'. You can relive much of that history at several local museums and exhibits.

SIGHTS AND ACTIVITIES • Catch a movie at the Historic Royal Theatre, an open-air theatre and museum • See the waterhole where Banjo Paterson wrote 'Waltzing Matilda' • Visit the Waltzing Matilda Centre • Discover Winton's role in the birth of Australia's national airline at the Qantilda Museum

VISITOR INFORMATION
Waltzing Matilda Centre, Elderslie Street (07) 4657 1466

TOURISM QUEENSLAND

MEET THE LOCALS

Few common names for many ants

Western Queensland is very familiar with insects, and there's always a trail of ants running over the kitchen counter. But did you know there are many hundreds of species of ant in Western Queensland, most of which haven't been named? This one is a red cocktail ant; keep an eye out for muscle-man tree ants, goblin ants, fierce gremlin ants and jumbuck sugar ants.

LOCAL KNOWLEDGE
Outback drive-in

It's pretty hard to find a drive-in around Queensland where you can still catch the latest double feature, and you'd think one of the least likely places to find one would be in outback Queensland. The Jericho drive-in opened 30 years ago and is still going strong. It can hold 36 cars and has further seating for 36 people at the back. It is now used for fundraising, and the community still snuggles up in the back of a ute to see the latest movies.

PETER JACKLYN

ABC North West Queensland

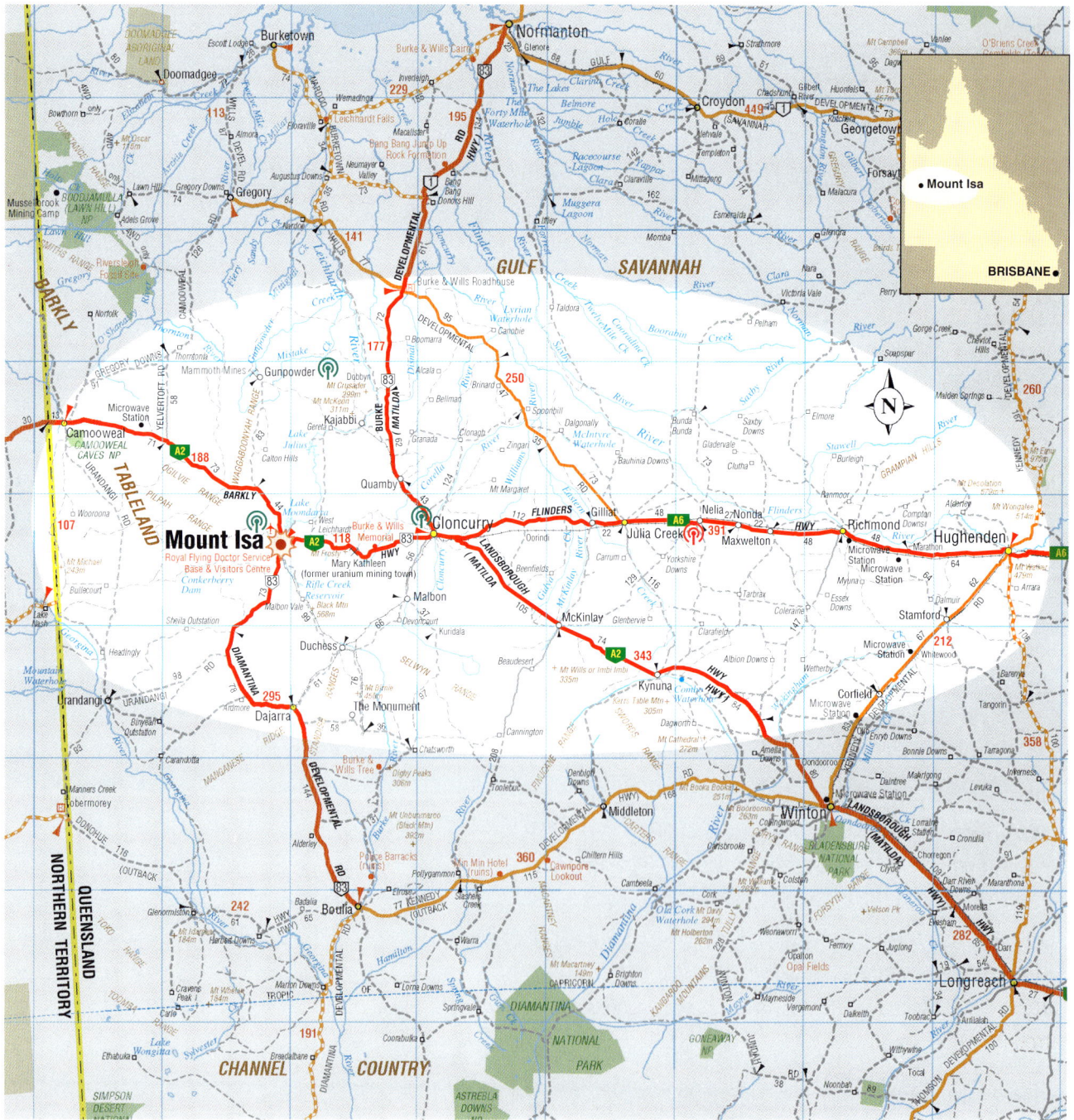

☀ Location of ABC Local Radio studio

Local Radio Frequencies

Burketown	567 AM	96.3 FM ABC Western Queensland
Camooweal	567 AM	106.1 FM ABC Western Queensland
Croydon	567 AM	105.9 FM ABC Western Queensland
Doomadgee	567 AM	97.5 FM Western Queensland
Georgetown	567 AM	106.1 FM ABC Western Queensland
Hughenden	567 AM	1485 AM ABC North Queensland 540 AM ABC Western Queensland
Julia Creek	567 AM	540 AM ABC Western Queensland
Karumba	567 AM	106.1 FM ABC Western Queensland
Kynuna	567 AM	540 AM ABC Western Queensland
McKinlay	567 AM	
Normanton	567 AM	105.7 FM ABC Western Queensland
Richmond	567 AM	540 AM ABC Western Queensland
Cloncurry	100.5 FM	567 AM 540 AM ABC Western Queensland
Gunpowder	106.1 FM	567 AM 540 AM ABC Western Queensland
Mount Isa	106.5 FM	567 AM 540 AM ABC Western Queensland

(◉) Julia Creek has the only AM transmitter in the region
(◉) Towns in green have their own FM transmitter

The popular Mount Isa Rotary Rodeo is held in August each year

TOURISM QUEENSLAND

ABC North West Queensland covers a large region of outback Queensland. The largest city, Mount Isa, has a population of just over 21 000 and is home to one of Queensland's largest companies, Xstrata Copper which operates Mount Isa Mine. The city is also the service centre for a number of other mining projects in Queensland's north-west. Other significant industries in the region include live cattle exports from Karumba and fishing in the Gulf of Carpentaria.

This remote and sparsely populated region extends from the northern lagoons and mangrove-lined estuaries of the Gulf of Carpentaria, south to fossil-strewn landforms punctuating the vast surrounding plains. Tourism plays a big part in this region, with attractions including the Riversleigh Fossil Centre, Kronasaurus Korner, John Flynn Place, the Royal Flying Doctor Service Base in Mount Isa and Lawn Hill (Boodjamulla) National Park.

NOT TO BE MISSED

- See the land through Aboriginal eyes at the **Kalkadoon Tribal Centre and Cultural Keeping Place**, Mount Isa
- Tour the World Heritage-listed **Riversleigh** fossil fields
- Visit **Lawn Hill Gorge**, the main attraction at the remote Lawn Hill (Boodjamulla) National Park
- Discover the history of the Royal Flying Doctor Service at the **RFDS Museum** in John Flynn Place, Cloncurry
- See some of the world's best marine fossils at **Kronasaurus Korner** in Richmond, on what's known as the fossil trail

TOURISM QUEENSLAND

Lawn Hill Gorge

TOURISM QUEENSLAND

Mount Isa

Mount Isa (population 21 751) is the most important industrial, commercial and administrative centre in north-west Queensland. Mount Isa Mine is one the world's largest silver-lead mines, and also processes and mines copper and zinc.

SIGHTS AND ACTIVITIES • Don't miss the Mount Isa Rotary Rodeo in August, reputed to be the world's third-largest rodeo, attracting rough-riders from all over Queensland and almost doubling the town's population • Be guided through town by the lead smelter stack – at 265 metres it is Australia's tallest freestanding structure • Visit Hard Times Mine and explore the mining tunnels and the town's history • Take a tour of the underground hospital built during World War II • Meet 20-million-year-old locals at the Riversleigh Fossil Centre.

VISITOR INFORMATION
Riversleigh Fossil Centre, Centenary Park, Marian Street
(07) 4749 1555

Pilot Bruce Waller (right) with RFDS Base Manager Steve Griffiths

MEET THE LOCALS
Royal Flying Doctor Service pilot
A 2.30am callout is probably the least of Bruce Waller's concerns as a senior pilot for the Mount Isa RFDS. The tough part is landing at a bush air strip for the first time in total darkness. 'When the area covered by the Mount Isa base is more than 500 000 square kilometres, there's every chance each trip will bring unexpected challenges', says Bruce. Find out more by visiting the RFDS base and visitors centre in Mount Isa.

MEET THE LOCALS
An old fossil
This toothy local is a pliosaur, a marine creature that thankfully prowled the oceans 100 million years ago. On a property just near Richmond, the best example of a fossilised pliosaur was found in 1989, and has been followed by numerous other superb fossil finds. Many of them can be seen at Richmond's Kronosaurus Korner, part of the Fossil Trail and one of the world's best marine-fossil museums.

QUEENSLAND MUSEUM

Cloncurry

An important mining town in the Gulf Savannah region, Cloncurry (population 2459) became the first base for the famous Royal Flying Doctor Service in 1928.

SIGHTS AND ACTIVITIES • Explore the history of one of Australia's most respected services at the RFDS Museum • Enjoy the cultural centre, outdoor cinema and take a stroll through Cloncurry Gardens • Visit the Fred McKay Art Gallery • See the town history and a comprehensive rock mineral and gem collection in the buildings at Mary Kathleen Memorial Park • Check out the Gidgee Inn, a new hotel made of rammed earth and local timber

VISITOR INFORMATION
Mary Kathleen Memorial Park, McIlwraith Street (07) 4742 1361

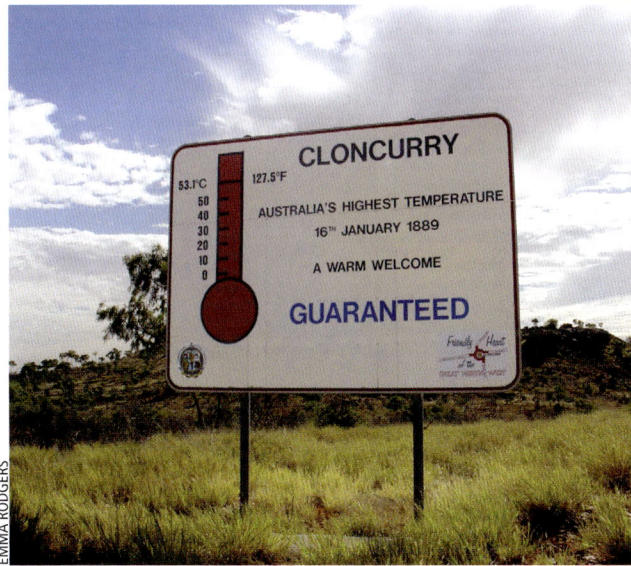

CLONCURRY

53.1°C   127.5°F
50
40
30
20
10

AUSTRALIA'S HIGHEST TEMPERATURE
16TH JANUARY 1889

A WARM WELCOME

GUARANTEED

EMMA RODGERS

Julia Creek

With a population of only 519, Julia Creek with its saleyards and trucking facilities is nevertheless a vital hub for the cattle industry. It's also the gateway to the Gulf Savannah country to the north.

SIGHTS AND ACTIVITIES • See the Duncan McIntyre Museum for local history • Visit the Dunnart Craft Store for regional art and craft

VISITOR INFORMATION
Council Offices, 29 Burke Street (07) 4658 6133

LOCAL TIPS

- **Richmond** is considered one of the most attractive towns in the region and is renowned for its ancient ammonite marine fossils
- The Combo waterhole of 'Waltzing Matilda' fame is just outside the town of **Kynuna**
- There's great **fishing** to be had in the Nicholson, Albert, Flinders, Norman and Gilbert rivers
- If you want to take the popular tour of the **Mount Isa** mine, book well in advance
- Moon rocks are found in many areas around **Julia Creek**
- There are accessible Aboriginal art sites in **Lawn Hill (Boodjamulla) National Park**

LOCAL KNOWLEDGE

Annual International Mining Challenge

Blood, sweat and tears are spilt at the International Mining Challenge in Mount Isa. With a $60 000 prize purse up for grabs, teams of five race against the clock to complete mining tasks such as gold panning, hand steeling, hand mucking and track laying. Strict rules apply, with some teams disqualified for failing to follow safety precautions such as wearing glasses and hard hats.

MEET THE LOCALS

The Freckletons

On the long road across the Barkly Tableland, break your journey at one of the most remote general stores in the country, in the tiny town of Camooweal. And while you're there, have a chat to Joseph Freckleton, who runs the store with his sister. They're in the best position to tell you all about Camooweal as they took over from their father, who ran the store from around the end of World War II.

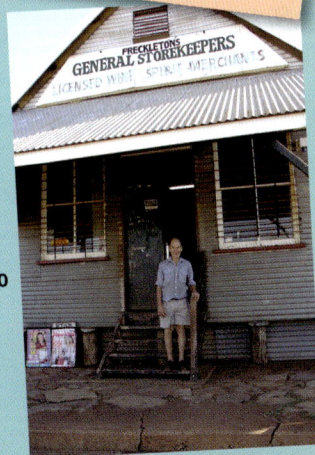

EMMA RODGERS

Index of Place Names

A page number set in **bold** type indicates the main text entry for that place.

Acknowledgements

Meet the Locals would not have been possible without the considerable efforts of the hard-working team who brought the project to fruition.

Writers: Evan McHugh and Kate Groth

Editor: Fran Church, EdInk Pty Ltd

Assistant Editor: Miriam Cannell

Art Director: Peter Dyson, P.A.G.E. Pty Ltd

Design and artwork: Sandra Coventry and Jenni Quinn, P.A.G.E. Pty Ltd

Cartographers: Chris Crook, Country Cartographics and Claire Johnston

Picture research and ABC liaison: Richard Johnson

ABC Network Editor: Anthony Rasmussen

The co-operation and support of ABC Local Radio staff around the country was crucial in providing information, obtaining photographs and checking details. In some cases that involved driving hundreds of kilometres, adding to already busy workloads. The ABC's staff in turn were just the tip of an iceberg of support from the ABC Local Radio audience, who also provided information, suggestions and photographs. Without all of them, this book would not have been possible, and their contributions are gratefully and warmly appreciated.

Photographs: Special thanks are given to the Australian Tourism Commission and Tourism Queensland for the use of their photographs, and also to the Australian Broadcasting Corporation, Explore Australia Publishing and ABC Local Radio listeners.

Explore Australia Publishing Pty Ltd
85 High Street, Prahran, Victoria 3181, Australia

First edition published by Explore Australia Publishing Pty Ltd, 2004

10 9 8 7 6 5 4 3 2 1

Printed and bound in China by Midas Printing (Asia) Ltd

National Library of Australia
Cataloguing-in-Publication data
Meet the locals : The ABC insider's guide to Australia.

Includes index.
ISBN 1 74117 088 5.

1. Radio stations - Australia. 2. Radio broadcasting - Australia. 3. Australia - Guidebooks. 4. Australia - Description and travel. I. Australian Broadcasting Corporation.

384.510994

Publisher's note: Every effort has been made to ensure that the information in this book is accurate at the time of going to press. The publisher welcomes information and suggestions for correction or improvement. Every effort has also been made to locate and identify the copyright holders of material. Write to the Publications Manager, Explore Australia Publishing, 85 High Street, Prahran, Victoria 3181, Australia or email explore@hardiegrant.com.au

Disclaimers: The publisher cannot accept responsibility for any errors or omissions. The representation on the maps of any road or track is not necessarily evidence of public right of way. Every care has been taken in placing transmitters and determining their coverage throughout this guide, however a range of factors may influence reception, such as local terrain, atmospheric conditions and sunspot activity. Readers should be aware that information is intended as a guide only. Should readers experience difficulties, the ABC Reception website: www.abc.net.au/reception/ may provide helpful information.

ABC Local Radio Stations and their Frequencies

New South Wales

Armidale 101.9 FM
Ashford 107.9 FM
Batemans Bay/Moruya 103.5 FM
Bega 810 AM
Bombala 94.1 FM
Bonalbo 91.3 FM
Broken Hill 999 AM
Byrock 657 FM
Central Western Slopes 107.1 FM
Cobar 106.1 FM
Cooma 1602 AM
Corowa 675 AM
Crookwell 106.9 FM
Cumnock 549 AM
Dungog 1233 AM
Eden 106.3 FM
Glen Innes 819 AM
Gloucester 100.9 FM
Goodooga 99.3 FM
Gosford 92.5 FM
Goulburn (town) 90.3 FM
Grafton 738 AM
Grafton/Kempsey 92.3 FM
Hay 88.1 FM
Illawarra 97.3 FM
Ivanhoe 106.1 FM
Jindabyne 95.5 FM
Kandos 100.3 FM
Kempsey 684 AM
Khancoban 89.7 FM
Lightning Ridge 92.1 FM
Lithgow 1395 AM
Manning River 95.5 FM
Menindee 97.3 FM
Merriwa 101.9 FM
Mudgee (town) 99.5 FM
Murrumbidgee Irrigation Area 100.5 FM
Murrurundi 96.9 FM
Murwillumbah 720 AM
Muswellbrook 105.7 FM
Muswellbrook 1044 AM
Newcastle 1233 AM
Nyngan 95.1 FM
Port Stephens 95.7 FM
Portland/Wallerawang 94.1 FM
Richmond/Tweed 94.5 FM
SW Slopes/E Riverina 89.9 FM
Sydney 702 AM
Talbingo 88.9 FM
Tamworth 648 AM
Taree 756 AM
Tenterfield 88.9 FM
Thredbo 88.9 FM
Tottenham 98.9 FM
Tumbarumba 92.5 FM
Tumut 97.9 FM
Upper Namoi 99.1 FM
Wagga Wagga 102.7 FM
Walcha 88.5 FM
Walgett 105.9 FM
White Cliffs 107.7 FM
Wilcannia 1584 AM
Young 96.3 FM

Australian Capital Territory

Canberra 666 AM

Victoria

Alexandra 102.9 FM
Apollo Bay 89.5 FM
Ballarat 107.9 FM
Bendigo 91.1 FM
Bright 89.7 FM
Cann River 106.1 FM
Corryong 99.7 FM
Eildon 97.3 FM
Goulburn Valley 97.7 FM
Horsham 594 AM
Latrobe Valley 100.7 FM
Mallacoota 104.9 FM
Mansfield 103.7 FM
Melbourne 774 AM
Mildura/Sunraysia 104.3 FM
Murray Valley 102.1 FM
Myrtleford 91.7 FM
Omeo 720 AM
Orbost 97.1 FM
Portland 96.9 FM
Sale 828 AM
Upper Murray/Albury-Wodonga 106.5 FM
Warrnambool 1602 AM
Western Victoria 94.1 FM

Tasmania

Bicheno 89.7 FM
Burnie 102.5 FM
Devonport East 100.5 FM
Fingal 1161 AM
Hobart 936 AM
King Island 88.5 FM
Launceston 711 AM
Lileah 91.3 FM
Maydena 89.7 FM
Orford 90.5 FM
Queenstown/Zeehan 90.5 FM
Rosebery 106.3 FM
Savage River/Waratah 104.1 FM
St Helens 1584 AM
St Marys 102.7 FM
Strahan 107.5 FM
Swansea 106.1 FM
Waratah 103.3 FM
Weldborough 97.3 FM

South Australia

Adelaide 891 AM
Andamooka 105.9 FM
Coober Pedy 106.1 FM
Cook 107.7 FM
Glendambo 106.1 FM
Leigh Creek Coalfield 99.3 FM
Leigh Creek South 1602 AM
Lyndhurst 88.7 FM
Marree 105.7 FM
Mintabie 88.7 FM
Moomba 106.1 FM
Mount Gambier 1476 AM
Naracoorte 1161 AM
Oodnadatta 95.3 FM
Port Lincoln 1485 AM
Port Pirie 639 AM
Renmark/Loxton 1062 AM
Roxby Downs 102.7 FM
Streaky Bay 693 AM
Todmorden 106.1 FM
Woomera 1584 AM
Yalata 105.9 FM

Western Australia

Albany 630 AM
Argyle 105.9 FM
Augusta 98.3 FM
Billiluna 105.9 FM
Bow River Mine 106.3 FM
Bridgetown 1044 AM
Brockman Village 99.3 FM
Bronzewing Mine 107.9 FM
Broome 675 AM
Busselton 684 AM
Carnarvon 846 AM
Channar Mine 92.5 FM
Cue 106.1 FM
Curtin 106.7 FM
Dalwallinu 531 AM
Darlot 105.9 FM
Derby 873 AM
Djarindjin 104.5 FM
Eighty Mile Beach 88.9 FM
Esperance 837 AM
Exmouth 1188 AM
Fitzroy Crossing 106.1 FM
Geraldton 828 AM
Goldsworthy 107.3 FM
Halls Creek 106.1 FM
Hopetoun 105.3 FM
Jameison 106.1 FM
Kalbarri 106.1 FM
Kalgoorlie 648 AM
Kalumburu 104.5 FM
Karratha 702 AM
Kununurra 819 AM
Lake Gregory 107.7 FM
Laverton 106.1 FM
Leinster 106.1 FM
Leonora 105.7 FM
Manjimup 738 AM
Marandoo 106.1 FM
Marble Bar 105.9 FM
Meekatharra 106.3 FM
Menzies 106.1 FM
Mesa J Mine 92.5 FM
Mount Magnet 105.7 FM
Mount Whaleback 105.7 FM
Murrin Murrin 92.5 FM
Nannup 98.1 FM
Newman 567 AM
Nifty 105.3 FM
Nimary Gold Mine 103.3 FM
Norseman 105.7 FM
Northam 1215 AM
Northcliffe 105.9 FM
Nullagine 106.3 FM
Packsaddle Village 97.7 FM
Palm Spring Mine 106.9 FM
Pannawonica 567 AM
Paraburdoo 567 AM
Perth 720 AM
Port Hedland 603 AM
Punmu 107.3 FM
Ravensthorpe 105.9 FM
Sandstone 106.3 FM
Shay Gap 107.9 FM
Sir Samuel Mine 94.3 FM
Southern Cross 106.3 FM
Telfer 100.5 FM
Tjirrkarli 106.1 FM
Tom Price 567 AM